THE FOUR OF US

THE FOUR OF US

A Holocaust Memoir

GOLDY HESS

Full Court Press
Englewood Cliffs, New Jersey

Published in the United States of America
by Full Court Press, 601 Palisade Avenue,
Englewood Cliffs, NJ 07632.
www.fcpress.com

ISBN 978-1-60643-025-5

Editing and Book Design by Barry Sheinkopf
Colophon by Liz Sedlack
Cover photo and back photo courtesy of the author
Cover photo, clockwise from top left,
Berta, Helen, Mina, and Goldy
Author photo by Barry Sheinkopf

Whoever injures a single person has injured the world,
For every man helps to complete the world.
Whoever saves a single person has saved all mankind.

—*The Hebrew Prayer Book*
trans. Ben-Zion Bokser

Tomorrow's dawn will robe our world tonight;
Our yesterday will vanish with the night.
But if our freedom should arrive too late,
The world should know the meaning of our fate.

—*The Song of the Partisans*

I Dedicate This Book

To my parents, who struggled so hard to survive and to give us
knowledge of self;

To my sisters, who have been there for me and still are, especially
Mina, who prodded me to finish my story;

To my children, Lawrence, Francine, and Aaron, who should
embrace our heritage and never forget the past;

And most of all to my grandchildren, Hillary, Benjamin,
Danielle, and Alexandra, who carry the names
of those who suffered most and for whom I wrote the book
so that they too may retell these events,
and in the hope that they never happen again.

I would be remiss if I did not thank my teacher,
Barry Sheinkopf, for encouraging me to capture the full story of
my Holocaust experience when I first began to take courses at
The Writing Center twenty-five years ago. Life intervened; I
am pleased that, at long last, I have completed this book.

PART ONE

HE WAS EIGHTY YEARS old, and once again I had to say good-bye to him. He lives fifteen hundred miles from us, in sunny Miami Beach.

I have never felt that the sun was shining upon those old wrinkled faces that I see each time I visit. I see a huge nursing home stretching from Fortieth Street to First Avenue between Collins and Washington. There they live, the retired ones, the sick and the lonely ones. They look older than their years. Some are crippled from arthritis, others walk hunched over, and others still are led by their companions because, alone, they could hardly manage. Some need the help of a cane to be able to shuffle along. Those who have been left without a companion just sit in the lobbies of their run-down hotels, which once were rated first-class. They while away the day by staring into empty space.

What are they thinking about? I wonder. About the good old days? Their youth? Their played-out dreams? They rock back and forth on the porches where they wait from one meal to another, doing nothing, going nowhere, waiting for no one. No one needs them any longer. It's become too much of a burden to keep them around.

Their children urged them to give up their homes and retire to sun-drenched Miami Beach with the promise of frequent visits. It worked for a while, and then the visits came less often.

Now they have become even older and needier. With some luck, they won't have to end up in a nursing home. Even the telephone calls grow rarer. I have seen these old parents and grandparents anxiously waiting for the mailman, at times even smiling for a while in anticipation, hoping that, maybe, that day there will be a letter or a card from their children, grandchildren, perhaps a nephew or niece—if nothing else, maybe the check they promised to send to enable them to get a few extras, or the overdue Social Security check that may have arrived.

Yet too often, those mailboxes remain empty. As usual, they call the mailman back to ask the same question over and over again. "Vait a minnit! Are you sure zere is nossing for me? Look. Look again, please, yes? Maybe someting you have overlooked?"

And as he has so often, he shakes his head and goes through the motions of checking his mail bag, knowing very well he has not overlooked anyone. His answer is always the same: "You'll see! Tomorrow I'm sure you'll get something. Tomorrow!"

How many more of those tomorrows will there be for them?

The old man of eighty I said good-bye to yesterday is my father. He wanted to stay in Miami Beach after my mother died. He could not be persuaded to leave while she was buried there with no one to visit or look after her grave. He thought the best thing to do was to stay. The climate was better; and even if all his children wanted him to come and live with them, he did not want to bother, or become a burden to, them. For us it was the most natural thing to have him come to stay with any one of us, whomever he chose.

I knew what was going on in his mind. Once, a long time before, I had overheard him talk to my mother about what he would do if he survived her. He said then he could never live with his children—in the long run he could not tolerate his daughters' deviations from his way of life, his grandchildren's even more. He is an orthodox Jew. He does not see eye to eye with his children's choices regarding the upkeep of what they were taught and saw in his home. He attributes their behavior to living in this modern world. They have drawn their own conclusions regarding religious practices and affiliations.

His younger daughter lives in the suburbs; their house, not being near an orthodox temple, joined a conservative one. When they go to services, they prefer to sit together as a family, opposing the orthodox tradition of separate seating of men and women. When the discussion arose, the children told him they did not see anything wrong in worshiping together. He did not want to ask but gathered that they also drove to temple on the Sabbath rather than walk, though it is not permitted to use any means of transportation on that day. They eat in non-kosher places. How could he expect to live with them in peace? They keep a kosher home, but that was not enough.

His other daughter lives in the city and does observe all the kashruth laws; on the other hand, she answers the telephone, warms up food, and watches television on the Sabbath, none of which are allowed in his home. He wouldn't have been happy with her either.

The other two children preferred to remain in Europe. How could they, he wondered, live in countries that had chased us out and wanted to exterminate us, among people who still do not like Jews? What will become of those grandchildren? he wondered. They will be alienated even more then the ones living here. No, he couldn't agree to stay with them either, not even on a visit. They'd kept even less then the ones here. He would stay on in Florida.

It's been eleven years since my mother died. She was a beautiful human being. It wasn't only her face that made her so, or her full, rich head of hair; her beauty shone from her big wide brown eyes. When she looked at you, you knew she saw you. Those eyes, which at times lost themselves in you when she thought no one was noticing, bored through you, deep into your heart, so that, subconsciously, she drew your attention to her gaze.

I remember seeing her cry when she was told her parents were dead, and the infinite sadness in her eyes when she heard how they had died. The Germans had invaded Poland and had marched into Warsaw. At once they had begun to persecute and murder the Jews of Poland, the way they had done in Germany and other countries they occupied. Her parents, with other Jewish villagers, had been dragged out of their homes in a little town near Warsaw and marched to the outskirts, into the wooded area that surrounded their town. Then the selections began. The young and healthy were ordered to step to the right and later designated for hard labor or deportation and early death, depending on the whim of the commander in charge. The old, the sick, and children who were too young to work were useless to the Reich. It was easier and simpler to dispose of them right there, and before the eyes of their families they were shot. At times their killers had to have some fun first. My grandfather had a long, beautiful beard. I don't remember him—my sisters have told me they used to play with it when they sat on his lap. They asked him once what he did with the beard at night when he went to sleep. His answer was, "I take it off and put it on my night table, so that it won't tickle your grandmother."

As my grandfather stood among the old people, pushing my

grandmother behind him to protect her from the blows the Nazis were dishing out while making their selections, the commander noticed him and took him out of the crowd. He set afire that beautiful proud beard that had become all white with age. While he was writhing in pain, his wife was shot to death in front of him. When they felt the old man had suffered long enough, they turned their guns on him, too.

We were in hiding by the time this news reached my mother. My parents had moved to Germany from Poland, because my father couldn't earn enough money to support a family or find a good job with all the restrictions the Poles had put on the Jews. They had started the war against us way before Hitler. Hitler had gone en masse, and with organization; the Poles and the Cossacks had done it by pogroms, whenever it suited some drunk. Since my father spoke German, he thought he and his wife would have a better chance if they migrated to Germany and at the same time escape the harassment of the Polish Gentiles living in their village.

Life wasn't so bad in Germany. He was able to support a wife and four children. He could even send some money home to the family they had left behind.

My parents were never involved in politics, so that when, in 1933, an unknown who was not even German but an Austrian named Hitler was elected Chancellor of the German Reich, it did not mean anything to them. It did not mean anything to them either that he had formed a Nazi party or that, on the night of his election, the Nazi storm troopers had paraded with torchlights through the streets to celebrate his victory. All this was not their problem. They were Jews who were involved in Jewish agendas. Their community did not raise an eyebrow when a new element was added to the German flag, the sign of the swastika that would, in later years, send shivers through most of Europe, especially the Jews. Hitler designed armbands with the black swastika to be worn by his followers, the storm troopers and their party members. It gave them an image, a symbol to bolster the morale of the masses who were still recuperating from the First World War. It had brought them economic disaster, high unemployment, disillusionment, and discouragement.

The Germans were ready for a Hitler, a new leader. He would see to it. No one was prepared for what unfolded thereafter. Between 1933 and 1937, everything started to change. Step by step, he poisoned the minds of the people. There was anti- communism, anti-socialism, anti-those who would not get in line with his philosophy, and anti-Jews. Hitler's propaganda became familiar through his inflammatory speeches filled with outrageous facts and innuendos against Jews, and with bombardment of newspaper articles against that "foremost enemy" of the German people. People began to lend these efforts credence, too: The Germans needed a scapegoat for all their ills. Hitler gave them one.

The Jewish community did not pay heed soon enough. Surely intelligent people would not go for that nonsense, they thought. Lots of their families had fought with the kaiser; their family trees went back for generations, proving their German ancestry. They had assimilated, intermarried, and felt those slogans were not meant for them. The craze would pass; no need for alarm.

Yet my father, with many others, saw the writing on the wall. He had known from experience what such tirades brought. He no longer felt safe. Jews were being discharged from high posts. Students were not permitted to enter colleges, and the ones already there were expelled. Jewish doctors could no longer practice in hospitals or have

German patients. My parents were no longer allowed to have their household help. No German was allowed to work for a Jew.

Some of our family members had migrated to Italy at the time my father left for Germany, and they persuaded him to come there instead and live in Milan. By then it had become harder to leave the country, especially with a Polish passport stamped Jew. My father thought that it would be best if he stayed behind, with me, and send my mother with my three sisters ahead as if they were going on holiday. It would not arouse suspicion. He would follow with me a while later. A man with a little child would also go unnoticed. Besides, he needed some time to sell their furniture and other household goods. He needed the money to make a new start.

Thus once again they were uprooted. My mother took very few belongings with her—it would have aroused curiosity in the border patrols that were checking railroad passengers had they seen too much luggage.

Since we were no longer allowed to have household help, my father had to put me in an orphanage for a while after my mother left. He could not take care of me and at the same time settle his affairs.

Everything went as planned. In Italy, my father managed to make a decent living for the family by becoming a door-to-door dry goods salesman. He had no papers, so he could not get a work permit. He went to the factories instead and bought whatever he could carry, and then he traveled by train to the countryside, visiting farmers and selling his goods to them. Sometimes, he would be stopped by policemen asking for papers, and when he could not show them a work permit, as penalty they would alleviate him of his merchandise, for which he hadn't yet paid.

Many a time there wasn't much food to speak of, but my parents never complained. There was always enough by the time the Sabbath came around—my father always found a way to get on his feet again and make up for his losses. Other Jews had to struggle too, because they too had left behind a homeland in which they could no longer find safety. Yet the Jewish community in Italy managed to thrive. My parents could send us to Hebrew school and pursue an orthodox life as they had before.

Slowly, though, ever so slowly, things started to turn sour in Italy, too. Mussolini had developed the Fascist Party and taken control of the government. They started by opposing communism and social-ism, tactics that had first been adopted by Hitler and the Nazi Party.

Italian Fascism never, however, much shared Hitler's concept of racial supremacy. It was a one-party system in which the individual was subordinated to the state, and control was maintained by military force, secret police, and rigid censorship.

Mussolini allied himself with Germany in all other ways, though, enchanted by dreams of conquest and Hitler's promises of a slice of the pie. As it does all dictators, power blinded him. He became a puppet of Hitler.

Before Mussolini's fall from power, his party was in full control. Fascism was flourishing. The "Black Shirts," as we called them because of their uniforms, were marching in the streets, waving flags, and singing all kind of national songs. They began to harass the Jews, throwing stones at Jewish-owned store windows, making them close their businesses, making it harder to go to public schools and be accepted at universities. Jewish students were dismissed without a cause. Italian Gentiles were afraid to be seen in the open with their Jewish friends. People began to be stopped in the streets to check if they had proper identity cards. Before the Germans occupied Italy, getting caught without papers meant being hauled to the police precinct for questioning and possibly given some papers of identification, or a date to come back with valid residence papers. Needless to say, those appointments were never kept.

The Italians never went as far as the Gestapo, but many collaborated, when the Germans marched into Italy, in return for food and other amenities. The Italians themselves also had to abide by new laws and rules. The Germans once again busied themselves with the task, as in other countries they had occupied, of eliminating the Jews and other traitors to their cause. But the Italians had never particularly liked the Germans, and after German occupation a resistance arose—partisans sabotaged railway stations, bridges, and other points of importance, anything that might delay the enemy. These "troublemakers," as the Germans called them, were persecuted and hunted with a vengeance, using any means of persuasion on anyone who they suspected knew something of their whereabouts. Italians who did not adhere to German commands were severely punished by imprisonment, torture, hard labor, or shooting.

This had all started in the spring of 1940; when Italy entered in the war as an ally of Germany, the plight of the Jews began, especially those with foreign nationalities. More and more raids occurred on the streets. The Fascists were no longer as tolerant when they caught Jews who had no papers; the time came once again when Jews were forced to evacuate their homes, leaving everything behind and taking only what they could carry in one suitcase per person, not ever knowing where they would be sent.

Thus, one day my father was picked up off the street. My mother went out of her mind when he did not come home, not knowing what had happened to him when days went by without a word of where he might be. She went to the authorities to ask if they knew anything. They humored her. They sent her home, telling her not to worry, that they did not know his whereabouts either, but that he would show up sooner or later. She waited in anguish, going back to the police station every day. Finally, the police summoned her to let her know what they had known all along, that my father was being held in prison and would be transported to a concentration camp in the south of Italy for internment. Immediately, she went from one authority to another to try to get him released, to no avail. After much pleading and crying, though, they finally allowed us to visit him before he got shipped out.

We were taken to the prison yard. When not in their cells, the prisoners were allowed to walk around in the barbed-wire court. That was the time when the inmates got to see each other. Every day more and more prisoners joined them. My father used to look for familiar faces among those who came in after him, in the hope that they could give him some news from us.

While he was held, he was not told anything about what was going to happen to him or his family. They did not tell him that all the prisoners would either be deported or interned in a camp. They fed him only bread and water once a day.

He had lost a lot of weight. His suit was dirty and wrinkled, hanging limply from his body. His eyes were sunk deep into their sockets from the sleepless nights and worry about us. When he saw us, he couldn't believe his eyes. Then, like a crazed man, he was pushing everyone aside to let him get through. He ran toward us, breathing heavily and gesticulating with his arms, then engulfed us all in one embrace. Mother was crying, nestling her face into his shoulder; as I looked up, I could see that he was crying too, stroking her hair with one hand and trying to hold us with the other. He raised his eyes to heaven and said a prayer of thanks that we were together. Then he asked her what had been going on in his absence. She told him what was going to happen, and about her choice to be deported with him when the time came.

He was silent for a while and then said, "You should have come to visit first and then decide if you would join me. I don't know if it was wise to volunteer. At least you and the children would have been free. The Jewish community would have looked after you. With the money we've been able to save, you and the children would not have been in need till my release."

He had no way of knowing that, very soon, there would no longer be a Jewish community, and that those who still were free would go into hiding or try to escape to a country that would accept them.

This time my mother was the wiser. "You fool!" she cried out. "Do you really think they would have released you? And do you think I would have ever known what happened to you? . . . And do you imagine we would have been safe for long? I chose to be with you, and whatever happens, it will happen to all of us, together!" She hugged him again.

". . . You are right, Dvora, you are right. I am worried about your welfare and the children's. I was going crazy not knowing how you were. God will protect us!" he answered, and once again lifted his eyes to heaven as he caressed her face.

Too soon, our visit was over. We left the courtyard after long embraces and tears. We walked away and around the corner, where we could look through the barbed-wire fence that enclosed the prison. As we stood there watching, guards came outside. They called each prisoner by name and proceeded to manacle them as if they were criminals. At the far end of the yard, the fence opened. Trucks drove in.

We stood staring horrified at what was going on. My mother screamed and called out to my father, who had not been aware that we were standing there and didn't hear us.

All this scared me so much, I pulled at my mother's dress. She picked me up but would not budge from the fence. A guard came by and told her to move on. She did not move, clutching me in one arm and the barbed-wire fence with her other hand. The men were ordered on the truck, packed together like sardines.

For a while, that was the last we saw of my father. My mother stopped sending us to school and kept hoping every day for news that we could join him. She cried often when she thought we would not notice.

Finally, a few months later, the order came: We were to go where my father had been interned, bringing with us only what we could carry. It was a gloomy day, yet my mother was calmer than on all those previous days of waiting; the uncertainty was over; at last she knew we would be together, and, therefore, she was prepared for anything.

She busied herself with the ordeal of packing. She did not know what was important, what we needed and what was superfluous, other than the few treasures she would not part with. She packed and re-packed. She supervised our packing and told us, here and there, what we should put or not put in our suitcases.

Soon enough, the time had come to leave. Autumn had arrived; we put on our coats and hats and walked out silently with our valises and backpacks, looking around for the last time, already feeling strange in that place where I had felt so happy. The walls were bare:

My mother had given away the wall hangings and pictures to some of our Italian friends, who could not believe what was happening to us. Then we left. She locked the door as usual when we went out, as if we would return shortly. But she knew in her heart we would never see that place again.

When we reached the prison, we were lead into a big hall filled with people just like us. I don't recall if they were all Jews or not, or whether we all went together. Many were sitting on their luggage, others standing holding hands with the members of their families. We saw familiar faces from our congregation. Everyone was asking whether anyone knew what was going to happen next. Some crying children and women were being comforted by others. The children who didn't quite understand the seriousness of the moment were greeting each other loudly across the room when they discovered that a friend had appeared. The commotion was in full swing.

I don't know how long we had been waiting when a group of Black Shirts appeared. At the sight of them, an immediate hush fell over the room. They told us we would be shipped to an internment camp, where some of us would join family members who were already there. They called our names one by one and told us to take our belongings and follow the guards.

A couple of hours later we were on a truck that drove us to the railroad station, where a train was already waiting. The rest remains vague in my memory.

I recall only certain things from that time in the camp. It was always hot and damp, and we were prone to fainting spells. The camp stood in a swampy area, and the mosquitoes were relentless. Quinine pills were given out to avert the malaria that was running rampant among the detainees. We slept in makeshift barracks with many other families and hardly any privacy, on beds that consisted of two wooden boards nailed onto four legs, with thin mats for a mattress. One could hardly turn over on one because it was so small. When it rained, the barracks were inundated with water, and till the water subsided we walked around for days in ankle-deep water and mud, since the floors consisted of hard-pressed soil.

There were daily roll calls, morning, noon, and night. Curfew was at nine in the evening, and permission was needed to leave the barracks after that. There were quite a few talented musicians among us. The administration allowed them to form an orchestra. Soon after everyone attended concerts, which for me seemed unending and boring, almost like torture to sit through those nights in the sweltering heat. I haven't been able to attend many concerts since then. My friends can't understand the reason, since they know how much I enjoy music. I've never explained the feeling I get in the pit of my stomach when I do get coaxed into going to one. I see the benevolent commander sitting in the front row in his black fascist uniform and, with a baton in his hand, following the moves of the conductor, nodding his fat shaven head once in a while.

Everyone was assigned to different work groups to maintain the camp in proper order. From what my family told me (as I said, I was too young to remember all the details of our confinement—I was only five then), life as such went on for eighteen months. More Jews arrived in the camp on a daily basis; they came from all over Europe. The camp was supposed to hold approximately 1,500 people and was ill-equipped, yet within months it housed more than 3,000. Water was scarce, dysentery widespread, and food became insufficient. As more and more Jews arrived and the camp became overcrowded, the option was given to whoever wanted it to leave and be transferred to another location. A few choices were offered.

My father welcomed this opportunity, feeling that we could only benefit from leaving the camp, since it was evident that things would become worse.

Many years later we found out that the camp was to be liquidated as soon as the Germans arrived, and all the inmates were scheduled to be shipped to various German extermination camps. The Nazis had knowledge of all those who were interned. Our names were on the list, among all those designated for the concentration camps (the Germans didn't realize that some had left). This list is among hundreds of thousands of documents reposing in the Holocaust Museum in Yad-Vashem in Jerusalem. As it turned out for us, and for all others who chose to leave, the greatest ordeal of our lives was just beginning. Many did not survive. There were not enough hiding places left.

THUS ACCOMPANIED BY two policemen, we arrived in Borgo San Giacomo, a small village in northern Italy. They took us immediately to the police station to register us as interned Jews who had no permission to leave the town, and who had to live in the village under surveillance. We had to present ourselves at the police precinct once a week, to make sure that we were still around, which was so foolish because the town was so small and we lived near the police station. My parents seemed relieved to find themselves and their family in such a small place, removed from commercial traffic, big roads, and a big city. They thought that it was safer for us to be detained in a place so unobtrusive that occupation by the Germans would be unlikely.

The village was inhabited by about a hundred families. It had a bakery, a butcher shop, a grocery shop, and a few other stores, which sold a little of everything, and an inn where only the men congregated in the evening to have some grappa or wine. They sat outside, at tables set up on the sidewalk, when the weather permitted. Young men liked to watch the girls walk by and make them blush calling all kinds of endearments after them. They knew almost every young girl in town. Other men played chess and checkers while they drank, slapping each other on the shoulder every so often after telling each other jokes, and then breaking out in boisterous laughter when they heard a good one.

It did not seem to bother anyone that we were Jews. They were mostly farmers. They worked on land handed down from generation to generation, where everyone knew each other and almost everyone was related to everyone else by marriage. For them, life had not changed much through the years. Politics was not their thing. Most of them had never seen a Jew nor heard of them.

We were given a vacant house near the parish, where Padre Giovanni was in charge of Borgo's flock. It did not take too long for us to establish ourselves within the confines of the village and the lives of the villagers.

They were quite helpful at the beginning. My parents had some money that they had been able to hide and take with them when we left the camp; it could sustain us for a while, until my father figured out a way to earn some more. Sometimes, when there was not enough food in the house, we would take some burlap sacks and, in the middle of the night, steal into the fields outside the town and scavenge for some remains of already harvested corn, or pick leftover ears of wheat. We would come back with sore feet, legs scratched from walking over the stumps of corn, and cuts in the palms of our hands from ripping off the stalks of grain. We ran hunched over from patch to patch like animals on the prey.

My heart would pound so hard against my chest I thought it would burst. My mouth dried out gulping for air; I was so scared someone would catch us. We returned furtively to our house, circumventing the village, using the back roads, falling sometimes in the stream that flowed alongside the fields when we were not careful enough, or got entangled in the fences that separated one field from the next. My mother would pound the wheat kernels to a coarse texture in order to use it for baking.

At last my father, with his entrepreneurial streak, began to buy chickens for the purpose of starting a small hatchery. Our house had a small pond in the back. I remember when, at times some small chicks wandered away from their flock and fell in the pond, my father ran to save them, hauled them out of the water, and frantically breathed air into their beaks to revive them. I used to laugh and make fun of it, not realizing that for him to lose these chicks was a catastrophe. If they didn't survive to become chickens, he would have less to feed us. From the poultry we had eggs, meat, and some dealing power with the peasants.

Mother became quite inventive, too. She used the feathers of the chickens to fill our pillows. Our meager home became a flourishing barter place: eggs and poultry in exchange for flour, sugar, clothing, and some makeshift furnishings. The peasants did not bother us, and we did not bother them; we co-existed quite nicely, other than on those few occasions when all hell broke loose.

We owned a few turkeys, too. One of them loved to go to church especially on Sunday mornings. When mass was said and songs echoed through the piazza, it invariably got the urge to follow the sounds, wander away from the yard, and to our dismay enter the church, the portals of which were always open. The turkey would waddle in and, lifting its wings, prance down the aisle, making its own sounds along with those of the singing worshipers. We could hear the gobbling.

I was always the one chosen to retrieve it. On those occasions, I hoped that the ground would open beneath me and swallow up the turkey and me. The bird never made it easy to be caught. Most of the time I launched myself on top of him when I thought I had caught him, he sent me sprawling in the aisle, eluding my grasp while everyone looked on, raising their voices an octave to show their displeasure. The little ones pointed fingers at me and giggled out loud. Most of the time, by the second try the bird caught on and, realizing he was not welcome, flew out the door with me close behind.

Needless to say, the wrath of the villagers following such displays had no limit. It took the intervention of Padre Giovanni to calm them down and explain how unfortunate the situation was, and that we would make amends so that it should not happen again, until the next time of course. . . .

My family and I loved Padre Giovanni very much. We took to one another at once. I used to tease him each time I saw him run, because he had to pick up his black dress (that's how I called his vestment) in order to be able to move better; then his hairy legs would show, and I'd compliment him on them, and he in turn would do a little dance, raising his robe, and run on. He never tried to convert us. As for me, I adored him because he was the first Gentile to tell me that the Jews had not killed Jesus, and that I should not feel guilty when the children taunted me.

We had to attend school and sit in for catechism lessons since they were an integral part of the curriculum. He used to call me into the sacristy, too, and let me help him prepare the altar for mass on Sundays. He used to tell me stories about saints and their lives that I so loved, and I dreamed of growing up to act as they did and maybe become like one of them.

My father made a few acquaintances through his wheeling and dealing, among them Mr. Migliorati, who owned a large parcel of land. He befriended my father, and we got to know his family. He had children our ages, so that we often went to his farm to play or help with some chores; in return, he gave us food. He had understood our plight and often helped us out. Mr. Migliorati used to come to visit us and loved to talk to my father. They used to discuss politics, religion and books. Among other things, he would ask my father why he didn't consider conversion so that we would have a better chance to survive. He felt that many more people would then be willing to risk their lives to save us thinking that they had assured themselves a place in Paradise by having been able to convert us. In their eyes we were heathen and possessed by the Devil, and surely we would end up in Hell.

The villagers were simple-minded people, good-hearted, hard-working, and rugged. They carried on in the same traditions their elders did, and they in turn as those before them. Schooling never went beyond the elementary grades. All hands were needed in the fields to help with the planting, harvesting and tilling of the soil. The girls were needed to help in the household. Only a few were lucky to be chosen to go to the big city to study when they recognized that one of their offspring had a good mind for learning and were urged by their teachers to study. Even then most of them couldn't afford to send them, or felt that the city was a bad influence. They lived on superstitions and handed-down old wife' tales. They believed that Jews had devils' horns and tails; they could not believe that we had neither. They thought we had some mechanism hidden away to be able to hide those features because we were ashamed; thus they strongly felt the need to convert us. Even Mr. Migliorati, who seemed more intelligent then the rest, tried to make my father see the light. Of course he did not believe that we were devils in disguise. My father, who did not want to insult him, nor cause ill feelings among the villagers—it would only have harmed us—used to answer, "We will see, who knows?"

Thus life went on with my parents trying to cope with the littlest of necessities, hoping that the war would soon be over and we could resume our normal lives.

I was always hungry, and in order to be able to get some extra food I began to appear at wakes in town. In the villages, people who were sick did not go to hospitals. The country doctor made home visits and prescribed some home remedies or simple medicine. They never died in hospitals; they died at home. There were no such things as funeral parlors or chapels. The dead were laid out in their Sunday clothes on a bed in their front parlors surrounded by candles. The vigil was held by their family members, which included children and even babies. The dead person would be visited by the inhabitants of the village and also by friends living near by. They came by foot and by horse-drawn carriages. The wake would last about a week. Homemade cheese and watered-down wine would be served for the occasion, sometimes even cake and cookies. I soon realized that it would be a good place to go to eat without appearing out of place or in need of food.

ONE NIGHT WE were awakened by Padre Giovanni, who came to our house accompanied by Mr. Migliorati and told us that the Germans would be marching into the village next day. He had received a telephone call from a friend who also was a priest, serving in another parish not far from us and had told him that the Gestapo had rounded up the few Jewish families who lived there and that our village would be next, so we should leave immediately.

It was past midnight; he urged my parents to wake us, to hurry and get dressed, leave everything as it was, take nothing with us—there was no time to lose. He told us that they had found a place where we could take refuge with one of their trusted friends, Mr. Savino, who lived alone in an old house, almost hidden from the road by overgrown bushes and trees, that wasn't easy to find. The padre thought we could hide there for a while till they could contact the partisans to find a better place to stay. Mr. Migliorati would take us there. We rode out of town in his horse-drawn carriage, across fields and small roads.

We did not reach our hiding place a moment too soon. At dawn, armored trucks and a whole motorcycle division of German soldiers roared into the square. The first thing they demanded was for us to come to the square, but we were gone. . . .

WE REMAINED IN hiding in that house for four months. Our main quarters were in a damp cellar hidden by a brick wall that could be moved only with a concealed handle that was in turn obscured by big vats filled with wine. Our host was the only one who knew about the passage. Since he lived alone with only one servant to do the cleaning and cooking, there was no immediate danger of being found out. As we were led into that sinister- looking place, we automatically held on to each other, feeling we were about to be buried alive. It took a while for our eyes to adjust to the darkness that confronted us. A few feet away was a small oil lamp hanging from a wet wall; the shadows it threw from the meager light made us children cry out. The flames seemed to dance and grin at us, bouncing from brick to brick. It was cold, and the cellar had a musty odor, and I was scared.

Mr. Savino apologized for the way we would have to live for a while. He had improvised a makeshift living room and bed room as best he could at such short notice. An old couch stood in the middle of a tunnel that was about twelve feet wide and twenty feet long. A simple wooden table with six chairs stood next to the lamp. Further down the cellar there were six army cots, one next to the other. He showed us where the bathroom would be. At the very end of the tunnel, an old water faucet was protruding from the wall; there was a hole under it where the flowing water would be caught. That same hole would serve as a toilet. Right there and than I decided that everyone could do as they pleased, but that I would never wash or go to the bathroom there. I'd rather be dead.

But quite soon those thoughts vanished; after a day or so of try-ing to keep from going to the bathroom, I started to have stomach pain and gave in. It wasn't so bad after all. We found a cover some-where to close up the opening when we didn't need it. In a way, the system was quite imaginative. We did not have to flush, and no one ever had to scold me that I had forgotten to do so—I had the tenden-cy to forget to flush the toilet. Under the opening was a river that flushed everything away into a common sewer of the villages spread about.

Food was brought to us once a day to minimize the risk of being surprised by the frequent house searches that could occur at any time. Every so often, we went upstairs to Mr. Savino's quarters to stretch our legs and see daylight.

I began to look forward to those little visits; they made me forget, for a while, the miserable existence we were forced to endure. Mr. Savino was a kind old man. He was short, with a pot belly, jolly eyes, and a bald head. He made me laugh.

Every so often we had little visitors—rats. I think I was more scared of the rats than the rambling noises of the approaching visits of the Gestapo, who never seemed to give up the search for us. I used to hear their voices and the sound of their boots when they came down the cellar to continue their hunt. My parents used to grab us and move to the furthest corner of the tunnel, blow out the light from the oil lamp that burned day and night, and lie in wait, huddled like lost sheep ready for slaughter. Meanwhile my father recited, almost inaudibly, the Schmah. My mother's eyes would burn like two coals in the dark. Her thin body would shake so violently that my father had to use all his strength to keep her down. She was ready to give up rather to endure such torments.

In these straits, the news reached us of my grandparents' deaths. A survivor of the massacre of the village where they lived found his way to the underground, which was trying to organize an escape route for us. Somehow, this man had managed to get away from Poland and make it safely there. He immediately volunteered to make his way through the woods and fields to get to us and let us know about the new plan for sending us to a safer place. Mr. Savino was sure that, sooner or later, one of the raids the Germans instigated would find our hiding place.

He arrived in the middle of the night. I was awakened by my mother's muffled cries. Things have a way of evolving: She had recognized that young man. He was the son of the rabbi from their village. Before any talk of our escape, he had to give an account of all that had occurred from the time my parents left their home-town—before anyone dreamed that something like this could come to pass.

That night, we never went back to sleep. The young man told us the sad news. His own parents had died the same way my grand-parents had. He had been lucky that day, had decided not to go to school and left with some of his friends in search of adventure. As they were coming back towards the village, some women who knew them stopped them from going further and warned them not to go back to their homes, that they would be killed. They would help them to get away.

My mother fumbled through her clothes and came up with an old yellowed photograph of my grandparents. She always carried that picture with her. How she came to salvage it, God only knows. As she stared at it, pain came to her eyes—a quiet, muted sorrow that was worse than if she had cried out.

"We should not have left them," she said quietly. "We deserted them," she continued. We started to cry at the sight of her grief. My father proceeded to recite the *Kaddish* and chanted the mourning prayer with the newcomer.

My parents sat on the floor for three days.

The young man never got around to laying out the plan of our escape route with my parents. They were too deep in mourning to have understood any of it. He conveyed it all to Mr. Savino instead. Then he bade us farewell.

We found out later that he had been shot trying to return to the partisans on the other side of the woods. Was he meant to have been spared the massacre and live just long enough to find my parents, to be able to tell them about my grandparents? Was this the reason he had found us?

It is easier to think of it in these terms; otherwise, the mind gives up under the stress.

While living in that dungeon, we also received the terrible news of Padre Giovanni. He was taken prisoner the morning after our flight. He refused to tell the Gestapo our whereabouts. The peasants did not know where we had disappeared, and when they were questioned they admitted that only the priest would have known.

The Gestapo tortured him, beat him, without result. He was held in prison for a few days to bring his strength back so that they could continue their questioning, which resulted in more beatings and torture. They had knocked all his teeth out, broken all his fingers one by one. He was blinded in one eye and was at the verge of losing his mind from all the pain he had endured. Yet he hadn't uttered a word. Finally, almost unconscious, he was tied up at the flag pole in the middle of the square, and they forced all the inhabitants of the village to witness his execution as a warning in case anyone else had ideas of defying their orders. When my parents heard of this new misfortune, they told Mr. Savino that this suffering and waste of life was enough. It was the will of God to give ourselves up and not to endanger more lives, mainly his. Besides they did not think we'd make it, that we would be found sooner or later, and why should we be spared when others were not. . . .

Our host did not agree. He argued that Padre Giovanni had not thought so either; if he had, he would not have gone through all that.

And what about the young man who'd been shot? It would all have been in vain. If for nothing else, we had to go on to give meaning to their lives.

Another *Kaddish* was recited, and the memory of those two was imbedded forever in our minds.

As my father chanted the Hebrew prayers, I turned away and recited a few of the Christian prayers that the padre had taught me. I knew them very well—and in Latin, too— *"Ave Maria gracias plena,"* I went on and on. . .I hoped he would have been pleased that I was praying for him to get to heaven, as he used to tell me often that, if one prayed hard and with sincerity, almost all wishes would be heard. I remember very often after that, when I was scared, having recited those prayers, thinking that if our God did not listen to our prayers, maybe their God would. Oh, how great the fantasy world of a child can be! Everything is so simple!

WHEN IT WAS my turn again to go upstairs to Mr. Savino to stretch my legs, I asked him, "Why do you think God let the padre die? If He is up there watching over us, why does He let all this happen? Wasn't he a good person? Praying all the time, like my father, too?"

I must have startled him. He stared at me for a while; I guess he was searching for an answer. He busied himself with some books, then rearranged his top desk, and finally could not avoid my eyes any longer; he made a few rasping sounds, as if to clear his throat. He sat down behind his desk and then, pronouncing each word slowly, he said, "Come here, child. . . ." I came close to him. He put his arm around my shoulder and said, "You are not the only one thinking this way, or asking this questions." A wistful and pained expression came over his face. "It's not easy to go on believing that all this has a reason, and that there is a meaning at the end." He paused, concentrating on his free hand, then staring out the window, almost forgetting I was there. I followed his gaze. Another reason why I loved to go to see Mr. Savino in his quarters was that I could look out the window once in a while. I could look into the garden and feel that, out there, was life. There was growth. There was sun and there was rain. Suddenly I loved the rain, too. I used to hate it when it rained. It kept me from going outside to play. Now I could just watch the drops come down and hear them at the window pain. I never heard them before. The garden was colorful. Green spruce, cypress trees, red roses and yellow sun flowers. I had never noticed these things before. They were there, just there, as a matter of fact. I could listen to the birds chirp, and make believe they were telling me a story that I had made up. I was allowed to go out into the garden only a few minutes each time; one could never know who was lurking in the garden and would see one of us.

I used to sit under an old tree on a stone bench that was shaded by the heavy branches, deeply inhale the fresh air that I so longed for, and exhale the foul air I'd brought upstairs from the cellar. It felt like being born again, and it made me feel good. It gave me a reassurance that everything would turn out alright. Weren't the flowers still blooming? The grass was still green and growing. I used to take off my shoes to feel the blades of the grass under my feet. It tickled me gently.

Wasn't nature part of life? If nature was part of us, then things would get back to normal. Otherwise everything would have been wilted. Something would have to happen to stop the madness. God could not smile benignly only upon the vegetation, and forget us. Mr. Savino regained his trend of thought and continued, almost apologetically, "I am not the most learned man, and at this moment, I have only one answer which makes sense to me." He sat back in his chair, massaging his chin, retrieving his arm from my shoulder. "Maybe God is sick and tired of the evil in this world, sees how the people he created have forgotten him, and the bounty he has given them. He's maybe figured: I'll produce a Hitler who will do terrible things, till mankind will rebel, they will remember all the good things that were created, all the commandments that were given and not obeyed, and finally realize the evil at last. His creatures will fight, will start anew."

He bent down to me and took my hands into his. "I know this answer is a bit too much for a little girl to comprehend, but you asked such a serious question, and I in turn am answering the best I know how, and may be once as you will grow older you'll remember and than understand, and make your own deduction. I must believe, my child—" he drew me close to him and continued in a low voice— "that the conscience of the people will not stand idly by while our freedom is taken. While people are persecuted for their beliefs or have different opinions. Tyranny has never lasted in past history." He looked at me, hoping that I had understood. "I am confident that good will win over bad, and as a result we will take stock of ourselves. It is simply put, but this is the only way I can answer you." He gave me a pat on the cheek, drew the curtain over the window, and said, in a lighthearted tone, "It's time to go, *colombina*." That was a pet name he had given me. It made me feel important to be called by a special name, since I had nothing else to call my own.

I left the room in better spirits, telling myself to bring this question up again, this time to my parents, since I really was not sure I understood what Mr. Savino had meant.

We did not indulge in long conversations in those days. It seemed we had to hide our bewilderment over what was happening around us. We felt we had to be brave, not to vent the frustration of helplessness, of the injustice, of it all.

The days went on without joy, without purpose or reason. My father tried to teach us some mathematics; we learned to recite the multiplication table backwards and forwards. (In later years, this proved to come in handy: I was the best student in my class when it came to arithmetic.) He taught us to read from the old newspapers and magazines that had been given to us by our host, and later go on reading the books he lent us to while away the time and keep our minds occupied. We learned to recite the daily prayers and read stories from the bible. But it was hard to concentrate in the dim and dreary atmosphere that surrounded us. We were cold, hungry, and weary most of the time. We preferred to sit huddled together for warmth.

At times, my mother gathered us around her to tell us about "the olden days," as my children call it when I in turn sit with them and reminisce about the past—a past that they vaguely study in history books—and about some things that have not yet been printed.

My mother's favorite stories were from her childhood. Her father was her image of all that was good—as my mother is mine— "Your *zeide*" (she referred to my grandfather by the Yiddish term) "used to bring home needy strangers every Sabbath Eve for dinner. He went to synagogue for morning and evening prayers. He derived strength and guidance to perform his daily work. Those were troubled times for your *zeide*," she told us.

"We were quite poor. My parents had eight children to feed and clothe." Tears would come down her sunken eyes. What had this sad period done to them, and her face? Her eyes never smiled as they used to. When she gazed at you, she seemed so far away, as if she no longer saw you. A haze had settled over them.

While sharing some of her favorite memories, she was thinking of her brothers and sisters. What had become of them? Where were they? The young man had not mentioned them. Had they made it to safety? She went on speaking. "Your grandparents used to bake bread in the back of their house. They only had one oven, therefore to produce enough bread the oven was used almost day and night. They sold their meager product to even poorer people then they." As she talked, the story became alive; we felt we were there. She spoke softly and low, as though not to disturb the savoring of the past events. "Most of the time their customers could not pay for the bread, yet they came back to buy more without having paid for the previous loaves."

Then, with a little smile that she could still master ever so often, she added, "Your grandmother would scold your *zeide*, tell him that they would end up in the poor house with the way he handled their business affairs. But," she continued, patting my hand and, alternately, my sisters', "he would put an arm around your grandmother and say, 'God will provide.' And do you know what?" Mother chuckled at the thought. "God really did provide. We never went hungry. We never were too full either—we could have eaten more if there had been some more to be gotten. We were sensible enough not to ask for second helpings, though, and there was always enough for a stranger in need." She paused a while, lost in thought, trying to think of some important moments she could impress in our minds, so that, if she were no longer there, someone would be around to remember. Her voice acquired some urgency. I felt that need in it to tell us all she could while we were all together, to let us know about a life and a time that she knew would never come back again, a life that had been erased from the face of the earth. There would never be a *statel* to go back to, or the people who inhabited it. Now more then before, she missed them. She too needed so badly to hear her father's reassuring words: *God will help!*

At times I find myself with the same need to tell my children what transpired, what The Holocaust meant to me. Maybe by remembering, and passing it on to them, they'll make sure it won't happen again. Maybe by being aware, by keeping it alive, the loss of all those loved ones will have been transcended.

"Children," my mother used to say, "always remember who you are." I find myself telling my children the same. I don't think they quite understand the real meaning behind it. They think they know what I mean. They live in America. They have an identity. But that's not what I mean. Will they be forsaken too, if such a catastrophe should again arise? What will the American gentiles do or feel about us? My mother continued, "If we should ever be separated, or one of us should not survive, you must carry on. Only if you do will their death have meaning."

The drudgery of our mode of living did not improve our disposition. We tried to lead a normal life as possible, but the dullness of the days that passed from weeks into months started to bear down on us. My sisters and I began to quarrel a lot with one another. At times, when nerves had reached their peak of endurance, we really spilled our guts out. When I think of it, I shudder.

One morning I woke up early. Something new had been added to our menu—bedbugs. They were everywhere; I was all bitten up. I jumped out of bed in despair, itching and scratching myself, drawing blood, running around in a rage, waking everyone up, making the roaches scurry to safety in the rotten walls and the rats disappear into the closest openings they could find. "Why must there be Jews, Christians, Hitler, and wars? Why? Someone tell me why!" I was screaming, beside myself, and sobbing. I woke my mother with my yelling. She jumped to her feet, trying to get a hold of me and soothe me. She brought me a glass of leftover milk from the night before. A fly had drowned in it. That was a reoccurrence that never bothered anyone. The fly, or whatever it may have been, sometimes it was a cockroach who was too nosy, was swiftly removed and the liquid drunk. It had ceased to bother us. There was so little food and milk that we would never think of discarding any of it, no matter what happened to the leftovers, which was very rare. On that morning it brought on one more uncontrolled storm. I pushed her hand away. "No, I don't *want* it! *You* drink it, *you* drink that filthy milk!"

I knocked the glass out of her hand, sending the glass smashing into a million pieces, splashing the milk all over. Mortified, I flung myself on the cot and hid my face in the pillow, not caring if there were bedbugs hidden in it or not. I felt ashamed of having made such a scene; I wanted to die. If only I had been punished or scolded, it would have made me feel better; I would have been able to justify my lousy behavior. Instead, my father told me in a stern voice to clean up the mess on the floor. "I'll talk to you later," he said, and told everyone else to try to go back to sleep. I made sure to take an extra-long time cleaning up. I wanted to defer the moment of facing him. I knew I had made him angry and sad. Such outbursts did not help our situation, and could be devastating for our morale already fray.

When I was finished, my father motioned for me to sit with him at the table. I hardly dared to look him in the face. I hadn't realized how much more gray had covered his reddish hair; his high cheekbones protruded out of his face more than usual. I had such an attack of remorse that I could no longer sit opposite him. I jumped up, almost falling over the chair, and ran to him, putting my arms around his neck, hiding my face in his shoulder. "Oh, Papa," I blurted out in one breath, "I am so ashamed, so sorry having made you and Mama upset. I know I should be grateful for being here, safe with you all. I know all this, and yet I don't know what happened, what came over me. I am going to apologize to Mama too. I'll tell her how very sorry I am!"

He stroked my hair and loosened my grip around his neck. "In any other circumstances, you would have been severely punished. You know that, don't you?" I shook my head, looking down at my toes, still unable to look at him.

"We are all under a tremendous strain, it is hard to control oneself at times. I understand." He cleared his throat. "You are the youngest and therefore hit the hardest. At your age, children should be outside playing, jumping, singing, and making noise." He was talking to me gently, almost absentmindedly, stroking my arm back and forth, staring into nothing. I was somewhat taken back by his words that to me seemed an outburst, though he did not show it. Even at five years of age, I had come to acquire a sixth sense about hidden emotions and silences that could say a million words. These things are never taught, they just happen; for some they never will—life will pass by without being touched. . . .

I stood there knowing that something was happening between us, something important that needed more maturity to be handled, a growth of a different kind, which in my awareness I felt I hadn't reached yet. At that moment I was shedding tears of regret for not being older (in the past, I had taken advantage of that fact: For the youngest of four sisters, it was a tactic of survival), for not having been able to say something appropriate, not having the capacity to feel the depths of the moment, which I knew even then I would never come face to face with again.

I saw him now in a different light. I loved him, not ever having given it a second thought. How else should a young child feel toward a parent? I thought of him as remote, not someone given to pry into one's feelings or make inquiries of one's state of mind. My mother was the one to cry and sigh to. She was the one to come to when in pain, the one to comfort us. When questions seemed to have no answers, when we were down, she lifted us, cheered us up.

Not my father. He was there alright, questioning our behavior, our intellectual forthcoming, pushing and cramming *religion* into us as much as he could, whenever possible, never letting an opportunity go by to remind us what he expected and what he wanted from us, bringing up examples from the bible as a for-instance. As young as I was, I began to feel the yoke rather than the teaching and need of it. Even in hiding he came across to me as stern, always expecting the utmost, no nonsense. I never played in front of him. If he ever caught me at it, he'd say, "Don't you have something better to do?" never stopping or making a remark about our growth. The changes from unknowing children to serious little adults.

For an instant, he had shown me he was vulnerable, too, shown his nakedness without embarrassment. He was sharing as he had never done before. A warm feeling came over me, an awareness that, even if he never said anything again, he knew me. It changed the significance of the words *I love you, Papa*, something which I uttered as a matter of fact. I never thought about it. I just said it whenever I wanted to say it.

He never again opened up to either of us, but those moments so long ago made the difference of knowing for the rest of my life that he had touched me, that he cared but did not know how to show it. How could he? He himself had never had a childhood. His mother had died when he was two years old, after giving birth to her twelfth child.

"I know," he continued the same way, "you had to grow up fast, faster than any five-year-old has a right to. More will be expected of you in time to come. You won't have the luxury of giving into feelings of pain, or be complimented for good behavior and wanting to be mothered. These notions have to be set aside for the time being. No matter what comes your way, you'll have to make the right decision on your own."

He pulled me down on his lap, giving vent to a bitter laugh that drew me out of the dreamlike state I was in. "At a time when my children, when *all* children, need guidance and teaching, when they should be shown love, taught the meaning of it, the joy of living, and we their parents should be experiencing the wonder of their life, I must teach them something entirely different— something we don't even know anything about. Nothing like this has ever been written in books."

He stopped for a moment, pushing back the black skullcap that had slid out of place, and continued, "I must teach you, Goldale."

My heart gave a jolt, and my ears seemed to stand up. My father hadn't called me by that name in God knew how long! For a split second, a vision from the past, which I had almost forgotten existed, appeared in front of me. My father had never made a big to-do about birthdays or anniversaries; thus we never expected anything from him.

Yet, on my fourth birthday—the last one I'd celebrated like any normal child, before the chaos started—he had walked in laughing, holding a package under his arm. I'd heard his call: "Where is my Goldale? Where is the old girl?"

Abruptly, the picture disappeared. His words once again etched themselves on my mind. "All those emotions, for right now, are signs of weakness. They will only stand in your way, they will make the difference between life and death." I started to tremble. I felt a knot in my stomach; it started to hurt. I became my old self again. I didn't like him this way. He was demanding again, expecting, pulling me away from something I was comfortable with. It was all I knew how to be, a five-year-old kid—it was too soon to grow up. I was the *baby*. It meant *protection*. . . .

My father shook me a little and hugged me tight and strong; it almost took my breath away. "Our only purpose in life right now is to survive. You must understand. I will put one more burden upon you."

He loosened his embrace and removed a strand of hair that had fallen over my face. He looked intently into my eyes; I could not avoid looking into his. They had filled with tears. I felt helpless, thinking desperately that he was crying for me. "*You* may be our strength to go on at times, to make it worthwhile to endure, to give us the will to live." He gave me a hug. "So. . .I think I've said it all. Now go on back to bed. Try to rest if you can." He coaxed me off his lap.

"And try to remember that bedbugs want to live, too!" He rolled his eyes, uttered a groan, sighed; he knew he had lost his little girl, and regretted those lost years when he did not partake in his children's games, songs, and playtime. Brought up by his sisters, whoever had time for him, he'd never known how to play. His father had been a sickly man not given to laughter, recreation, and displays of affection, his days were filled with studying the Torah and prayer. When my father was old enough, he was made to go to *cheder* (Hebrew school), where he had to study and learn the Torah, too. His growing years were hard, so how was he to know how to pass time with his children? That was his wife's job. He was the provider, and now he realized he had missed out on something special.

He turned to the table, took the prayer book, and started to leaf through it. I heard him talk to himself, or to God as I always assumed. "Is this what you are giving us? You made a covenant with Noah, remember? No more floods. Is this *instead*? Is this *better*?" He began to weave back and forth, back and forth, chanting psalms, never losing faith. I knew I had lost the moment, but a memory was born that I would draw upon—oh, so often.

THE DAY ARRIVED when Mr. Migliorati felt there had been a breakthrough and came excitedly into our roach-infested hiding place. With the passing of time, it seemed we were getting more crowded by the minute. The additions were all kind of bugs, mice, and rats when their hunger brought them out of their holes. To this day, when I see a roach, I feel the skin curl up on my back and immediately start to scream like a maniac (yes, now I can indulge—I have earned the right). I find myself paralyzed before a scurrying bug that is more scared than I. I will run away, to return only if someone goes with me to make sure it's no longer there.

Mr. Migliorati came to tell us that a new commandant was taking over the region; the old one had been recalled to Berlin. While this transition was taking place, the Germans would be busy putting their papers in order, polishing up for their new chief. There would be a goodbye dinner in the school hall, with lots of food—food which they periodically took away from the peasants, leaving them hungry—and there would be lots of drinking. No one would want to roam around the woods in search of fugitives. It would be a perfect time to make our escape through the forest and on to where a group of partisans was working for the underground, on the other side of the valley. The partisans at that point could no longer send some of their people to get us. It had become too dangerous. We would have to cross the valley by ourselves. The Germans had already entered Milan and were marching south. We would be caught right in the middle. We had to make the move and try to reach our friends as soon as possible.

We were given old but sturdy shoes to be able to cover the forty-some kilometers. Summer was gone, and a cold winter wind had taken its place. We had no heavy clothing; therefore, we wrapped blankets around ourselves to keep from freezing. The few possessions we had managed to bring with us into hiding could not be taken along. We had once again to leave the few possessions we had behind. Mr. Migliorati promised to hide my mother's silver candelabra till we returned and do the same with the few prayer books and the prayer shawl my father had kept with him, the only treasure he had never thought of parting with. It had been given to him on his bar mitzvah. (That beautiful hand-woven relic with the collar embroidered with gold and silver is still in our family. Mr. Migliorati kept his promise. He saved it for us. Now, we have all been married under it, held up at the four corners by four ushers. My mother's first grandchild was also married under it, and, hopefully, the others will, too.)

It was a December night in 1941: In a few weeks I would be six years old. In a few days, it would be Hanukkah. We wouldn't be able to celebrate this festival of lights. My parents wished me a safe birthday rather than a happy one. We did not know if we would make it together; we were already pretty lucky to have made it so far as a family.

I had forgotten my father's words; I was holding on to my mother, scared and apprehensive once again. I didn't want to leave if it was so dangerous; I had become accustomed to my dungeon pretty well. So what if, among other things, the place stank with bad air!

My father reminded me of our talk and told us that our host had run out of food too, and soon we would be more hungry than now, and get weak, and we would not be able to walk such a distance any longer. We would become sick living under such conditions and ultimately endanger the life of Mr. Savino, too. Who knew whether we would starve to death?

That scared me even more. I knew that the dead did not move, and very often we *had* to move, jump up and down, when we saw rats scurrying about; it would scare them away, and we would not get bitten by them. The thought of lying there and not being able to chase them away, and the rats having a feast, gave me some courage. I had a vivid imagination, as all children do.

That evening, we had a warm and a good meal to sustain us through the trip. For good measure our friend gave us a thermos filled with chicory coffee. We would need it to keep warm. Mr. Migliorati stayed with us through dinner; he'd been able to bring some food along, so that we really had a party.

After dinner, he showed my father a map, pointing out the road we had to take. If we zig-zagged toward the south, we would cross the woods. At the end, we would come to a clearing where the valley lay in front of us. We would turn east, the long way around, where there would be some protection from stray trees and mounds of stones so that we could take cover from time to time and not be seen. Finally we would come toward the south once again, approaching a large farmhouse. That would be our place of destination. We had to arrive not later than five o'clock in the morning, before it became light. The door of the barn would be open for us, and we were to hang a white kerchief over the window as soon as we arrived. This was a pre-arranged signal, so that the partisans would know we had made it. Someone would come in due time to give us further instructions.

Mr. Migliorati gave my father the map so that he could study it and remember all the details marked on it—he could not take it along, since it would be a dead giveaway in case we were caught. He gave him a small compass and embraced us with tears in his eyes. "*Andate con dio, miei amici!*" he declared in a horse voice. "Go with God, my friends, and may He watch over you. God willing, this mess will be over soon. We will meet again. I will be waiting here for you."

My parents thanked him profusely for all he had done for us. "There are not enough words for your deed. Whatever we may say to you, Mr. Migliorati, it will never be enough!" We were all in tears. He and Mr. Savino took us to the back door, assuring us that it was the best way out. Mr. Savino unbolted a thick, heavy latch, and embraced us quietly. He turned to me and whispered, "Remember our conversation. All this will pass soon. There will be a new beginning." He put both his hands over my head, as if he was about to give me a blessing, but Mr. Migliorati pushed us out the door and pointed us in the right direction, and then both vanished behind the door. We took a few steps before looking back one more time, staring at the proud old walls that had given us protection and shelter for such a long time, and then we too faded into the night.

❀ PART TWO ❀

My mother took my hand and walked silently behind my sisters, to be able to watch their every move while my father took the lead. The fresh cold night air was almost too much for us. We hadn't breathed fresh air in such a long time, it nearly took our breath away. Our lungs had to get used to it.

We were in luck otherwise; the full moon was hidden behind dark clouds, so that we were sheltered by the darkness. Our steps had to be light, so that we would not make unnecessary noises. At the beginning, everything went smoothly. We were still refreshed from the dinner we had eaten and still felt comfortably warm. Having listened to so many bible stories, I imagined the exodus of the Jews from Egypt, wandering through the desert. We were wandering through these woods to find safety and freedom as they had.

We walked listless and mute, trudging to keep up with my father's brisk pace, passing through without notice or record, each lost in our own thoughts. We were all thinking the same. Would we make it? If not, what would happen? Yet no one gave vent to these fears. The path took us through underbrush and thickets; strange sounds and rustles emerged from the dense bushes.

Meanwhile, the cold became more severe. A wind started to whistle around our ears. We had no hats or gloves. We pressed the blankets tighter around our bodies to give us more warmth. Silently we blessed Mr. Migliorati for having urged us to take them along. My father stopped ever so often, looking back to assure himself that his brood was still following him and were not lagging behind, then, with a vague smile, nodded and went on.

We must have been a strange sight for the animals living in the woods. It seemed they were transmitting it to one another, because their sounds seemed more animated than usual. Some of the sounds were kind of scary. Then a horrible thought came through my mind, and a shiver ran down my spine. If the Nazis did not get us, maybe the wolves would. I quickly touched the rosary beads that Padre Giovanni had given me. Maybe that would protect me. I had kept them hidden all this time from everyone, and I had put them on furtively under my clothes before we left.

A few moments later, what had been a fleeting thought became reality. We heard a crackling sound and a fierce growl out of the dark; then we saw rows of teeth and the glowing eyes of a pack of wolves ready to attack us. My father had to make a quick decision. He yelled, "Run! Run as fast as you can! Your lives may depend on it!" He pointed straight ahead. He turned around and threw the empty thermos as far as he could into the woods at the opposite direction, hoping the animals would think it was food, and run after it, which would give us some headway toward safety. His thinking paid off. The wolves disappeared, rampaging and howling after the thermos.

We ran as fast as we could, scampering over rocks, fallen branches, and left-over corn stalks. My mother started to fall behind; we could hear her heavy breathing and dry cough. She managed to yell, "Go, go on, no need to endanger all of us. I'll manage." With that she fell to the ground, exhausted. We stopped running—we too felt exhaustion creeping over us.

My father had figured out that we had another two hours of walking to do. Our shoes were torn; our blankets had become moist from the night's mist and were no longer keeping us warm, just becoming heavy. We had reached the clearing indicated on the map. My father realized that, with my mother feeling sick and us being so tired, we would never make it in time by going the long way as Mr. Migliorati had suggested. He decided that we would cross the valley. It would take a shorter time and therefore give us a little time to rest and regain some strength.

He ran to my mother to help her, knelt at her side, took her in his arms to give her some warmth from his body. He motioned for us to come near. As we bent down to see how she was doing, he spoke. "Children, this is almost the end of the line. We are in an open area. We could be spotted at any moment unless we start crawling the rest of the way." He pointed straight ahead, "You see down there across the meadow? That is the place we are to meet. Here, take this white kerchief." He pulled a crumpled rag out of his pocket and handed it to Berta. "Hang it over the window once you enter the house. It'll be the signal that we have arrived. Hurry! I'll stay with your mother a while longer. She needs a little more rest. Then we'll join you."

As we were ready to follow the instructions that my father had given us, we realized that we had company. Two men had noiselessly approached us from behind. We tried to rise from our kneeling position but were stopped by two guns pointing at us.

"*Nessuno si muove!* No one moves."

All the blood drained from our bodies. We went limp. One of the men grabbed my father by the arm and pulled him up. His blanket fell off; he stood there helpless in his torn jacket and ripped trousers. I wanted to get up. What where they going to do to him? I thought. *Please, God, don't let them hurt him!* I prayed silently.

Dawn had approached. We could see the men. They were dressed in dark sheepskin coats; big heavy boots covered their feet. We could not see their faces clearly. They wore fur caps that came down over their ears. All we could see were the glaring eyes and the rifles pointed at us.

The man who had pulled up my father spoke roughly to him. "Who are you? Tell us, or we'll shoot."

My father tried to say something, but nothing audible came from his lips. The man pushed him down again and grabbed Berta, who struggled to free herself from his grip.

"You, who are you?" He roughed her up a bit. The white kerchief fell from her hand. Before she could answer, the stranger bent down to pick it up. He looked at it, looked at us and said, "You came from Signor Migliorati? This is the signal, *si?*"

My father nodded his had.

"*Mio dio!*" The man's voice had, in an instant, grown gentle. "You are the people we were waiting for!" he exclaimed. "It was getting late, and daybreak was approaching fast, and no sign of you. We decided to go looking for you. You were not supposed to have come this way." He made some apologies. "We had to make sure it was you—one never can tell. Many of our men have fallen into traps."

They shook hands with my father, took off their coats, and handed one to him and the other to Berta, who was standing there shivering in her tattered dress. Her blanket had fallen off, and she was too afraid to bend down to retrieve it.

They fished some more coats out of their knapsacks, enough for each of us. "Well, now. We'll leave all the talking for later. We must hurry to the house. You are late. It has become light now, and dangerous. I will help the Signora while you crawl after my partner. It's not that far anymore." He took the blankets and shoved them in their sacks. Then he said, "*Avanti,*" and took charge of my mother while the other led the way in front of us, crawling on his belly, bidding us to do the same.

It wasn't easy, crawling with those heavy coats over us; we were laboring under the weight of them. But soon we realized how handy they were, as we crawled like animals on all fours through hollows of water and mud, toward the rendezvous.

Finally, after what seemed an eternity, we'd made it—reached our destination. . .for the time being, at least.

Our leader gave a whistle, and the door opened. "Get in," some-one whispered. We stumbled into a semi-dark room, fell to the floor, and lay there for a while to catch our breath.

The men helped us up and helped us toward a lit fire-place. "Come, sit here for a while and warm yourselves up. We prepared a fire while we were waiting for you." Chairs were standing invitingly around the hearth. Big logs of wood sizzled in the flames. How long had it been since we had all sat around a fire? The warmth of the room, and the crackling sound, gave such a feeling of well-being that I could almost have forgotten that danger was still lurking around us.

The men helped us to take off our drenched coats and dirty shoes. "Soon we will have to shut the fire down," said one of the men. The smoking chimney may attract attention. We'll let you warm up first. We don't want you to get sick."

I looked around and was surprised to find the place empty. There was no furniture other than a table against one wall. I wondered who lived there.

As my eyes became used to the dim light, I saw another man we hadn't seen in the field. He was standing guard by the window with a gun slung across his shoulders, looking through the half closed blinds. The other two men were leaning against the opposite wall, waiting for us to regain our composure. They had taken off their hats and coats. They no longer appeared so mean and scary as when we had first met them. They were young men, maybe in their late twenties. One could not be sure—they had unshaven faces. They were tall and thin with black curly hair. Though they were smiling at us, their eyes were serious and dark. The three of them were wearing knickers, the ends tucked into heavy boots and turtleneck shirts.

One of them approached us and, as if he had read my mind, said, "This is all what's left of what used to be a fine room. This house belonged to friends of ours." He fell into silence again, seating himself on the floor. Then the other man joined him, and said, "My name is Pietro, and this is Carlo."

"Where are your friends now?" I asked.

"Mario, Dino, and Paolo used to live here with their father Pepe," Pietro answered, looking back at the third man, who was still at the window.

"Well, where are they?" I asked again.

My father, sitting near me, seemed annoyed at my insistence. "Can't you see the *signori* are tired and need their rest as we do?"

"But, Papa, all I asked is where they are," I answered.

"Oh, please don't be annoyed at the little one. It's a child's privilege to be inquisitive." So he told us. "We were all friends as long as I can remember. A year ago, a group of foreigners arrived here. They'd been placed on this farm by the mayor of the town. They were Jews detained here under surveillance, never allowed to move about freely without permission from him. Pepe's farm was the largest around, with enough work to keep them busy and lots of spare rooms for living quarters."

Inadvertently, we looked around, trying to find another doorway or extension of space we might have overlooked. All we saw was the room we sat in; there were no other openings except for the door way we'd come through and the crooked window. "Oh no, you won't see anything else but this room. This is all that's left."

He turned around and pointed next to the table at the furthest corner of the room. A large board was secured to the wall, with slabs of wood nailed across it for support. I hadn't seen that barricade in the darkness.

"About three months ago, the Germans passed through here and made their headquarters in town." The young man ended his narration for a moment, watching the man moving from the window across the room toward the boarded area. He leaned his head against the wood, clenched his fists, and abruptly began to beat heavily against the boards. "*Merda, merda!*" he screamed, "*Animali*, beasts, all of you!" He continued to pound the boards and then the wall; deep sobs joined the rhythm of the blows. Pietro jumped up, crossed the room, and put his arms around his shoulders. And the man stopped. His raised arms fell limply to his sides; he stood staring at the nailed boards, all his fury, all his anger, exhausted.

I felt so terribly sorry for having insisted to be told. I no longer felt comfortable and warm. I was cold.

We all sat up straight, bracing ourselves for the blow we felt was going to hit us. I felt worse and worse. It was my fault having brought it up. Why couldn't I keep my mouth shut once in a while? But I loved stories and thought this would make a fine one to cheer us up.

My mother took my father's hand. "Chaim!" she whispered—his Jewish name (my father's Christian name was Abraham). We had stopped calling each other by our Jewish names. We did not want to draw more attention to us by our foreign sounding names-but now involuntarily she had called him that, as if to identify ourselves with those who had lived here just a short while before. "Dvorah!" he murmured understandingly.

The man continued to talk to the wall. "How many more will have to die? How much longer can we hold out?"

Pietro came back to sit down near us again. "Should I continue?" he asked.

"Yes, go on." My father had risen and was pacing the floor with his hands behind his back. He always did that when he was upset or thinking.

"Va bene," Pietro said. "Everyone thought that the papers containing the whereabouts of those people staying here had been destroyed. Quite a sum of money had been paid to have them removed from the archives of the town hall. The mayor, a lifelong friend of Pepe's, was bribed too, to keep quiet about the fact that the foreigners were Jews. All that was known about them was that they were displaced people from Poland looking for work and a place to stay. Meanwhile, the underground movement was notified of their presence in the region and had started to work out a plan to get them out of here safely."

Pietro went on to describe how badly Italy had been doing since the Germans had marched into their country. Il Duce had led them to believe that the Germans would protect them from the Allied forces, and that the alliance with Hitler would bring them victory.

As the war went on, Der Füehrer betrayed them, too. The Italian soldier found himself working for the glory of the Reich. Those who were not sent to the front were rounded up. All able-bodied young men were put to work in ammunition factories, to produce more firearms and ordnance. They needed to replenish the arsenal that was dwindling fast. They needed more supplies if Hitler was to go on to successfully conquer all of Europe.

Mussolini had become Hitler's puppet. Too late was he to understand that he had lost. Meanwhile the Italian army was in disarray. They started to resist the Germans. Some deserted and joined the Allies, who had entered from the south. Many escaped and joined the partisans. Underground they could retaliate and inflict the most damage.

Food had become scarce. The Germans demanded all of their surplus, leaving them with barely what was necessary to survive. Farm animals and horses were confiscated. Anyone caught gouging was either shot or sent to working camps. "Before help could reach the farm, the mayor's teenage boys were snapped by the Germans, to be shipped further north to rebuild roads and bridges that had been blown up by sabotage. The mayor bought his boys back—for a while, anyhow—by trading the documents, which he had never destroyed as he led them to believe. He'd kept the papers hidden, thinking they might come in handy someday. You can almost guess what followed next." Pietro's shoulders slumped. His throat had tightened, his eyes were burning, and he couldn't finish the story. He looked at his friend.

"Please go on, you must tell us the end," Mother insisted, almost yelling. "I hope you understand, Pietro, we must know what happened. There must be a reason for our being here. Maybe we'll be the only ones left to remember them by, and mourn for them. Please. Do go on."

So the young man did, his voice almost inaudible. "The Gestapo arrived three months ago, at night, while everyone was asleep. Those *banditi!*" He raised his voice and clenched his fists. "No one heard their trucks. They surrounded the farm. They pointed glaring lights at the building, so that anyone trying to escape would be seen and blinded. Then they announced through a megaphone that they had the place surrounded. They were ordered to come out as they were, with their arms over their heads. As the first few people walked out, barefoot and sleepy eyed, stunned by what was happening, they were met by a fusillade of bullets."

"I'll tell you the rest," said the man from across the room, coming closer. "You, Pietro, watch at the window." He sat down, taking Pietro's place. "...The first few to be shot were the lucky ones. The bullets hit them, and they died instantly. They were free from bondage after only a hail of bullets. But the others... the others, realizing that they were trapped, decided not to give up so easily. In fact, they never gave themselves up. With guns they had kept hidden, they barricaded themselves. All knew it was hopeless, but at least they would go down fighting. The Nazis hadn't expected to be met with a counterattack. Those *bastardi!*" He grinned maliciously. "They did not go down in vain, they took a few of them along." We looked at each other, breaking out in a sweat; the heat was becoming unbearable. We were crying silently as he went on.

"There is not much more to tell. The Nazis, maddened by the audacity of their captives, set the house on fire. Everyone burned alive in that inferno. The neighbors told us that they could hear the screams and crying of babies. My father Pepe, my brothers Mario and Dino, perished with them. If only I could have reached the underground in time, they would be alive."

He bowed down, covering his head with his arms, and cried. His sobs shook his body. He looked like a little boy.

My mother got up and tried to console him. As if there was something to say to sooth the pain, to alleviate one so grief- stricken, but she had to try. She knew the feeling. She told him that she too had lost her parents, and that there was a reason he had to go on, for their sake. "Paolo—" she brushed her hand through his hair— "don't you think it odd that you and we were spared? At times there are reasons for things that are happening. Not clear at first. But we have to continue. To struggle harder to stay alive, because all of them must be *remembered*. We must be the *witnesses*. We must not let it happen again. Whoever stays alive has the duty to bear testimony. Do you understand, Paolo?"

If he did, I couldn't. Mother was exhausted. She sat down. The moments passed by quietly, with only the sound of Paulo's sobs and the crackle of the burning wood.

"You were supposed to have come back with that young man we sent to Mr. Savino a while ago," said Carlo, who was standing. "For some reason he did not take you back with him as ordered. Do you think he may have had a premonition that you wouldn't make it with him?"

Paolo lifted his head and looked at my father.

"Oh, Paolo! Who knows the *why* of things. Maybe. . . ."

After a long silence, my father rose and began to chant the prayer for the departed; when his prayers were finished, we all answered, "Amen!"

Paolo summoned the fellow called Carlo, who so far hadn't spoken one word to us. He came closer and shook hands with us, then went on to apologize for having scared us out there in the meadow. "We have spies among us. As you have heard. On occasions, the Nazis have set traps for us. We have lost quite a few men. We also have good people. Look what the neighbors did. They rebuilt some of the house for Paolo to come back to." He stopped talking and shrugged.

We were startled when a rooster crowed. It was the beginning of a new day. We looked at each other and felt that we had come one day closer to freedom and hope, because without it, where would we be? "Someplace around here, you should find some clothes to change into." Pietro walked around the room. He seemed to be the nervous one, because he was always in motion, never sitting down for one minute. Sure enough, in the corner next to the window we saw some bundles lying on the floor. He picked up a few things and handed them over to my mother. "Here, *Signora*, find what is suitable for you, for the *signore* and your children. Meanwhile we'll prepare something to eat. We have some food in the knapsacks. We must get ready and go soon. After we have eaten we will discuss the next step." He nodded to his companions, picked up the knapsacks, and turned toward the table, showing us his back so that we could change unwatched. Mother sorted out some garments and distributed what she thought suitable for each of us.

Soon the story that had just been told us, the dead people, and the fire, were forgotten. All an animal needs to be quieted down, at times, is a bone. We had been reduced almost to such. All we needed to get us back into things was the sight of freshly washed clothes and food.

THERE WAS A moment of pleasure putting on those old hand-me-downs. They did not fit very well, but in wartime no one is well dressed, nor does one look at what others wear. As the war went on, the clothes one owned were worn out, repaired over and over again, and everyone had to make do with what was left.

Berta could finally discard the old lady's dress she'd had to wear for so long, for all we knew, it might have been lice- infested. The facilities for washing properly in captivity weren't exactly the most modern. Soap had long since run out, though poor Mr. Savino had tried his best to come up once in a while with some homemade gook that could hardly be used or called soap. Most of us broke out in a rash after washing with it. "Well, how do I look?" Berta asked us spinning around excitedly, making a ladylike curtsy. She sported a coarse tan woolen sweater that itched the hell out of her. She kept on scratching her neck and her arms. This was a homemade article that would last much longer than the Third Reich. The farmers wove their own cloth and spun their own wool. (Which was, of course, no longer being done. By then, the Nazis had confiscated all animals for their use.)

I used to witness the lamb-shearing quite often. It was an affair in which the whole population of the town and farms worked together in unison.

The wool was a very important commodity. The sheep would be gathered together in makeshift stalls in the marketplace. Each owner had a brand mark on each of his sheep or lambs, so that some order of ownership was easily established. A row of men would be sitting along the square on three-legged stools. I often wondered with what skill those farmers sat without falling off them, when they were holding those poor animals between their legs, wincing, thrashing, and bleating. It amazed me over and over how quickly and skillfully they performed the job. When the shearers were through with them and released them from their grip, they pranced back to their stalls in search of their companions. The noise, mingled with the sweet music of mandolins, swooning melodies rising in the air, children roaming around up to their usual pranks with each other, and church bells ringing for the matutine and vesper prayers, all rose as one sonorous force.

By nightfall their task was finished. The owners arrived in wagons pulled up by sad-looking horses. Once they must have been sassy-looking animals, fit to prance around with elegant carriages. The good horses had been taken by the Germans, and the old ones left for the menial tasks such as transporting the wagons full of wool back to the farms and a dry place. There it was packed tightly in sacks and once again pulled to the market to be sold. Each household had a spinning wheel, an heirloom handed down from generation to generation, a diadem no woman could be without. It was part of a bride's trousseau. On those winter nights, the farmers used to congregate in the stables, where it was warm; amid the smell of horse and cow manure, the women sat busily spinning night after night at the wheel. Some men brought along their harmonicas, some others their guitars, from which they could wring the most beautiful and saddest tunes. In such surroundings, a hand in marriage was asked and everlasting love was sworn. Listening to those melodies, I would forget the stench and the flies. At times a melancholy sound from an approving cow would join in on "O Sole Mio" or "Torna a Surriento." Slowly, timidly, and then with confidence, voices began to accompany the players. A baby cry would join in. The infants slept in cradles handcrafted by their grandfathers and their fathers before them. Those too were handed down from generation to generation. Every so often they would be rocked back to sleep by a grandmother's foot; if it wasn't sleep they needed, the baby was handed forthwith to the mother, who stopped spinning long enough to empty her breasts of the milk the child so greedily sucked.

Berta wore a black skirt with that sweater, which was a little too big on her. But who cared! Dark gray knee socks with brown walking boots completed the look. Mother smiled. "Now you look like a young lady."

Then it was Elena's turn, the second oldest. She had light brown hair that used to be curly. It annoyed her at times when she would brush and brush to try to straighten it out to look like that of Dina, her best friend from across the street. It bothered Elena to see Dina's neatly combed while her own was unmanageable. Now it had grown limply down her shoulders. Mother had found a red button-down dress for her with a little white (rather yellowed) Peter Pan collar. It had long sleeves. Elena was pleased because it hid her crippled left arm. Elena had to thank Hitler for that.

My mother had had a housekeeper then. Lore had been with us for quite a while and seemed to like the job with us. She began to change her nice disposition when Hitler started to spread his propaganda. After she became a staunch follower of his, my mother let her go. The last chore Lore performed before she left was to bathe us. Esther, as she was called at the time, was fussing a bit, and apparently gave the maid a hard time. In times past, this had never bothered Lore; she had always known how to handle us with patience and care. Yet this time, annoyed, she yanked Esther angrily from the bathtub by her arm, then twisted it behind her back, scolding her for having been such a nuisance. Esther was horrified and ran to her room. Her arm was hurting and she was fussing about it. The next day, the arm was swollen and, due to all kind of decrees and restrictions imposed on us to get medical help, the arm healed improperly. My poor mother never stopped blaming herself for that mishap, thinking she should have fired the girl sooner. My sister learned how to cope with the abnormal arm but never wore a short-sleeved dress from then on whenever she could help it. She was so elated to have been given a dress with long sleeves. There were dark blue knee socks for her and the same walking boots Berta had. She looked at herself pulling at the sleeve of her left arm and said, "Isn't this dress and everything else just fine?" We all laughed and complimented her.

Mina, the shiest of us all, had reached her ninth year and was like a little mother hen, always concerned about others, always cleaning after us so that my mother would not be displeased.

Even in those hard times, she came through for us, managed to devise something to give us when we asked, whenever we needed it. She still is the most giving and thoughtful person I have ever known. She was outfitted in a dark gray jumper with a black linen shirt. She touched the clothes she had on over and over again, as if to assure herself she was really wearing them. "Does it look good? Better then the ones before, huh?"

I hugged her, and my father lifted her up. "Yes, definitely! Yes, much, *much* better."

It was my turn. I was dying to hear what the others would say. Everyone knew how much things meant to me. Even a small ribbon counted for a lot—I could cherish it for as long as it would last. I would use it over and over again.

Someone up there must have known that I would be coming along, because the dress my mother handed to me to change into was lilac, with a big bow at the collar—not a very proud-looking one, a little wilted, but a bow nevertheless. My mother undid it and made a double bow out of it so that it looked fluffier. "There, pigeon. . . ." Our smiles left our faces: For a moment, we all thought of Mr. Savino, our dear old friend. Would anyone ever discover what he had done for us? We could not foretell the future then, so all we could do was keep on thinking lovingly of him and pray for his safety.

My father had gotten dressed too, though his outfit left him somewhat bewildered. Knickers in his old age! He thought. He wore heavy corduroy knickers like the other men, with heavy boots and a black sweater. "Now you look like all the farmers around here, Papa. You don't look Jewish at all!" Berta said, smiling.

At this last remark my father quickly turned to her, his eyes ablaze. "And what is this supposed to mean?" he asked curtly. He didn't bother to wait for an answer. "So, you too finally think that we are different! The evil tongues have set your mind working, huh? Soon you'll believe that there is something wrong being Jewish, or maybe you shouldn't be one. Maybe you also believe that all the ills of the world stem from us Jews! Tell me, smarty. . .how different do we look from the others? Soon you'll tell me we should convert to save ourselves. Do you really think that'll satisfy them?"

There was no stopping him; he finally was giving vent to all that had been kept inside him for so long. "In all the history books, have you ever read or learned that we produced evil in this universe? Did we ever incarcerate people because of their belief, or come up with an Inquisition? Did we produce an Ivan the Terrible, or invent the ghettoes?" He went on and on, stunning us into silence. No one could have silenced him, even though my mother tried over and over—he had to let it die out by itself.

When he had said it all, he sat down in exhaustion. He took his head between his hands and muttered, "I don't know what came over me. Berta is right, of course, we are dressed to look like the peasants around here. Forgive me!" He rose and went over to my sister, who was standing as if someone had thrown a bucket of cold water over her. He lifted her chin and kissed her on the forehead. "I guess I am entitled to be irrational at times, too." He smiled apologetically at her.

Pietro came toward us and handed my father a dark beret. "Here, wear this at all times. All men wear one around these parts." He turned to my mother to give her a black shawl. "You wear this over your clothes. No woman would be caught dead without one. It's the fashion. When it's cold, put it over your head. He smiled, looked at her approvingly, and told her to comb the loose hair she was wearing into a bun. "You'll look more authentic, *Signora!*" He winked with one eye. "And now, we must change your names. For you, *signore*, it will be Alberto. Abraham is too conspicuous. For *la Signora*, it will be Maria, since Dvora is out of the question. Now we need one for your little one." He meant me. He scratched his head for a moment. "It will be Olga. Goldy will only raise questions."

"What's wrong with my real name?" I asked, almost insulted.

Pietro grinned. "Nothing, nothing at all, *signorina*. It's a lovely and unusual name in these parts, but too foreign sounding. Your sisters Berta and Mina can retain theirs. Esther's must be changed, too. We'll call her Elena, like our queen."

While we were at it we had to assume a new last name, too: Silbermann would have been a dead giveaway. They gave us a good old Italian name, Fermi, instead.

All agreed to our new names and identities.

WE SURVIVED THE next twelve months running from place to place, always one step ahead of the Gestapo. There were closed- in rooms, more cellars and attics; they remain vague in my memory. Bits and pieces have managed to creep into my mind at times, especially when I watched my children grow up. It always came to mind that I had lost my youth. I never went through being a child to adulthood. I remember myself always as an adult. I never played.

Life is such that it constantly repeats itself. Today you live it, tomorrow it is history, and in a while it makes news all over again, only depicted in a different hue.

In my idealistic folly, I had always hoped that, from the past, a much better future would arise. We would grow into a much wiser genera- tion, come to recognize the pitfalls before we stumble into them. I real- ize that was only a fool's dream.

I do remember that, from the day we met the partisans, we start- ed to work at our survival. We learned what real fear was, though we'd thought we had experienced it already. No more lengthy hideouts. No more becoming acquainted with our helpers, or establishing some kind of human bond. We became vagabonds, wandering from one place to another because, after a short while, it became unsafe. A pattern established itself soon. We proceeded from one obstacle to another, from one phase into another. Always a step ahead of the hunter.

I can recall thinking, at the time when the young men took us to the next place to hide out, that I gave it a name. . .I called it a *station*. I had already realized that, for a while, there would be many stations we would be stopping at, till the time would come when it would be the last stop, dead or alive. Till then, there would be no home, no address, no friends, only images, passing moments of reflections of once upon a time. . .like now, when I tell my children.

Some things are vague, especially the faces of people who helped us while passing through. Vague are the innumerable places, rooms, hidden behind fake walls and closets, except for the few that left a mark through occurrences that may or may not have helped to shape the writer's mind or outlook on things.

I can still remember the horrible burden of having to walk out in the open after so many, many months in hiding and furtive walks. It was time to leave the farm house. Pietro went first with my parents, toward a new location in town. We watched.

For an unsuspecting onlooker, the picture appeared so loving, so serene and heartwarming—a son strolling with his parents—while it took all the strength they could master to make it appear so.

Then it was Paolo's turn. He left with Mina on one side and Elena on the other—a charming brother or friend taking his sisters to the market. Each of the girls had a basket hanging from her arm. People passing by smiled at the sight.

Then it was Carlo's turn to go with Berta and me. She must have developed a crush instantly for the taciturn young man. He really looked like a young lover escorting his intended with a chaperone alongside. In those days a young girl would not have been allowed to go out alone with her boyfriend. It was not proper. A few old peasant women dabbed at their eyes when they passed us by—if young love could still be born in times like those, surely not all was lost. They could not have guessed what it took to walk along so calmly, smiling carelessly into the crowd, when every fiber of your body was telling you: *Run while you can. Now surely someone will recognize you for what you are, branded like Cain after killing Abel. They'll see the sign of a Jew. They'll point at us.*

I had to learn to walk all over again. It was one of the hardest things I had to do, to walk straight with my head up and show no fear when the occasion arose. Yet, if they came after us, we had learned to run. We had learned to scrunch our bodies to make them almost disappear when needed. But to have to walk freely, when you wanted to run, that had to be learned all over again. My knees were shaking, my legs stiff, as if they had come out of a cast. Pearls of sweat appeared on my forehead. "I'll give us away," a voice was saying. "You look scared, you'll blow it!" the voice kept on, hissing in my ears.

Carlo must have sensed my secret battle. He took my hand and squeezed it gently. "Come, come now, little one. I'll teach you to dance when this is all over. We'll fly. You'll see—trust me, let's go." And thus my first love was born. And I walked.

Oh, God, what captivity does to the human spirit. How strong we can be. Strength is within us, without us ever knowing the capabilities we possess, until something of a magnitude confronts us. Yet we are so frail! It is such a thin line, the *in between.* The walk to the new rendezvous was not too far, even though for me and surely for the others too, it felt like a hundred miles—the strain would have been the same.

We met each other in an attic that Lucia had made available to us. She was our ghost hostess, since we never actually met her. It was thought better for her not to get to see or know us. In case things went wrong, she would not have a description.

Signora Lucia was a seamstress who owned the shop she was working in. She was kept busy by the army, cutting trousers and repairing uniforms. A bell would ring each time someone walked into her store, which summoned her from the back room where she was busy sewing on an old machine that she pedaled at furiously to make the needle move up and down.

By lying on the floor, pushing our faces to the ground, and squinting hard through a few loose boards, we could watch her movements without her knowing she was being observed by us kids. It whiled some of the time away.

Lucia must have been quite a beautiful girl when she was young; she still had traces of it. She had that aura about her. She appeared to be in her late fifties. She was tall, with a hint of matronly maturity settling onto her well-put-together figure. She had an oval face, dark eyes, and an olive complexion. Her graying hair was pulled back in a bun. She seemed to be the most sought-after of seamstresses, because that bell was the busiest performer. Every other minute someone came to the shop in need of her services.

In the attic, meanwhile, the sound of each chime wrought unsettling disturbances on our nervous systems. It was as if an electric shock would go through our bodies, putting us on alert:

Maybe this one is for us!

We had to change our living habits once again. Nights became days, and days became nights. While it was business as usual downstairs, we had to refrain from moving about, so as not to give ourselves away; the floor of the attic was wooden and it would squeak easily. At day's end, when Lucia locked up for the night, we could move furtively about. It was quite easy to fall back into that surreptitious existence, with the same familiar fear of being heard by someone who shouldn't have. Every step taken needed a second's contemplation before we took the next. Had we made too much noise? Had a board made a squeaking sound? How far did our vibration carry? We had our work cut out for us, to move about our waking hours as quietly as possible. The easiest way out at last was to stay in bed as much as we could stand it.

The attic consisted of a bare room just high enough to stand upright under the center post. Its sloping ceiling permitted us only to sit against the walls. We had a table with wooden stools and the luxury of two king-sized mattresses on the floor, with a few loose springs which had to be padded with some old rags so that they would not carve holes in our backs when we lay down.

The cold kept us shivering most of the time; since the room was not insulated, frigid air found more than enough crevices to seep through. But we soon befriended the colorless chamber whose only light was from an old kerosene lamp. In any case this attic seemed luxurious compared to Mr. Savino's cellar.

The nights were for eating. Lucia left food for us at the ladder that she pulled down from the ceiling every evening before she left her shop.

We took turns to crawl down the attic ladder, which led to a dingy hall adjacent to the seamstress's back room, to reach the bathroom. We had to stumble about in the dark, in stockings, to prevent any sounds. The dim, flickering light from the lamp that was placed at the head of the stairs had to be enough to reach the hall by. In the beginning, we tapped and groped along the walls; in time we became acquainted with the dark and quite easily found the unlatched door to the bathroom.

I never had a chance to see how that room looked. We never dared to switch the light on or flush the toilet. Lucia did that in the morning when she came to work. We washed ourselves at the sink, making sure not to turn the faucet on full force—the sound of running water could also carry. We washed ourselves as best we could with water trickling from the tap.

My memories come back at the oddest times. I find myself thinking of that bathroom, especially when using someone else's. I visualize how it may have looked. Did it have wallpaper, or were the walls painted in that drab faded pink or blue one encounters so often in gas stations? Was the sink made of marble, with gilded faucets, or did it have an old enameled basin with rusty water stains?

How odd that such silly things find a way to linger on in one's thoughts for the rest of one's life. How such trivia imprints itself in the mind, when so many other important and painful experiences have been made to vanish from memory.

Yet *they* really never are. *They* are present, indeed, because they have been integrated, have become part of you. I guess it is easier to try to visualize how that hole in the wall may have looked than to answer puzzling questions that still plague me: "How could it have happened?" or, better yet, "How could we have allowed this to be done to us?"

Our idyllic way of life ended sooner than expected. The Germans had fully occupied northern Italy. We were caught in the middle. The partisans hadn't found a safe way to get us out of the country yet. Meanwhile, the underground guerrillas were stepping up their counterattack against the enemy with greater tenacity and accuracy, which brought upon the citizenry the full vengeance of the Third Reich.

House searches became more frequent, punishments more severe for aiding the terrorists. The Gestapo was buying spies by taking innocent victims at random into custody and sending them to forced labor camps. Their release was promised as soon as the prisoners, or their loved ones, collaborated. It happened that, overnight, one could not tell who was a friend or foe.

Lucia became frantic. She sent word to the underground to move us out. We left our attic two weeks later on a cold and dreary November afternoon in 1942. The seamstress had whispered to us behind our locked door that we should get ready to join a burial procession that would soon pass by. We were to accompany the mourners taking the coffin to the cemetery, which was outside the perimeter of town. More instructions would follow on the way.

We tiptoed awkwardly downstairs through the back exit while she was watching the procession pass, headed by a priest and two servants. They were followed by four young pallbearers who were carrying their fourteen-year-old brother to his rest. The deceased had been shot trying to escape the clutches of the Gestapo, who'd caught him on a clandestine mission to deliver important maps to the partisans. Someone had given him away.

It was customary for the whole populace to join a funeral procession. Living in as small town without ever moving away (not so common today), everyone knew each other; most likely half of them were related to one another through the years, and they wanted to show their final respects. People were joining from everywhere, from alleys, buildings and stores, like silent silhouettes in the waning day.

As the line filed in orderly array past Lucia's shop, we mingled among the people. My mother wore her black shawl over her head like all the other women; my father pushed his cap deeper over his eyes; the four of us followed them silently, looking down at the ground, feeling naked and unprotected. At that point there was no time to think of fear or panic, no hesitation whatsoever; we knew the moment had arrived when each of us would have to be on her own if something were to happen, no matter how painful. We'd had to promise that to our parents before leaving the attic; besides, we had spoken about it very often.

All of a sudden, all hell broke loose; from the alleys came German soldiers surrounding the procession with pointed guns, while in the forefront the priests were stopped by a barricade of soldiers positioned to shoot if their orders were not followed. "*Halt!*" one of them commanded, raising his arm. "It has come to our attention that among you there are traitors, Jews, and spies. We shall seek them out one by one!" His voice was like thunder shattering in our ears.

My mother brought the ends of her shawl to her mouth to muffle her cry: "*Chaim!*" all caution forgotten, her new identity disregarded. She was ready to grab us and run, terror in her eyes. My father quickly put his arm around her shoulders and said sternly under his breath, "Maria, be still." The sound of that hissing command, and her new name, put her in her place once again.

The German soldiers pushed the priests roughly aside, pointing with their guns at the casket. "*Auf machen!* Let's see what you carry there."

The clergymen protested, "This is sacrilegious!" but, before he could finish, the Nazi slapped him hard across the face. The impact of the blow made us all wince. It sent the padre sprawling to the ground.

"*Du schweinehund!*" the German yelled down at him. While the soldiers were distracted from guarding the rear by what was happening in the front, three men broke away from the formation and ran toward the nearest side street. At once, attention shifted to the attempted escape. The Nazis started to shoot after them.

It did not take long for the troop to return with their captives, pushing and kicking them back to the street while we stood still, at a loss what to do next.

"*Weiter.* Go on, march on to the cemetery. We've caught what we were hunting for. Be gone!" growled the commander like a dog. He turned to the prisoners and grinned savagely at them, already feeling the honor that would be bestowed upon him for a job well done.

Out of nowhere, Paolo appeared at our side. He looked haggard, unshaven, and tired. He put a finger to his lips, motioning us to be silent; meanwhile the procession was on its way again. The priest, helped up by his companions, started to sing a psalm as he tried to stop the blood gushing from his nose and mouth. Everyone joined in.

Paolo whispered to us, "Soon the procession will make a right turn before the woods start. This will be your cue to leave by twos. Others will be leaving too, not wanting to go to the burial, so that you won't be conspicuous when you leave. Go slowly, don't run. You will make your way to the forest. Don't look back. Keep on going. The woods are full of our men. They will pick you off the path."

Before any of us could make a comment, he vanished between the mourners.

Soon after, the woods came into sight. My father gently pushed my mother and Mina out of the line as soon as the procession made the turn. This time my mother was in full control and walked away with my sister, head bent like a mourner's should be, very slow, ever so slow. . . . A few seconds later, he took me by the hand. It was our turn to leave. He whispered to my other two sisters to follow a few seconds later. We never looked back. No one seemed to have noticed or cared, it being natural, as Paolo had predicted, that everyone would not continue to the cemetery. Besides, everyone was still shaken from the previous occurrence—only now they had more to grieve about; not only were they burying the boy in their hearts, they were burying those three men, too.

I walked away holding my father's hand, without thought. I am trying hard to remember what I felt, whether I was horrified or scared by the events that were unfolding. I can't say; it remains a blank, and only my imagination can take over, trying to conceive the state I may have been in. . .I can't recall how we reached the woods, or how long it took, or how we found ourselves in a desolate cabin.

I remember living for a while in that cottage shared by two brothers. One of them seemed to be not altogether, somewhat retarded. I recall that he used to run around like a madman, at times menacing us with an axe, sending us scurrying behind the stairs, were we found a broom closet big enough to hold us all safely till his brother came to coax him away and calm him down.

Children can always find some fun, even if the world is in chaos around them. On one of those occasions when we were scampering behind the staircase, I could not help but notice a filled burlap sack. On one of the quiet afternoons when everyone was napping I went to investigate its contents. Lo and behold! It was filled with hazelnuts. Before I ran to tell my sisters, I made sure to fill my belly. I found a hammer in the closet and cracked them open. When I thought I'd had enough, I went to tell my sisters. They thought I was kidding, but they came with me. Sure enough, they too appreciated the nuts.

After that, ever so often, we found occasion to sneak away and feast on those hazelnuts. It's one of my favorite memories, sitting hunched behind the dark stairwell, giggling with my sisters and eating.

The fun stopped soon after.

The other brother noticed that his sack was getting pilfered. He summoned my parents and gave them a lecture on the meaning of gratitude. My parents scolded us; we had to apologize and promise never to eat those nuts again. As for myself, I did; for whatever reason, when I had a chance to, I ate them or, better said, devoured them, and after that they gave me a stomach ache.

I don't remember how long we sojourned in that place. I do remember something else, though.

One day, watching from the window, our unbelieving eyes caught two parachutes plummeting from the sky into the thicket. The two brothers must have seen them too; we saw them hurrying toward it, the crazy man holding his axe as usual. After a while, waiting in suspense, we saw them return with two men at their sides. The strangers were tall and blond. They were wearing the nylon uniforms of paratroopers. From downstairs came the voice of one of the brothers calling to us. "Don't worry, they are *Inglesi!*"

A sigh of relief came over us. We'd already thought of running up the crawling space above the room, which was a hiding place for us in case the Gestapo came calling. We ran downstairs.

We were informed that the landing had been an accident, that the soldiers were not supposed to be there; their plane had had engine troubles and had to force-land. They assured us they would radio the underground to lead them out of there, so that they would not cause us any trouble.

We formed a friendship at once—a friendship of circumstance, a friendship of a different nature. It was not developed by people who had found a liking for one another under the usual conditions, experiencing things in common, to ultimately come to trust and derive pleasure from each other's company. It was more like an instantaneous bond. Here were men who had come to liberate, to reinforce their belief in freedom, to give their all, to fight for what was right. There was an idealism that emanated from them, and it gave hope to our spirit; at last help was on its way! Humanity was not lost. Mr. Savino's words came to my mind—"the conscience of the people will not stand idly by while our freedom is taken away. Tyranny has never lasted in past history." I think I started to understand what he meant.

These two young men looked so innocent and so young. Nothing had touched them yet. Their zeal was intact. They were going to conquer the world. They were going to show those krauts a thing or two. . .I was thinking of Paolo and the others, the same age and yet already old.

I think often of Paolo as a long-lost brother because he was connected with us through the same experience, by being hunted, having to hide, by feeling pain and having to endure. This does not bear a friendship, but ties you to another; there is a mute understanding that runs as thick as blood.

The only difference between us was that they were free to fight back while we were a people taught not to fight but to achieve. Since we had been dispersed among the gentiles, we had become foreigners over and over again, taught to survive, never having had a chance to settle down in a country long enough to call it our own and learn the art of soldiering and defending what was ours. Wherever trouble arose, we'd been made the scapegoats and had chosen to move on. To start over and over again. Only now, after a new and free generation has been born, after reclaiming our land and proclaiming ourselves as a nation through hard and tenacious battle, have we come to realize that we too can fight, and the bitter question has arisen: arose; *Why did we let it happen?*

I see Paolo standing there—tall, dark, lean, strong, and angry. If we could only have told him how grateful we felt. How often do we dwell upon things that should have been said, feelings that needed to be expressed and never were. We come to reproach ourselves for the silences. Since I was so young, such thoughts couldn't have entered my mind. Yet when I think back, I realize I never embraced him. Why? I never held his hand to show him my trust. He was a person who has left behind the meaning of what life is all about. He was a *mensch*; he did what he did, put his life on the line, not for political reasons, not for gain or recognition, but for pure essence. He had an ideal, a reason, a cause. . .freedom.

The Gestapo caught him returning from an expedition as he often had and volunteered for, smuggling Jewish children into Switzerland, finding safer places for Jewish people they were hiding. His captors wanted to know the secret passages he and his men were using, whom he bribed, and who the leaders were. It pains me till today to know how death was so unkind to him.

It was fun to try to make the Englishmen understand us, and ourselves to understand them. They spoke a little of everything—some German, some Italian—and we knew some English, too. In the evenings at the fireplace, while roasting chestnuts, they sang their songs. For a while, we lived knowing we were creating a memory that would linger on after all this was long past. We were making believe that all was well. It felt as if we had not a care in the world. We had a hearth to be warmed by, food, good friends, and beautiful songs. We were free and high on our own sails. I still know the songs they taught me—"My Darling Clementine" and "My Bonnie Lies over the Ocean" and many more. (Those Englishmen, like Padre Giovanni, still hold a special place in my heart; they remain vivid in my thoughts.)

Shortly after, *il pazzo* (the crazy one) went to town, to the inn. It was the local pastime for the older folks to get together, have a drink, and talk. *Il pazzo* went to quench his thirst with some *vino*. He drank himself into a stupor and began talking nonsense. The people in the inn were used to his drunkenness and never paid attention to his incoherent talks. That annoyed him quite a bit; to make them listen up and feel important, he blurted out the story about people falling from the sky. A few Germans were taking their nightcap near his table and overheard him. One of them understood Italian. He promptly went to his superior, who thought it wise to investigate. The next day, they came driving into the woods in an armored truck full of soldiers.

Once again it must have been fate; the Germans found the two Englishmen alone, without us. They were taking a stroll nearby, while we thought it better to stay indoors. As we heard the rambling of the armored truck, we scampered to our hiding place in the attic. Peeping through wall cracks, we saw our friends for the last time as they were herded in the truck after having been manacled, their young lives played out in front of us.

At times I still think of that incident, which leaves me so sad and a void in my mind. I also think of Paolo and the others, of friendships we had made along the way and lost. Paolo came the same afternoon, as soon as he had heard. He told us it was time to move on again. We were lucky that the Germans had not surrounded the house and made a search. He told us that we were no longer safe there. No one could tell when *il pazzo* would get drunk again and divulge that he was hiding some more people in his house. This crazy man didn't understand that he had put himself and his brother in jeopardy already for having it be known that they had hidden the Englishmen. The Gestapo could have come back for the brothers.

PART THREE

FINALLY, THE SCATTERING of our family began. Within a few days, my parents walked away with Paolo. My sisters and I each went to stay at separate farms, on to different lives. We were not told where either one of us would be going, as a matter of precaution.

I was placed with an elderly couple who owned a huge farm. They employed a lot of people to help with the place and run the compound. The help was made up of older people and minors, who were exempt from going to war. All the young men had been called to the front; some others ran away to join the partisans. The farmhands lived with their families in cottages scattered all around the main house.

My new keepers were parents of two grown children. They had a son in the army and a daughter who had become a nun. They were very proud of the fact that she wore a habit. Not a day passed without a mention of Sister Maria Angela. Her parents depicted her as only parents could. She was an angel of goodness and piety, sweet, warm, and loving.

I lived in awe of the unseen nun. Pictures of her were all over the house. I used to look at them very often, musing over those features staring out of the frame of a black gown covering her young figure, leaving only a cool face with hard eyes exposed, the rest surrounded by a heavily starched coif and bib. I was looking for some warmth and sympathy in those features. I was looking for that sweet angelic portrait over which the parents swooned. They must have been hidden, because they surely did not come through.

I was given Sister Maria Angela's room. She did not need it, since she no longer lived at home and never would again, having chosen the order of the Ursulines. Once in the convent, these nuns take a vow never to leave the cloister, never to see their parents, relatives, or friends again. Ever so often there was a visiting day, but they were not allowed to see the faces of their visitors. They could talk to as to a priest in confession, each on one side of a partition, heard but unseen.

Her room had the same barrenness as the features of her face. I could not understand how her parents could idolize her so. Glancing at her pictures, something cold always gripped me. Somehow I had already made my acquaintance with her: unseen, unknown, I knew there was no love lost between us; we were enemies.

Her room, small and rectangular, was directly under the roof of the house. It had a single bed standing in the darkest corner. The walls were whitewashed and without decoration, except for one solitary picture of Jesus hanging over the bed and a simple cross on the opposite side. The floor was bare, too. A small night table with a large oil lamp stood next to the forlorn-looking bed. The single window stood desolate along one wall; no flowers graced the empty window sill. Yet in all the other rooms one could feel that life was going on. Flowers were on the tables, colorful rugs adorned the heavily polished floors, curtains were hanging from the windows.

I was put immediately to work; I had chores to do. I had to gather wood to kindle the fire every morning at six o'clock so that, by the time the workers came in for breakfast at seven, the kitchen was warm and the coffee ready. All life was lived in the kitchen, the most spacious room of all. The parlor was in use only when the priest, doctor, or teacher came to visit, many a time for weddings and wakes.

The farmers had no gas or electrical stoves; all cooking was done in big, heavy cast iron pots hanging in a big fireplace. I shall never forget the round one they used for polenta, the staple food of the Italian farmer. Polenta is made out of yellow corn meal. You bring water and salt to a boil and gradually pour maize into it, stirring constantly with a big wooden stick (i.e., an undersized broom stick) to prevent lumping. One has to keep on stirring slowly and evenly for thirty minutes or more, till it no longer sticks at the sides of the pot.

Besides making the fire and the coffee, they delegated to me the preparation of the polenta almost every day to me. The farmer's children were quite adept in this chore ,since they were almost born with the know-how, while I had a hard time with it. The sweat used to run down my forehead as I stood over the boiling pot; my hands and arms managed to get burned quite frequently. I was small and not strong enough to properly hold the long club to stir the polenta with. I had to grasp the handle as low as possible with both hands, bringing them very close to the heat. I couldn't readily stop the stirring, least the mass stick at once to the sides of the pot and burn. I was too scared to tell them that I had never done it before, had only watched others doing it, thinking they might find me lazy and unwilling to work. I was often scolded because I had stopped long enough to wipe the sweat off my face and tried to cover my arms and hands with the sleeves of my dress so as not to feel the heat so intensely, and caused the polenta to form lumps. Only much later did I master the tricks one used to become good polenta maker. Yet ever since I left that place, I have never made nor eaten another piece of polenta. That episode of my life returns vividly in my mind whenever I find polenta one of the main courses on an Italian menu.

When the food was ready, I was helped to bring the pot to the table, where the head of the household turned it over onto a large carving board to which was attached a thick string. He would then expertly slice the polenta with the string as soon as the polenta had cooled off and hardened a bit. Usually there were about twenty people at the dinner table. All the workers and their families ate their evening meals together, while breakfast was taken at random whenever one wished to step into the kitchen; lunch was eaten in the fields. The men enjoyed that time with each other—they had lots to talk about, mostly the evolution of the war, the latest events in the lives of friends and neighbors, captures, sicknesses, deaths and births of the surrounding farmers. Sometimes they were somber evenings, and at other times some laughter erupted. Wine was invariably served with the meals, and although watered down since the war to make it go further, it was thoroughly and gratefully enjoyed.

While the men seemed to enjoy each other's company, the women took turns serving them and made sure to replenish their plates; only after the men were finished and left the table, belching and slapping each other at the shoulders, were the women able to finish the remainder of their dinner in peace. The men went outside for a smoke, which they rolled themselves. Cigarettes and tobacco had become a scarcity and were shared. Sometimes they even went for a quick visit to the nearest inn to hear the latest news.

Apparently the women did not mind. No one ever complained. They, in turn, could talk about their affairs and give vent to their intimate thoughts, sending us kids to the other end of the room so as not to overhear something that was not meant for children's ears. After having cleared and cleaned the table, washed the dishes, scraped the pots, and scrubbed the floors (also one of my chores), they all went to join the men in the stable for the social hour. There was no radio (even if there had been, it was forbidden to listen to it), telephone, or television to while away the little leisure hours they had.

Most of the time, though, they finished the evenings in the barn. I did love those evenings in the smelly stall. At first the presence of cows, horses, dogs, flies, and, worst of all, the horrible smell of cow manure, did not entice me at all. I used to excuse myself and go up to my room instead, where I would cry myself to sleep thinking of my parents and sisters, not knowing where they were or what had happened to them. I felt so lonely and so out of place. I had no one to talk to, and no one felt the need to talk to me, other then to tell me what to do. What used to hurt the most was when the children from the other families made fun of me, mimicking my walk, my talk, and at times bumping into me, making believe it was an accident. Signora Maria used to tell me not to mind them. But it hurt nevertheless.

I noticed that the people around me gave me side glances, but no one questioned my presence. Everyone thought that the owner's wife was getting on in years and needed some help around the house; therefore, she must have taken in a poor child from the neighboring town. One would often see strangers coming by, adults as well as children, asking to work for a day or two for food that was badly needed at home.

Signora Maria was known to never send anyone away. They were left with not much, but she always found something to give to the hungry. In time people even came to think of me as one of the poor relations she had taken in. She never said anything to the contrary and let people think what ever they wanted.

In time I became tired of the loneliness of my room and joined the others gathered in the barn. After a while, I even started to love and look forward to those evenings, when they soon invited me to become one of them. I was prodded to join in their singing, and there was loads of that. I was taught how to spin at the spinning wheel. I was even allowed to hold their babies in my arms and, with soothing sounds, get them to sleep when neither the gentle lull of the cradle nor the warmth of the breast milk of their mothers would help.

I also loved to listen to their superstitions about things that came to pass because someone did not believe in the evil signs. How Signora Maria passed under the ladder and would not go around it as she should have done. She had not believed that nonsense and only laughed. Soon after, she'd slipped and broken her hip, losing her first child that way. How Filomena, the daughter of the inn keeper, let a black cat pass in front of her without making the sign of the cross to banish the evil spirit the cat may have brought with her, and there-after never grew as tall as the other girls her age, and most likely would never marry. These stories kept me on guard all the time, lest something terrible happen to me as well. I started spitting right and left when I saw a deformed person. I was crossing myself before a black cat, I made sure never to go under a ladder but around it, and I was petrified when I broke a mirror.

At least these memories bring a smile to my face, and I remember those tales with warmth rather then sadness and tears.

WE HAD REACHED the first week of November 1942. Some sadness had touched the household of Signora Maria. Some of the young men had disappeared, whereabouts unknown—vanished as soon as it became known that the Germans were in need of more men for their labor detail. The few able men and young boys left went to join the underground. The older men who were left behind no longer felt like talking or laughing at dinner, or spun tales of past adventures, outdoing each other in quantities of conquered hearts in their youths. The songs no longer had the vibrancy of those evenings gone by. Nothing seemed to matter. The young men had gone, and now they felt old and worn. Some of those men were their sons, nephews, and sons-in-law. The war, which they had tried to keep from their door-steps as long as they could, had finally reached them, too. They all felt lost and tired, worn out from worry, overtired from the double shift of work load they had to take upon themselves since so much manpower was missing and the fields could not be left idle. The land had to be prepared for the spring. They worried it might not give them enough harvest, because it was impossible to work all the land. They worried because the Germans were constantly demanding more food and came around more often. My new family was fearful for me, and I was more afraid then anyone else.

They came one morning without warning to search for some missing men. For the first time I stood face to face with the *invincibles*. They stormed in, breaking down the front door, posting themselves at once in front of all the entrances and exits, yelling, "*Heraus!* get out everyone." In seconds there were soldiers all over, opening doors, shoving people down the stairs, pushing them out in the courtyard like cattle, pointing their guns, ready to shoot at anyone who dared to make a wrong move. Oh, yes, they were very fast on the trigger, always ready to shoot, to prove over and over who the masters were.

"Where are the young *Schweinehunde?*" they demanded. Some soldiers went into the barn and, with pitchforks, poked through the hay stacks to feel if anyone was hidden in them. Hay was flying all around. It had taken such a long time to gather it and stack it in a certain way for the winter, and now it was all over.

I was caught standing in the kitchen. It never occurred to me that I would ever be in such a situation, face to face with the enemy. Even though the possibility was always at hand, the mind never truly accepted it. It would happen to others, not to me. A helmeted soldier, garbed in a gray-green uniform, with steely blue eyes glaring, looked at me with rifle pointed. "*Du.*"

I backed away.

"You, come here."

I'd always thought, in fact I was sure, that if the time ever came to face a German soldier, I would surely run. Yet I stood there motionless, wondering when he'd fire, or what would happen next. I didn't even understand what he wanted.

My whole family flashed in front of my eyes. I was glad that they were not with me, especially my mother. I still did not move. Impatiently the soldier yelled again, "*Out* with you." He shoved me outside, where everyone else was standing huddled in support of one another. We were all bewildered. The Germans continued yelling, cursing and poking their guns at us.

"Where are all the young men of this place?" the *oberleutnant* demanded, staring at us in disgust. Some of the men had been caught in their underwear and not been allowed to dress; some others had come out in bare feet; some of the women were in their nightgowns, shivering in the cold. He planted himself in front of us with spread-out legs and hands at his hips; there was no question that he meant business.

Signora Maria's husband stepped forward. A small man with gray hair and a long mustache a little yellowed above the lip from smoking a pipe, he replied without a tremor in his voice, "All the young men were taken away by other Germans long ago." He did not bat an eye.

At the same moment, a soldier came from the main house holding a picture in a frame in his hands, which he handed to the officer. The *oberleutnant* grabbed it away from him and asked who it was by showing it to the crowd and pointing at it. "*E il mio figlio!* It's my son!" Signora Maria cried out.

The officer seemed to have been satisfied looking at the uniformed young man posing in the photograph. "We will be back if we find out differently. We are warning you." He threw the picture to the floor, shattering the glass of the frame into a million pieces. He ordered his men to gather some food and stock and whatever else they could lay their hands on. They did, breaking and throwing around anything they did not want. They regrouped at his command with their loot, boarded their trucks, and drove away—but not before telling us that, when they returned, they would check all our papers.

Some women had fainted and had to be revived by their men. "Let's go into the house and recuperate from this ordeal," Signora Maria said softly, kneeling beside the broken picture frame of her son, tears streaming down her face. She picked up every single piece of the broken fragments and placed them in her apron before she too entered the house. She did not allow any of us to help her gather the broken pieces.

I was still trembling and could not stop. She took me in her arms and whispered to me, "I won't let anything happen to you. You are safe with us. The underground will see to it," and held me close to her till I stopped shivering. "Let's get dressed and have something warm to eat," she said to the others. "If anything is left, that is, and then try to clean up this mess." The whole house had been left in shambles.

From then on, everyone lived in fear of retribution. Sooner or later, the Germans would find out that some of their men were no longer serving in the army but had gone AWOL to join the partisans. Meanwhile life had to go on. We lived in the shadow of another Gestapo visit.

December arrived, and Signora Maria did not let the tradition of Santa Lucia go by, nor the preparation for Christmas festivities go unobserved.

In some European countries, as in the United States, Santa Claus, or Sanct Nicholas, is celebrated; in Italy Santa Lucia and comes much earlier then Christmas. She too is never seen; she just leaves presents for all children, for the ones that were good all year, that is. In turn the children prepare themselves by being on their best behavior for weeks in advance so as to become worthy of her gifts and not to be passed over. The gifts were not elaborate in those days. Not much was to be had in the stores. Toys were mostly handmade.

Santa Lucia thought of me, too. She brought me a little white chick. It was just a few days old. I woke up to its pipsqueak next to my bed. It had been placed in a basket and left with a note that said, "Cici is all yours. She needs much loving care from you. She will be your pet." I couldn't believe it. I carried that basket around with me the whole day. I showed my present to everyone. Finally in the evening Signora Maria came to me and said, smiling, "Olga, don't you think it is about time to take Cici out of the basket and put her in the chicken coop with all the other chickens?"

"But I thought Cici was all mine!" I answered, almost crying at the idea of having to give her up.

"Of course Cici is yours, but she belongs in a place where she can roam and grow. Do you think the basket is a proper place?" She laughed. "We'll put a ring around her foot to tell the difference among the others."

I hadn't thought of what to do with her. All I knew was that I'd been given something alive, something warm to love and to care for. I didn't want to let her go. I realized, naturally, that Signora Maria was right, that I couldn't keep the chick in the basket in my room forever. I went to the chicken coop and let her out, but not before a ring was put around her foot. I visited with her every day, dressed her up with ribbons, notwithstanding that, as soon as I put them on, they came off. It did not matter. I gave her extra goodies each day when I went to feed the chickens. I was sure Cici recognized me as her mother, because she started to run after me whenever she saw me. I became a mother hen. I measured her; I weighed her to make sure that she progressed. I spent all my free time with my newly acquired friend. I did not want to insult Santa Lucia and kept the name given to the chick, but I gave her a second name, "Colombina," "Little Pigeon," as Mr. Savino used to call me.

A FEW WEEKS later, the nun in whose home I was living arrived unexpectedly. The convent had closed its doors. The mother superior, afraid the Germans would overrun the cloister and harm the nuns, had decided to dispense for the time being with their cloistered lives and send them home to their families; those who had none were sent to other countries.

I got up at dawn that day as usual, to prepare the fire; while immersed in my chores, I suddenly felt I was not alone in the room any longer. I went on with my work, thinking all of a sudden of Sister Maria Angela. I had a feeling she was there. I turned around slowly to find her standing outside the picture frame, watching me in cold silence. She seemed etched in stone, the black tunic that enveloped her figure making her look taller and thin; tired from the long journey, she had dark circles under her eyes.

Every object in the room seemed to recede into the background. She took hold of the whole ambiance as if she were a force larger then life.

Our eyes met: We transmitted to one another a mutual understanding of dislike without uttering a word. We didn't know each other, yet we knew. . . .

Signora Maria came into the kitchen, throwing her arms up, first shocked, then delighted, to see her daughter standing there. She ran toward her, embracing, and hugging her over and over again, then let go, embarrassed. She had forgotten whether it was against the rules or proper to come so close. She hadn't touched her daughter since she had made her vows ten years before; from then on, she hadn't belonged to them any longer. She had been so proud and happy when her daughter announced her decision, but saddened when Angela decided on one of the strictest orders. She never thought of having to give her up so completely.

Signora Maria bent down and kissed the cross that was hanging from the sister's belt, took her hand, and directed her to a chair near the fire. "Rest a while. You must be exhausted." She looked at her daughter, wondering if she was happy, wondering if Angela ever thought of her life before the cloister. "Maybe, after a good breakfast, you'll lie down for a while," she added.

Signora Maria remembered my presence at last and, with great excitement in her voice, said, "Olga, how do you like this surprise? My Angela, here in the flesh!" She clasped her hands together and, without waiting for my response, turned once again to her daughter. "I forgot to introduce you to Olga. I wrote to you about her, and the last time we visited with you we explained all about her. Remember?"

So, I thought, she already knows all about me.

I was still standing at the fireplace, feeling happy for Signora Maria. She was so excited, her face flushed, her eyes afire with joy at seeing her child. Lately she'd had nothing to be happy about, and this made up for it. Sister Maria Angela, seemingly untouched, unfeeling, without a sign of warmth, sat on the chair, acknowledging all her mother's fuss with a thin smile. I don't think her mother noticed that coldness as I had. I curtsied and said, "*Buon giorno.*"

She sat there, still not letting her eyes off me. "Didn't you forget something?" she asked me. As I had anticipated, her voice was pure ice. I looked at her questioningly. "Well, don't just stand there. Where are your manners, child? Come here and kiss the cross!" she demanded.

An astonished look passed over Signora Maria; then, somewhat embarrassed, she looked away from me. She knew she had mentioned to her daughter the fact that I was a Jewess hiding out with them. What had gotten into her?

What would have been natural to do, to please Padre Giovanni—I had kissed his rosary many a time—did not come easily or voluntarily to me for the nun. Since no one else was around to put me in danger, I brazenly said, "I don't kiss crosses."

I excused myself and was ready to walk away, but Sister Maria Angela was not ready to be discharged like that, nor would she forgive me so easily for not having bent down to her. She would show me and let me feel her displeasure and authority. "We shall see about this," she said. "From now on, you'll do what you are told. My mother must have spoiled you."

With those last words, she got up and glided stiffly out of the room. I stood there listening to her skirt rustle.

Oh, yes, Sister Maria Angela was going to teach me and there was nothing anyone could do. I had, all of a sudden, become her ward.

For starters, she moved back to her room, insisting that I shall share the room with her. Her parents told her that it would be better for both our privacies that I should move to her brother's room. "Olga would have a nice bed for herself. In your room, there is just one," they pointed out.

The nun wouldn't hear of it. "Olga should be happy to have a roof over her head. No need to spoil her by giving her her own room. We'll put a cot in my room for her."

No one could talk her out of it, and so I became her roommate, like it or not. She also let it be known that she would take over my education, since I did not attend school with the other children. It was thought wiser to keep me home rather than risk a lot of questions about me on registration forms.

While I wasn't too happy with the new arrangements, I had no other recourse but to play along; at least I had Colombina to talk to about my mishap, and that made me feel better.

One morning, however, when I went to feed the chickens as usual and visit with my pet, I could not find her. I ran around the chicken coop, frantically looking and searching for her. Since there was no sign of her there, I ran into the yard—maybe she had strayed away or was looking for me. But I could not find the chick anywhere. Tears welled up in my eyes, and something cold gripped my throat.

"Cici," I called out. "Colombina, *pee-o, pee-o*, Cici, here." There was no response, no sign of her.

I was standing disconsolate in the yard, feeling as lonely as ever, when Sister Maria Angela came into sight. "Don't you have work to do?" she asked coolly.

"No, not right now. This is my free time, free to visit with my chick as usual!" I started to cry, not being able to contain my unhappiness any longer.

"You stupid girl, to cry over such frivolous nonsense." She turned to go back to the house. Halfway toward it, she looked back at me with an ugly smile on her face that for one moment seemed like a devil's victory. "By the way, I had to remove your silly bird from the others. You spoiled it so much that it started to fight with the other chickens and became a nuisance." She pronounced every word slowly and distinctly, to see the effect it would have on me. "Therefore I had to give it away. You should be pleased it went to people who needed food and are not as lucky as you!" Before I grasped what she had said, she was gone.

I was too proud to show my pain to the nun or complain to Signora Maria. My crying stopped at once. There would be time for tears later. I clenched my fists until the knuckles turned white and the nails dug themselves into the skin of my palms. It felt good to feel the added pain. I'll show you, I thought, I'll show you, knowing of course that there was nothing much I could do to hurt her in turn. But it made me feel better. At least, for a while, something had made me happy in the midst of madness—another moment and cherished memory to be stored.

Sister Maria Angela continued the routine of her cloistered life even away from the convent. She prayed, she fasted, she did penance and prostrated herself on the floor to show how humble she was. The only difference was, that while in the cloister she had done all that in the privacy of her lonely cell, now she did it with me. She drilled prayers into me. She dished out punishment upon punishment on me for whatever reasons she could devise—because she felt I hadn't prayed fervently enough, or long enough, because I'd been too frivolous in my thoughts on the few occasions I gave an opinion, or maybe because I was daydreaming too much. She always found an occasion.

Among many chores which I disliked, I also had quite a few that gave me pleasure, like feeding the animals or walking the horses around (the few that the Germans had allowed them to keep); she made sure that those chores were given to someone else. She found different chores for me to do, less pleasant ones.

I couldn't keep up with the many misdemeanors she accounted me for. Sometimes she made me lie down on the cold floor in the freezing room half the night, face down, reciting all the prayers she had taught me. At other times I had to kneel for hours while she questioned me about the catechism she had drilled into me. At times, she thought me impertinent: For that great sin, I was not allowed to eat breakfast and given only a meager lunch and half my dinner. She told me over and over again that all this was for my own good. I had become spoiled. I had to do penance because I was not of her faith, and she did not want me to go to purgatory when I died.

Thank goodness she did not know how little not eating affected me; if she had, she'd have made sure to punish me with something more severe. I'd had worse times behind me, though. On those days when I went hungry or felt hunger pains, I tried very hard to remember how much worse it had been when I really had nothing to eat.

I don't quite know why it made me think of Yom Kippur. My parents used to fast. They spent the whole day in temple. After a while, when us kids could no longer sit quiet, we were allowed to stay outside with our friends and play. My older sister would take us home to eat (children under thirteen did not fast). I'd remember the sounding of the *shofar* and my mother's explanation for each prayer. I had been very young then, but somehow I remembered. The sound of the ram's horn in the evening meant that the holiday was over, the fasting had ended, and with it my mother used to say, "Goldale, a new year is starting and a new beginning, a new page in the book of life, and all sins forgiven. Isn't it marvelous how God is giving us always another chance to be good?" I'd nodded, feeling happy that she'd taken me into her confidence and talked to me as if I were a grown-up. But as hard as I tried to think it out, I didn't understand what she meant about pages in the book of life.

We always had other family members and friends coming home with us to break the fast. I loved listening to the grown-ups talking about how the service had gone and how everyone had fasted well. How, some years before, some of them had had a headache towards the end, but how this year everything was fine. How I wished to grow up fast so that I too could partake with the grown ups and tell them how I had fasted. . . . My mother loved to talk to us about Jewish traditions.

I could never understand the hatred that Sister Maria Angela bore toward me. It was like an obsession. The more I tried to stay out of her way, the more she seemed to seek me out, to find fault and unleash her wrath upon me.

Maybe she thought she had found an opportunity to be of service to the church by preparing me for Christianity, hoping that my parents would never come back to claim me. Or maybe all that anger was just a cover-up for a real reason that I couldn't guess and that, most likely, she too may not have realized. I was sure that she was starting to care for me quite a bit; as a nun, she had sworn to leave all her worldly feelings behind, to fill her heart and soul with Jesus and the church only.

She may have felt that she was betraying the allegiance she had given. Maybe I had brought back forgotten images; had she not become a nun, she could have had a child my own age already, to teach things to, to love, and to share. Was she fighting, through me, the arousal of feelings that she had had once upon a time?

As I understood from the gossips of the others, Sister Maria Angela had once had a lover, and because he did not want to marry her she'd become a nun.

One night I thought that I had the proof that she cared about me after all. The wind was blowing fiercely, finding its way to our room, making it colder than usual. I was cold, moving about on my cot to find a little warmth under the thin blanket she allotted me. I was too proud to ask for another cover; she would only have told me I was spoiled. At times I went to bed almost dressed, to keep warm. Thinking I was asleep, she got up, tiptoed downstairs, and brought up a down quilt, which she put gently over me, then stood looking at me, stroking my hair, and left. The coziness the quilt brought made me fall asleep at once. At dawn, when it was time to get up, the quilt was gone.

A while later, she relented and let me use her brother's room.

I thought I would never want to think about her ever again. Most of the time she does escape my memories, but oddly enough she comes back to my mind on Yom Kippur, and especially on Hanukkah.

When I watch my children excitedly unwrap the gifts I bought them, I can't stop thinking and wonder, Are these gifts going to be as important and make them as happy as Colombina made me? Will they remember a particular gift in years to come that made them extremely happy to hold, as I have? It maybe unfair, needless to say, to think this: These are different times. . . .

WE HAD SURVIVED another winter, and with it, Christmas. Celebrating Christmas with the farmers has made a lasting impression on me. Every Christmas since, I have relived that occasion.

One week before the holiday, a manger was built in the barn. A beautiful life-sized baby carved from light wood was set on a bed of straw and hay, wrapped in a blanket. It looked almost real. Its arms were spread out as if it wanted to welcome the whole world. Beside the baby, Mary and Joseph were kneeling. They were carved life-size, too, and their clothing was painted on . Before him, standing, were arrayed the three kings bearing gifts: those were more like statues. Tall candles in heavy wrought-iron holders flickered and shone warmly upon the scene.

Every night until Christmas the villagers flocked into the stall to admire the display and sing carols. When the holy night arrived, I was taken along to midnight mass. Horses were harnessed on to the carriages and the children seated in the back, covered with hay to protect them from the cold. It was one of the most beautiful and memorable hayrides of my life.

Jingling out on to the unpaved roads toward the village, we saw other carriages join us. After a while, we had a whole entourage following along as if on a pilgrimage. Every wagon had an oil lamp hanging in the back; looking up and down the road, one saw in the stark night a row of little flickers swaying back and forth, moving along the rhythm of the trotting horses. The majestic trees alongside the winding road seemed to join hands with neighboring outstretched branches. The night was silent, interrupted only by the solemn chanting of prayers coming from the riders. I looked up into the most splendid firmament, sprinkled with dancing stars. The big North Star was pointed out to us; it was leading the way. After a while the singing stopped. I felt such quiet, such stillness around me, such wellness, such comfort.

Have you ever heard the silence? Has the stillness ever had anything to say to you? At times, it scares me with what it has to say, and at some other times it gives me such comfort, I've learned not to be afraid of it anymore. I often seek its company, for it replenishes me.

It took an hour to reach the square—I wished it could have gone on and on, everything had acquired such beauty, such immense tranquility; all seemed well; all seemed loving, as the words in the carols declared.

Inside me, a little voice arose, asking if this feeling was alright. I was enjoying something that was alien to me, a festivity we did not partake in at home. I thought of my parents and sisters. Where were they? Did they celebrate *Natale,* too? Tears formed in my eyes. I didn't know anything anymore. I wanted so much to enjoy the night with everyone and not feel different. I think the child in me won. I lay back and looked up at the sky and told myself my parents wouldn't have minded, and that all of them were alright.

We were greeted by the ringing of one lonely bell—the only one left. Once there had been five. The other ones had been confiscated by the Germans to be melted down and made into artillery pieces. It is amazing to think that man can reach such greatness in his art and yet sink so low when he is out to conquer.

The bell was calling the people one and all to gather, to reaffirm the birth of their savior. The priest, dressed in holiday surplice and red tunic, was ushering his flock into the large church lit only by candles.

Every church in Italy is a museum. The altars are built of the finest marble, covered with silk and velvet coverlets embroidered in gold and silver thread, and appointed with silver chalices hidden from the enemy and only displayed on such rare occasions.

The church displayed beautiful carved crosses; they adorned the top of the altar. Heavy oil paintings covered the old walls. They were lucky the Germans had not yet confiscated those, too. Slim pews were lined up at each side, leaving a carpeted aisle open for the worshippers to kneel on and wait for communion. The priest, with the altar boys at his side, moved down the aisle to distribute the Eucharistic sacrament to the worshipers, who came forward one by one to receive communion. I was not included in this ritual; I was too young.

The ceiling of the church was painted with angels forming a circle around a child, holding a crown over his head. The walls were dominated by large stained glass windows depicting the various stages of Jesus' life and those of his disciples. Later on, those windows, and the ceiling, came crashing down in the shelling.

The majesty of the church was enhanced by a choir that filled the air with the most beautiful rendition of "Ave Maria." I knew I was a

Jew, and once again I wondered if it was all right for me to be there, though I had no other choice. Once again I felt guilty to find such pleasure in partaking in that solemn celebration. My eyes joined glowingly with the others. I tried not to linger on too long on those feelings. I decided once again to forget all the turmoil; after all, the moment was there.

With spring coming on, the victories of the Germans were manifold. Paolo appeared with my family one evening. I looked up, and everything, all those lonely nights, vanished when I saw them. I realized how much I had missed them.

No one was surprised to see Paolo—apparently he was known to them. The peasants saluted him, hugged him, and patted him on his shoulders, shaking hands over and over again. They asked questions—mainly if he knew where any of their sons were.

I had leaped up toward my family standing quietly at the door. Now the farmers quieted down and looked quizzically at Paolo. Caution immediately dampened the excitement of his arrival. A few youngsters were sent out to the road to keep watch for any approaching soldiers, strangers, or vehicles.

"*Mamma!*" I cried out, "Papa, Berta, Mina, Elena!" I hugged and kissed them, holding their hands as if to make sure they were really there, calling their names over and over again, still not believing my eyes. My mother covered me with kisses, her embrace so tight, telling me, "I'll never let you go again."

"We missed you," my father said.

"How very much you'll never know," my mother added. "My, how you have grown in these past months!" She held me away from her to be able to take a better look at me. Her eyes shone with pride. My older sister Berta had filled out a little. She was fourteen and had grown, too. She did not look so scrawny any longer. She was pink-cheeked and blossoming into a nice-looking girl. I couldn't talk. I was almost choking from the emotion.

Paolo, who had been waiting till our emotions settled a bit, said, "Now I will introduce you to these lovely people." Signora Maria in turn shook hands with my family and, with a warm smile, invited them to sit at the table. "I didn't realize that our Olga had such a lovely family. She never talks about you."

She asked the workers and their families to go to the barn, realizing that something serious must have occurred to have Paolo come there with my family. She didn't want the others to be involved in anything. "We'll join you later after we chat with Paolo a bit," she told them.

"I'll give you something to eat. You must be hungry," she said as soon as everyone else had left. I finally took hold of myself and started to make myself useful.

"Mamma Maria," Paolo said, "take that worried look from that lovely face." He went toward her and lifted her in his arms. She started to giggle like a young girl and blushed.

"You rascal, you always managed to sweep me off my feet."

She planted a noisy kiss on his cheek. Paolo laughed, putting her gently down. He told us that this was his second home. "I love these people as if they were my family. They took over when I lost everyone." He was the one who had persuaded them to take me in.

After teasing her a bit and making small talk with her husband, he became serious. "Well, now, I will tell you what is happening." It had occurred to me too, that something had gone wrong; otherwise they wouldn't have been there. "The underground has decided it is time to move this family on. A plan has been made to get Mr. and Mrs.

Fermi out of Italy." It seemed so odd to hear my family called by their new names, I had almost forgotten. "We have been lucky to provide them with false papers. They will be going to Switzerland. Any day now the Germans will return to your farm. No need to endanger you any further. Besides, the farmers hiding the others felt they could no longer take the chance. In time it will become increasingly more difficult to keep the peasants from talking.

"We were lucky to get false passports for the parents. They will be able to travel as citizens to the border, where they will be met by our people and taken across."

Paolo was pacing the kitchen floor. My eyes filled with tears. I was disappointed—I'd thought we would be reunited again.

My father got up and came over to me. "Don't cry, Olga, it's a good plan. Berta will travel with us to the border. When her mission is over, she'll come back and, with some luck, you children will be able to remain together until all this is over. This war can't last forever with the Allied forces moving in. Hopefully, we'll find a way to send for you soon."

Paolo nodded. "Mr. and Mrs. Fermi are no longer safe around here. Their accent will surely give them away one of these days. Tomorrow morning, Berta will go to the train station with her parents. She knows everything she has to do. She will accompany them because she will be the speaker in case the border control asks questions on the train regarding their traveling. Meanwhile, if you people don't mind, the other children will remain here and wait for her return. I hope you won't mind putting them up. Will you?"

Paolo turned to Mamma Maria with questioning eyes. It had never occurred to him to ask them first. He knew that, no matter how short the stay would be, it would put them further into danger.

Without blinking an eye, Signora Maria said reassuringly, "Of course not. You know we'll go along with anything you think safe for these people." Yet you could tell from her looks that she was obviously worried.

"Berta will be back within twenty-four hours. After that, they will be picked up by a truck and taken to a convent. I really think that it will be better to leave all details for when Berta returns," he concluded, and sat down, his mission completed. He looked at us, his eyes lingering on each one of our faces to try to remember us thus; he was leaving now for good. He had been called upon to perform other, more dangerous tasks. He hadn't mentioned them, not to worry anyone. An overwhelming sadness came over him, and he put his head down. He felt very tired .

Did he have any premonition that this would be his last goodbye?

Signora Maria had quietly prepared coffee and put it on the table with thick slices of bread and cheese. No one spoke. What was there to be said? Our hosts were thinking of the new burden. Even though it would only be for a short while, no one ever knew what was going to happen next. They hoped not too many questions would be asked by the people around them.

Paolo had regained control. After drinking his coffee, he bade us all Godspeed and walked out with Mamma Maria.

That was the last we ever saw or heard of Paolo, till the news reached us of what became of him. He, like so many others, died tortured by the enemy without having given away a single soul.

We were left alone in the kitchen. We had nothing to say to one another, yet I felt an unspoken conversation going on—questions flying across the table.

"*How have you been?*"

"*How have you been treated? Are they good to you?*

"*Did you have to work hard?*"

I looked at my parents; they were exhausted. I had almost forgotten those days when we could laugh together. It seemed inconceivable that there had *been* those days, when they had other worries, like my sisters' school grades, their lack of motivation whenever those grades were not up to par. Oh, and I couldn't memorize the alphabet. They used to complain about how we managed to get all that dirt under our fingernails; and mother scolded us about our eating habits. Quite often we heard, "Why do you children eat like vultures? Where are your manners?"

Those lessons had seemed the ultimate in importance in our lives, yet how meaningless they were at that moment. I wondered, looking around the table at my family, would the Gestapo care that I knew the sequence of the alphabet now? I even thought of chicken soup that my mother used to cook, with lots of fat on top. Mother did not know about skimming the fat off the top—that would have been sacrilegious. Every Friday, the house acquired that holy smell of chicken soup full of *kneidlach* (I've never been able to make them like hers) and a plump chicken on the table, with *schmaltz* to spread on the challah. The house smelled of home-made bread, two loaves made into braids on the table, covered by a beautiful hand-stitched cloth.

Signora Maria came back into the room. She looked sad and had red, swollen eyes from crying. "Paolo is gone," she said simply. She lifted the big apron tied around her waist to wipe her eyes. "I can't seem to stop crying. I love that boy like my own," she stammered. "Now we must get some rest, we have difficult days ahead of us." More tears came to her eyes. This time she didn't bother to hide them, letting them flow freely, though every so often she swished them away with the palm of her hand. She busied herself with the clearing of the table. She needed something to do at that moment. She motioned to me to stay put. "No need to help me, I'll be done in a moment." We sat quietly watching her.

"Olga," she said after a while, "you won't mind giving up the room to your parents for tonight? You girls will sleep in the barn. There's lots of hay to make you comfortable." She continued to putter around while her husband quietly puffed at his pipe. He never said much, but he always was there at her side. Now he said, "I'd better join the others before they wonder what happened to us. I'll see to it that they leave soon." He shook hands with my parents, wishing them good luck, and left toward the barn.

"I told Sister Maria Angela to get some blankets for you children, and to freshen up the room for your parents," Signora Maria said after a while. "Mr. and Mrs. Leoni, you must be tired."

Yes, they were. We were all tired. They had a long walk behind them. It was showing. Mina could hardly keep her head up and was falling asleep at the table. Elena and Berta were constantly trying to subdue their yawns.

Sister Maria Angela entered quietly. She had not been present when my family arrived, since she had chosen to stay in her room that night to fast and pray. She had changed from her black habit into a housecoat and moved to her brother's room.

She did not look so austere that evening. I thought I detected a softness in her voice and behavior. She bowed her head to everyone as I introduced her to my family. She already knew what had happened. Signora Maria had taken a moment out to go upstairs to inform her.

"I'll show you to your room," she said to my parents, "and you, Olga, take these blankets, and off you go, girls. It's late. I saw the people leaving the barn." She handed me the covers and watched us go out the door.

My father called after us, "Don't forget to say a special prayer tonight! Hopefully you haven't forgotten the ones we taught you."

I turned to look at Sister's face. She had raised her eyebrows. Was she hoping I'd forgotten them? She would have been right. I was taught the *Schmah*, "Hear Us, O Israel." I only remembered the first line. Later on, Berta recited it aloud with us, and I remembered it once again. We added a few more words to it: "And let Mama and Papa cross the border safely tomorrow, and keep us all safe."

"Amen," we answered.

Sleep did not come easily after all, that night. We huddled close to one another, talking about what Berta had to do with my parents the next day. We gave her courage, assuring her that everything would go well—after all, we had come so far. . . .

We reminisced for a while about the past, about those short years we had already lived; for some, they might have already encompassed a whole lifetime, while for us they were only the beginning. We had stored up so many feelings, fears, and thoughts that should have never occurred in our young lives. Would we ever grow up alright? What mark would they leave on us?

There were so few *memories*, especially for me. I had not much to remember. Events had started to fade away, and only yesterday's were vividly with me—and those did not seem to cheer me up or comfort me. I lay shivering, listening to my sisters, who were talking of the old good days and the new experiences they had gone through while we were apart. I wanted to make them mine, too.

Finally, we all fell asleep. It did not matter that the hay was not as fresh and did not keep us warm as Signora Maria believed. She was wrong—the hay was not clean, someone had urinated on it, and it smelled. Cobwebs were hanging from each corner of the barn; I was imagining all those spiders at work spinning webs to trap their prey. Flies were racing between the cows and us.

I FELT A GENTLE tap on my shoulders. My mother was bending over me, calling me gently. What a nice dream. I wanted to dream on. But the touch became stronger, I had to wake up, to let the dream go. I opened my eyes. It wasn't a dream at all. "Wake up, my love, wake up." Mother was so close to me, I flung my arms around her. She whispered, "it's time to say good-bye." She took me in her arms and cuddled me to her. It seemed so long ago that she had done so. I promptly snuggled closer to her, trying to make myself as small as possible, wanting to stay there forever. I remembered how very often I used to crawl into my parents' bed early in the mornings when everyone else was still sleeping and find a comfortable spot between them, to fall asleep all over again feeling secure and protected.

"I should have done this more often," she said, mussing my hair. I could have gone on sleeping that way, but she shook me gently again and pushed me softly out of her embrace.

"Sleepyhead, there's not much time left. I too would love to sit here with you some more, but everyone is waiting for us. I just wanted to have these few more minutes with my little one alone."

The sleepiness vanished. I was fully awake. I embraced her again tightly. There were so many questions I would have loved to ask her, but I held them back; there was no need to add to the distress of that moment. This embrace, the feeling of her, had to last for whatever time it would take till we saw each other again. I would have to remember her thus. She must have had the same thoughts. She untwined my arms from her neck and looked silently at me, then, placing both her hands around my face, kissed my forehead and my hair. "We missed a lot, you and I," she said simply. I looked at her. She had grown thin; small nets of wrinkles had formed under her eyes, and there were deep furrows on her forehead. Two hard lines had carved themselves into the sides of her mouth, making her look older and harder, not as I remembered her—smiling, with rosy cheeks. Her hair had thinned out a bit, and it was all gray now. She had it combed straight back and twisted it up in a bun. She did not look like the mother of young children. She picked off a few stubborn straw stubbles nestled in my messy hair. She was trying to smile; she would cry later as I would. The now was for me and her.

"Mamma—" I hesitated, then continued— "*Ti voglio tanto bene.* I love you. I. . .I am sorry for all the troubles I caused when I was little." There, I'd told her. I was relieved. I'd thought about it for such a long time. I had told myself that, when I saw my mother again, I would let her know I had missed her so much.

She got up and lifted me up with her. She smiled that old smile of hers that I knew so well. "I know, Goldale, I know. You were so little then." (She still called me by my old name; She couldn't get used to "Olga".) Two big tears rolled down her cheeks. She straightened out my clothes, folded the blankets, and took my hand. "Let's go. Everyone will wonder what happened to us. We'll go and have something to eat. We'll both feel better afterwards."

We looked around the barn one more time. Then we left. I asked her to go in by herself. I felt I needed that cry. I wanted to be by myself, needed a few minutes alone, wanted to memorize those few moments with my mother. I was not yet ready to meet the others and make believe it was a good morning.

Mother went into the kitchen while I sat on the outside steps. I looked around the courtyard; it was quite early yet—I could still see a few stars fading in the dawn. They had lost their luminous look against the lightening sky.

I pulled my knees tightly up to my stomach, put my arms around them, and rested my chin on my knees. I started to ponder my tomorrows. I felt lonely and desolate. I remembered that I too wouldn't be here for much longer. I had finally gotten used to the place, to the people, the work, Sister Maria Angela. Now I was thinking about the convent we would be going to. I had never seen the inside of a cloister. It always made me wonder what went on behind those quiet walls. We'd used to live around the corner from one. Now I was to spend some time there. Sister Maria Angela ought to be pleased: Maybe I would ask her what went on in a convent. I'd rather have stayed on the farm. Tears came to my eyes again. The unknown scared me. what if my parents would never come back? Where was Switzerland, and how far was it? What would we do without parents? It frightened me to remain alone with those feelings; I rushed into the kitchen to be with the others.

The kitchen looked gray, the dim light from an oil lamp standing on the table hardly brightening the surroundings that morning. The shadows it threw along the walls made the day look even grimmer. My entrance apparently did not make a difference, because the five people who represented my family seemed in a trance. They were automatically eating what Signora Maria had placed in front of them. She was the only one who noticed me coming into the kitchen. She smiled at me with sorrow in her eyes. She too understood what my family and I were going through at the moment. She motioned for me to sit down at the end of the table, where she placed a plate of cheese and bread, and a cup of boiled milk, in front of me. I sat down without making a noise and ate silently so as not to disturb the stillness of the hour.

Breakfast seemed endless. Wasn't there anything to be said, I thought, in these last moments of togetherness?

As if my father could read my thoughts, he stood up. "It's getting late. It's time to go. Let us pray, and give thanks for having been able to come thus far. Let's thank God for having found these people to help us and place themselves in great danger to save us. Let's ask God to bless this house for having sheltered us and my little one, and that he should keep on watching over us all." He sat down again. We bowed our heads in silent prayer, each asking for a miracle, while my father chanted the appropriate prayers in Hebrew.

Signora Maria knelt in a corner, crossing herself, looking up at the picture of the Holy Mother that hung at the far corner of the kitchen. "Mother of Jesus, we are all God's children. Help us in this hour of need!"

She brought my mother's shawl and father's cap; without a word, she shook his hand, then kissed my mother's damp cheeks and handed her a small basket filled with food covered with a linen napkin. "Just a little something to eat on your journey. You won't find any food along the road," she said simply and turned away, drying her tears with her apron.

We all rose and rushed toward my parents to give them our last embraces. "God bless you all, my children. We'll be together soon," my father said hoarsely, placing his hands over our heads to give us his blessings, while my mother held us tight.

"Be good, my children. Remember what we taught you," she finally managed to say.

Berta stood there as white as a sheet, lifting her arm to wave to us, "*Ciao!*" That's all she managed to say, then turned briskly and walked out, with my parents following behind. The door shut behind them. A thirteen-year-old child had been given the responsibility of taking her parents to safety. What a world!

I never realized until that moment what a resounding finality a shut door can mean. Would it ever be opened again by those people who had just left?

We ran to the window to watch them disappear out of the court-yard like thieves not wanting to be caught in the act. We wept silently as we stared through the windowpanes long after those shadows had moved on.

Signora Maria had stayed in the background, busying herself, not wanting to intrude in our pain. A knock at the front door brought us back to reality. We looked startled and quickly wiped our tears away. Our hostess did not seem surprised to have such an early caller; she nodded to us and went to the front parlor to open the door.

A gentleman, of medium size and well dressed, stood at the entrance. He took his hat off and introduced himself as Signor Lucca.

"I hope you were expecting me, Signora," he said in a soft tone. "It is quite early. I was afraid of disturbing you," he added apologetically, twirling his hat in his hands.

"Oh, no, don't worry," she assured him. "I was notified of your arrival." She wiped her hands on her apron and shook his extended hand. "I did not have the chance to inform the children, nor explain why you have come." She took the hat and asked for his coat. "Please take a seat." She turned toward us and told us that he had important matters to discuss with us. She excused herself and left the room.

"What I have to tell you," he said, "will come quite as a surprise, but let's sit down first, and then I'll explain." He waited till we were seated; after having given us ample time to look him over, he sat down opposite us. He asked our names and then, as an afterthought, went to the door, opened it, and looked up and down the hall. "I wanted to make sure that no one is spying on us to overhear our conversation. One has to be alert at all times these days." He sat down opposite us.

"First of all, greetings from Paolo." Our hearts jumped when we heard Paolo's name mentioned. We already felt more comfortable in the presence of this stranger. He knew Paolo, and that made it all right. But before we could ask him about Paolo, Mr. Lucca continued, "I know you must be wondering why I am here and not he. Paolo has to stay in hiding for a while. The Gestapo is looking for him. He did not want to be tracked down coming here, and endanger all of you. Since I am not yet known to collaborate with the resistance, I was the best choice to become your guardian from now on. The farmers with whom you were staying had become afraid to keep you on any longer. Luckily, we found a way to send your parents to Switzerland. Eventually we will find a way for you too to join them. Meanwhile, we've found a safe place for you children to hide out for a while." He got up and started to pace up and down the floor as he unfolded the future of our lives. He didn't know that we already knew about the convent.

"I will take you to a convent where my sister is the mother superior. The nuns have agreed to hide you there for as long as it will be necessary. You will be staying here until your sister returns. If everything goes according to plan, she will be back by midnight. I shall leave now and return at dawn with a milk truck. We'll ride along with the milk man, as his helpers, bringing the milk kegs to town for delivery."

As soon as he had finished, Signora Maria came back into the parlor. "Well, did you tell the poor lambs the whole story?" she asked. "I want you to know," she lamented, turning to us, "I'll miss you. You have become dear to me like a daughter." She started to cry and took me in her arms. It saddened me too, to have to say good-bye to this lady whom I too had become fond of. I felt sad to have to leave this place that I had become accustomed to.

Mr. Lucca took his coat and hat, and bade us good-bye, instructing Signora Maria how we should be dressed in the morning for our journey while she accompanied him to the door.

It was to be a long day. No matter what we set out to do, the hours passed ever so slowly. Our thoughts were constantly with my parents and Berta. Sister Maria Angela finally came down from her room. Silently she went about her chores. Mina and Elena whispered to me that they did not like her: How could I have stood her for so long? Annoyed, I whispered back, "What choice did I have?"

Mina pulled my sleeve. "Sh! She'll *hear* us."

She made me think of the nuns we would be living with at the convent. Would they all be like her?

I asked permission to take my sisters to the barn to show them the horses. I proudly exhibited the expertise in milking a cow that I had finally mastered. I recalled when, at first, the cowhands taught me how to do it, how repugnant it felt to touch those hanging things. I used to fall off the stool each time I tried to sit on it. When that happened, the cow moved and made the pail under it topple and spill all the milk. I would be scolded for that and called stupid. The cow's tail used to hit me in the face at times when she swung to chase the flies away. In short, it had been a disaster, though after a while, I mastered the art and in a merry fashion learned to pull gently yet firmly at those pulsating udders. I derived a mischievous pleasure in watching my sister's disgust, how they recoiled at the sight of me milking a cow. They would not touch the animal, let alone try to feel one of the udders. They could not understand how I could perform such a ghastly chore.

Once again my darling sisters had forgotten, of course, that I'd had no choice in the matter. I hadn't been on that farm for a vacation and had to do as I was told, working alongside everyone else, disregarding my age. I soon understood that I had to be good, that, once taught something, I had to perform better then the other children, though they worked much less than I did. After all, they belonged there with their parents. I made sure that no one had anything to reproach me for. My keepers knew I was a Jewess, and the others thought of me as a foreigner, and no one was going to get a chance to attribute a misbehavior to me. I was constantly on my guard.

In the course of the day, I found out that my sisters had not had to deal with those feelings. The farmers they were staying with had not needed the services of my sisters. One family had no children; therefore, they adored Mina and kept her as if she were a princess. Elena had been with people who needed her as a companion to an elderly sickly mother who could hardly see. Elena's job had been to read to her, help her to get around, listen to her chatter, and keep her occupied so as not to impede the others from going about their chores.

We were left to ourselves most of the day. Signora Maria did not want me to help her in any way; she wanted me to keep my sisters occupied and try to enjoy the last day on the farm.

Finally, the evening approached. Signora Maria served us dinner before anyone else. "I think it's better this way. We don't want the others to ask too many questions. Besides, you seem exhausted and scared. I understand the worry about your sister's return," she said while serving us. "After dinner you'll go upstairs and lie down. You will all sleep where Olga slept. I put up some cots. I'll wake you as soon as Berta arrives."

After dinner she kissed us and pushed us gently out of the kitchen. We were glad that we did not have to join the others; we would have felt awkward under their scrutiny. The long day had tired us out at last, so that it did not take us long to fall asleep.

THE NEXT THING I knew, someone was waking me up, telling me it was time to get going. It was already dawn. I jumped up, startled. Didn't I want to stay up and wait for Berta's return? Had she come back? Was everything alright?

I didn't have to wonder any longer, since it was Berta who woke me up. I just sat on the bed looking at her. She was really there!

"Come on now, we must hurry and get ready. Signor Lucca will be here soon. We can't let him wait. Let's go, sleepy head." She pinched my cheeks as she'd used to do whenever she teased me; I hated it then, but now I embraced her, loving it. Way back, everyone pinched my cheeks when they came visiting my parents and saw me. I had rosy pink, round cheeks, a real invitation for everyone to pinch as they told my mother, "My, has the child grown, and look at those cheeks!" followed by another squeeze.

Berta had picked up on that, and whenever she wanted to upset me, she used to mimic them. "Oh, my, get a hold of those fat cheeks! Let me have a little pinch!" It used to infuriate me, and I'd run straight to my mother, whining and complaining about it. Now it seemed such a welcome touch. I smiled and did not let her go. "Oh, Berta, you are back, you are back, you are here! Pinch me some more so that I can believe it," I laughed, offering my cheek to her.

"Oh, no, you'll start whining at once and run to the others to complain that I hurt you." Immediately I realized it wasn't mother I could run to and bowed my head in sadness. "None of that. I know what you're thinking." She became serious. "Mama and Papa got off all right. Everything went well. Let's concentrate on *us* now."

"All right, children, here I am with your clothing." Signora Maria had walked briskly into the room. "We must hurry. The milk truck will be here shortly with Mr. Lucca. There is no time to lose!" She handed us old pants, shirts, jackets, and heavy work boots. By the time we were dressed, we really looked like experienced laborers. "Mr. Lucca will be quite proud of you. You look the part, which is of the utmost importance. You look like the milkman's helpers."

She tucked in my clothes a bit, then helped my other sisters; she had to make sure we looked exactly right.

Just then Sister Maria Angela came flouncing in, garbed in a white robe and a night cap gathered at the edges and almost covered her forehead. I was used to seeing her like that in the mornings, but to my sisters she appeared as if she were from another world. They stopped doing what they were doing; they put their hands over their mouths to keep from laughing. Then dead silence came over the room while she stood looking at us coldly, holding her rosary beads in her hands.

"I think we have forgotten our prayers this morning," she said. Olga, let's kneel down and show your sisters how we say our prayers." She let herself down the floor. She handed me a rosary and started to chant the Ave Maria. I was not about to antagonize her and did as I was told. My sisters stood watching us with open mouths. After the Hail Marys were over, she recited another prayer, asking Jesus to watch over us. As soon as we were finished we got up. "Keep the rosary as a remembrance," she said.

She kissed my forehead and made the sign of the cross on it; then, as she was offering me to kiss the cross hanging from her beads, Berta grabbed me. "You must know that my sister is Jewish. You have no right to make her pray your prayers. We have ours." Sister Maria Angela turned toward the door and managed to snap, "You ungrateful infidels!" and marched out.

Berta shook me by the shoulders and in indignation demanded, "How *could* you? Did you forget what Papa and Mama said? You shouldn't forget who you are!"

I freed myself from her grip and cried out, "It's easy for *you* to say! I had to do what she ordered me to. If not, she would *punish* me. What was I to *do?*" A flood of tears rushed to my eyes. I wanted to tell her that all those prayers did not mean anything to me, and that, anyhow, I didn't understand any of them, but sobs shook my body, and I could not utter a word.

Meanwhile Mr. Lucca had arrived, and Signora called us down. He was dressed as we were, in heavy trousers and boots. He wore a cap over his eyes. This time he did not look like a well-to-do gentlemen, as he had on the previous day, but like any other peasant in that area. "Let's be off. There's no time to waste," he said seriously.

Signora Maria quickly handed us some bread and cheese with a cup of hot milk, which we gulped down in a hurry. She stood wiping her eyes and kissed me over and over again. "Remember us, my child. God be with you," she said and propelled us out the door.

Another door closed, another opened. How many more doors would we have to go in and out of? How many would shut us out, for our and someone else's safety? And how many would lock us in?

❈ PART FOUR ❈

We walked briskly after Mr. Lucca toward a truck waiting in the courtyard. It was already getting cool. The beginning of an early fall making itself felt. We pulled our worn jackets closer to our bodies; as we reached the van, I turned around for a last look at the house and waved to Signora Maria, who was standing forlorn at the door, watching our departure. My eyes wandered up to the window of what had been my bedroom. I thought I saw a figure lurking behind the pains. I could have been mistaken, but it looked like Sister Maria Angela.

I never saw them again. When the war was over, we went back to look for them. We found out that Mama Maria and her husband had died within a short period of one another. Their son was killed while trying to join the partisans. No one knew what had happened to Sister Maria Angela.

Mr. Lucca sat in front with the driver while we found space in the back between the milk kegs. The engine started. We drove away. We took the same road as we had taken that Christmas Eve. How very different it felt now. We were driving towards the unknown, towards a new chapter—once again, another station.

We drove through country roads and side streets, trying to avoid highways and busy intersections for fear of being stopped and having our papers checked. The ride took a few hours and was quite bumpy. We had a hard time keeping the milk kegs from falling over us. We kept them out of harm's way with our feet propped against them. Not a word was exchanged. Whatever questions we wanted to ask would have to wait. If we were lucky they would be answered soon enough.

The driver seemed to be mute; he made it a point never to get acquainted with his passengers. It was easier to remain strangers and not get involved. That way everyone remained a nameless, faceless entity; it would also be easier to forget them. Otherwise, his task of transporting human cargo would have been impossible. He never even asked whether his risk was worthwhile, or if anyone ever made it. What would have been the point? He had lost enough relatives and friends to mourn over; it would have become unbearable to grieve over these strangers too, so he had resolved to keep his distance and detachment.

We were tense and pensive. We whiled away the time by concentrating on the countryside. As we came closer to the city, we noticed some shelled houses standing like ancient ruins. We passed bombed-out towns; it was the first time we had come upon such sights, and we could not believe that such destruction was possible. Living in the country, away from the city, the shelling had not hit us yet. We saw work groups bare-handedly clearing the shelled areas. "Oh, mio dio!" Berta exclaimed. She took my hand and held it tight. "Look, they're wearing band around their sleeves with the Star of David on it! They're being guarded by soldiers!"

I didn't understand and looked back at them.

"They're *our people*, don't you see? They're *Jews!*" Berta said with difficulty. She rose from her cramped position and pulled at Mr. Lucca's sleeve. He turned around. "Mr. Lucca, those are Jews that were caught, right?"

He didn't have to answer. His pale and anguished face said it all. "Will they eventually die?"

"Maybe. Some will, and some may survive, escape, get shot. Who knows, my child? Now we have to concentrate on saving *you*," he added harshly and turned around.

We saw other people disconcerted by the scene, scavenging around, trying to retrieve some of their salvageable property. They came with sacks on their backs, they came with carts, wheel barrels and old, beaten-up bicycles to transport their few belongings to some other place they had found refuge in, until another shell sent them running to another shelter. Some would just go on living among the rubble that remained of their homes. They hung burlap curtains around the crumbled walls. Their whole life was falling apart in front of them, they barely were surviving themselves, they had lost everything; how could they think about those workgroups under surveillance? They hardly noticed in their state of shock. All they knew was that they might die from lack of food, from exposure when the cold set in, especially the older ones and the wounded.

Mr. Lucca turned to us again. "Remember that, in times of need, surprisingly enough, everyone develops a genius in the art of survival. Meanwhile they too are paying the price!"

He didn't know why he had said that to us. We didn't know if he wanted to encourage us or felt he had to say something. Anything. He was suffering, too. His country was falling apart. He saw his people broken in spirit and body, joylessly and aimlessly wandering from rubble to rubble, pondering their fate, questioning how they would survive without food or shelter. Their leader had made them such grand promises. Those words, those speeches—they were impressive. I remember listening to the sonorous voice of Mussolini coming over the radio, accompanied by wild applause, jubilant greetings, and always ending in patriotic songs.

What had happened? Where was the prosperity they had been assured? After every speech that they listened to on the radio, Signora Maria used to mutter, "Traitor, you sold us out! You will burn in hell!" and cross herself, while her husband tried to calm her down and caution her. I was too young to understand any of it.

It is amazing how people fall over and over again for men who give beautiful speeches, swelling rhetoric, and if the time is ripe are even compensated with leadership. How gullible people are for want of more and better. The human mind has soared to such heights that it can only lead us to destruction; it has mastered the unthinkable without being in charge of where that will take us. We keep on listening to well-meaning promises. Will we ever learn? Thank God that, with it all, we still have a great wealth of hope; because of it, I believe, there is still a chance.

We had arrived. The truck turned into an alley and stopped. Mr. Lucca jumped out, came around the back of the truck with the driver, hauled down the kegs, and told us to get off and lend a hand. We lugged the kegs across the street and halted in front of an old house that looked like a school; behind it rose a tapering structure that looked like a steeple of a church. The building was surrounded by a wall that ended at a gate. Before we could ring the bell to make our arrival known, the gate swung open to let us in.

A nun came out of the portico. "Welcome. We have been waiting for you. Come with me—I'll show you to the kitchen." She led the way. She was short and plump; two dimples formed on her rosy cheeks when she smiled. She was swinging her hips like a boat on a wave-tossed sea; it made her look comical but very pleasant. She seemed to be a jolly sister. It took us only a second to recognize a warm and happy human being. Not at all like Sister Maria Angela.

I gave a sigh of relief. This nun was humming to herself while she led us around the building. She put us at ease at once. "I am Sister Antonia." Her words came like bubbles. Her voice was warm. We were at the entrance of the kitchen from where an aromatic smell of baking rose to our nostrils. The kitchen door was wide open.

"Sister Margerita, I have a delivery here," she called out to a figure hovering over a stove. We entered a huge kitchen big enough to hold an entire army. We looked about. A huge stove took up almost the whole length of one wall. Big cast iron pots covered the burners. A long wooden table filled the middle of the room.

"God bless you folks!" Sister Margerita called out, covering a steaming pot before she turned toward us. "Oh, Lord, how we've waited for this milk. All our children in school have had to do without for so long!" she sighed. We had to look up at her; she must have been six feet tall and was very thin. Big feet protruded from the long black skirt of her habit. The white bib contoured a long, olive-skinned face from which two dark, sad- looking eyes greeted us.

The driver lifted the kegs on to the opposite end of the table and handed a receipt to the nun. She glanced at it quickly, signed her name, and handed it back to him. "You are not our usual driver," she said. Then she remembered, realized the stupidity of the remark, and put her hands over her mouth as if to shut it up. Of *course* he was not the usual driver—*he* had been paid off not to take the route that day, and to let the other man drive for him, in order to pick us up on the way. How foolish of her—we all looked at the door automatically, hoping that no one else had overheard her and become suspicious. We had learned never to be off guard, never.

The driver turned around, tipped his cap, and without a word disappeared. Sister Antonia broke that awkward silence. "Let's go to our mother superior. She is expecting us."

"Yes, let's," Mr. Lucca said, still annoyed at that slip of the tongue. Thoughtless little things like that could sometimes end in disaster after painstaking hours and effort spent to save lives.

Apparently he knew his way around, because without waiting for Sister Antonia, he had already crossed the kitchen leading to another door into the corridor of the convent. It was a long, carpeted hall with dark wooden walls waxed to a sheen. Paintings of famous popes and saints covered its length. Our steps sank deep into the carpet, giving us a feeling of floating rather then walking. It had been a long time since we had walked on rugs; we did not allow ourselves to step to hard on them, so we tiptoed after Mr. Lucca. He stopped in front of a broad double door and knocked. "Enter," a clear voice called out from inside.

We walked into a spacious study. From behind a massive mahogany desk, a tall, slender figure arose and, light-footed and smiling, approached us. "*Buon giorno*, Giorgio!" she said in a melodious voice. She embraced Mr. Lucca, quite obviously thrilled and happy to see him. "How are you, how have you been?" she asked, eagerly examining his face. "God, am I happy to see you!"

"*Bene, bene, grazie*," he answered laughingly. He had taken his cap off and planted a kiss on her right cheek and then on her left. "Ah, you look marvelous, Benedetta! You look like a rose." He swooned over her, bringing a blush to her cheeks. Hers was a world where no compliments were given; all nuns were alike.

Her eyes were deep and dark, her skin pale and fine. One could have called her pretty. I noticed her hands—long, beautiful fingers, well manicured and delicate. She wore, like all the other nuns, a simple wedding band.

She pulled him down on the seat next to hers. "Tell me about Mother and Father. I have not had any news from them lately. All visits have been canceled for the time being." A cloud seemed to pass over her face when she thought of her aging parents left alone. But she soon dismissed these thoughts and held his hands in hers, eager to hear news about the outside world that she had given up so long before.

It had taken her years of painstaking sacrifice and penance to achieve complete detachment from the outside, even though she had always wanted to become a nun. As a child, she'd used to love to go to mass with her mother every day, while her friends preferred to go elsewhere. Then she had chosen parochial school with the nuns while her friends went to public school. She had always felt so safe and peaceful with the sisters. Their serenity was what she enjoyed the most. The outside world was always in chaos. She had not known how hard it would be to become a nun, that it was a life of sacrifice and self-denial. But with patience and an immense love of Christ, she had to come to love her chosen path.

"Mother and Father are quite well, even though they are getting on in years and it's showing. They have their usual pains and aches. I have insisted of late to hire a housekeeper full time so that they wouldn't be so quite alone. My work has not allowed me to visit them as often as before. I didn't want to jeopardize their safety because of me. These times don't make it any better for them. I have moved them to the countryside for safety. Now, enough about us," Giorgio said seriously. "Here, meet your new charges."

He introduced us to her. At once she resumed her position as Mother Superior. After the formal introduction was over, we took our seats opposite her. Mother Superior measured us discreetly while I let my eyes wander about the room. Her desk stood in front of a big sliding door leading to an outside patio that overlooked a beautiful garden surrounded by a high wall, excluding almosot all sound from the outside world. Vines were trying to take hold of the bare bricks. The sunlight poured a warm brightness into the room. One wall was filled with shelves of books; on the other side she had erected a personal altar, a life-sized Madonna and child stood in a niche, at her bare feet a big vase of fresh white lilies, reaching upward as if to touch the child. Two lit candles stood watch on either side.

A small wooden pew sat before the altar for Mother Superior to sit on when she needed to contemplate, or pray when she needed to be alone and ask for guidance. She was responsible for forty nuns, although just then there were only twenty-five. The others had chosen to return to their native lands when the dispensation came allowing them to leave the cloister for the duration of the war, for their safety.

"You will be treated as if you were nuns," she said after a long silence. "This brings with it a great burden." She spoke slowly and distinctly, to make sure we understood every word she said to us. "You will live inside the enclosure, where no one else has ever been allowed to enter. You will abide by the silences we have." (Those proved the hardest of all.) "In time," she continued, "you will learn all the rules of this order. You will have assigned nuns to tutor you in different subjects. We can't neglect your education, can we, now?" She smiled, winking. "You will also learn to sew, cook, and become helpful where needed. You will follow us for prayers in the chapel at matutine and vespers. You'll eat with us in the refectory, a privilege to you children only—no one other than the monsignor, who comes to give us communion every Sunday and performs mass on the holy days, has ever been permitted to eat with us." She explained a few more rules by which the Ursuline nuns abided by as well. "You will have free time and be able to while it away with the sisters in the recreation room, or do whatever you may feel like." She paused for a second to make sure that she still had our attention, and then went on to tell us about the do's and don'ts.

"While you are allowed access to almost everyplace, you will not be permitted to enter the nuns' sleeping quarters. Your dormitory will be in another wing. . . . Now, a few very important musts which you will have to make your priority," she continued, just when I thought we had heard everything. It started to sound like a recital. My head began to spin. "I know this is a lot to absorb," she said, as if she knew how I felt, "but it is very important that you understand the precarious situation we have put ourselves in. We have children coming here from the orphanage. They are being taught by our sisters. You are *never* to be seen by them. *Never!*" she emphasized. "During those days, you will remain in your quarters,where you won't be seen by them. You'll be given work assigned to you there. I must stress, that if only one child sees you—" she signaled the "one" with her right index finger to give it more importance, while her voice acquired a tone of urgency— "you will be inviting a disaster. It would be a catastrophe if anyone were to ask who you are and find out you are hidden here. This would surely reach the ears of our enemies, and this convent would be subject to a search immediately. You very well know the consequences. All the rest, you will be told while we go along." She paused to think of whatever else she might have forgotten to tell us. "Oh, yes, there will be no light after dark because of the blackout. You'll make sure that all your windows are covered by the dark blinds hanging above them."

I had thought the ten commandments were long and a bit much, but these regulations topped them all. We looked at each other in bewilderment. What if we forgot some rules? Mother Superior sensed our consternation. "Now, now, children, it won't be so bad. Don't look so unhappy. Just remember how lucky you are, while other children like you are being deported and never heard of any more." (We were to hear that remark quite often). "You are safe here with us. If God wills it. Come, cheer up!"

She got up and turned to her brother, who had been sitting quietly all that while. "Giorgio," she said, "these seem to be nice children. Everything will go well. We have to trust in God."

Mr. Lucca rose, too. "I hope so. I wished we could have found another solution. I would have preferred it!"

"I know, Giorgio." Mother Superior embraced him. "We all have to do our part. We thank the Lord for having chosen us to do his work," she concluded softly, holding his hands in hers once again.

"*Arrivederci*, children. Things will work out. This war won't last forever. I only beg you all to be careful."

"And you, too," Mother Superior added.

"Don't worry about me, I'll do my best not to get caught. I am needed too much. For once I feel alive. I am not just a lawyer sitting behind a fat desk, listening to those Nazis giving me orders about how to run my affairs. I was despondent and afraid of my skin for much too long. I'll see you soon." He kissed her again then turned to us once more.

"I'll be coming ever so often to see you. Hopefully I will have some news from your parents." He kissed us on the forehead, and then he was gone.

For a moment the nun stood looking sadly at the closed door, and then she sighed deeply. "God keep you safe," she whispered. "And now to you children. First of all, you must get out of those terrible clothes. I will ring for Sister Antonia. She will show you to your quarters, where you will find all you need." She rang for the sister, then, as a second thought, added, "I would like you to know that this door is always open to you. Feel free to come and talk to me any time you are troubled or need to have a chat." She smiled and patted Berta's head, then lifted up my chin. "This must be hard, especially for you. You are the eldest."

Before she could continue, there was a knock at the door. Sister Antonia came in. "Ah, sister, here you are!" she greeted her gladly. "Please show these children upstairs. I'll see them again later when they meet the rest of the sisters."

We rose from our seats, thanked Mother Superior, and with a curt-sey followed Sister Antonia out. It seemed as we had sat in that room for hours. My body felt stiff, and my bones were aching. I hadn't real-ized how tense I'd been all that time. I had not moved a muscle for fear I would do something wrong. We trudged after Sister Antonia like lost sheep.

We were led onto the same corridor we had walked along before. The convent was enveloped in a deep silence, as if no one lived behind those closed doors we were passing.

Later we learned that the nuns did everything in silence. They had learned to go about in humility; only in the recreation room could one hear them talk and laugh. We were to learn what Mother Superior meant by silences. No one was allowed to talk at meal-times, or after vespers, till the following morning. We were to learn the signs the nuns made to one another when they wanted something at the table.

We came upon a large staircase leading to the upper floor. We followed like shadows after the gliding sister. All one heard was the rattling noise from the vibration of the wooden beads making up the rosary that hung from her belt. We climbed up the stairs; involuntarily, I started to count the steps. Five, six, seven, eight. . .we came to a landing where Sister Antonia stopped for a second to bend her knee and cross herself in front of a statue of Jesus with long brown wavy hair, in white-and-blue robes. We passed by, hardly looking up at it, unsure of what we were supposed to do. The staircase divided to right and left. We turned left. Eight more steps, and we reached the upper floor. We continued down another hall, which led to our dormitory, a room neatly lined with rows of beds on each side, and whitewashed walls. Two plain windows allowed in some light. Above each bed hung a crucifix. Each place had a chair and commode standing next to it—no frills, no superfluous bric-a-brac to interrupt the evenness of the surroundings. Yet so many young girls had passed through and lived there. It had been a boarding school before the war. No impression of them was left.

"You choose any of the beds you wish to sleep in," said Sister Antonia invitingly. "I'll be off now. I will be back later to pick you up and show you around. I suggest you rest a while first."

Without fuss, we fell on the beds we happened to be standing nearest to and let out a long, loud groan. Yes, we were tired. We took her suggestion and fell asleep without much ado.

We awoke startled by the sound of a bell. It rang a few times, as if to summon us. We had slept through lunch and most of the afternoon. Sister Antonia had come to call us for lunch, but, seeing us so deep in sleep, decided we needed the rest more than the food. She knew that, when we had enough rest, we would wake up by ourselves.

We jumped up; for a moment we had to think where we were.

"Oh, God," Berta exclaimed. "We must have slept the whole day! They must think we're lazy. Let's hurry up and find a bathroom. We'll get dressed and find the sisters."

The bathroom was next door; it encompassed five stall showers, five wash basins, and five toilets. Pretty nice, I thought, until I took a shower. The water was like ice. No matter how much I turned and twisted the knobs, the temperature did not change. It seemed to become even colder. I heard Berta screech from the other shower, "Shit, there's no warm water!"

"Hey, you'd better watch your language. Do you know where we are? This is a *nunnery*," Elena muttered through chattering teeth. "My shower has cold water, too. Mina, how is it by you?"

Mina had jumped in and out as fast as she could when she realized that there was no warm water. "Well, I guess this will do for now. It's freezing. Let's get out of here." Berta grabbed a towel and disappeared into the bedroom.

Later, we found out that we would have to get used to cold showers. There was only cold running water. The nuns did not allow themselves the luxury of whiling away their time under a warm shower; therefore, neither could we. Besides, we were in the midst of a war. For the moment we had forgotten that a cold shower was better than none, as we had many a time done without washing properly when we were in hiding.

We found new clothes for us, enough to choose for size: dark blue jumpers, white blouses, long white cotton stockings, and blue shoes. We looked prim and proper, uniformed as in a private school.

No sooner had we dressed and straightened out our beds we heard a knock at the door. Sister Antonia had come for us. "Oh, how lovely you all look." She clapped her hands in sheer delight. "You must thank Sister Regina, our seamstress, for these lovely outfits," she hinted. "Do you know you have slept through the whole day, girls?"

"We are very sorry, Sister," Berta told her.

"Never mind, you must have needed it. Let's go and join the sisters for dinner. The bell has already rung to summon us to the refectory."

We went downstairs. The nuns were already seated. I felt that all eyes were upon us. Unconsciously, I bowed my head. I felt hot flushes creeping up my face. We took our places at the end of the table where Mother Superior directed us.

It was a very austere room, containing a long plain wooden table with a simple bench on either side. There was a big wing chair at each end—one for Mother Superior, the other for guests, such as when monsignor would stay for dinner, or a visiting mother superior from another convent. There was no tablecloth, no china dishes, but wooden bowls and plates. Sister Margerita, whom we had already met in the morning, was handing the food through the window from the kitchen. The sisters took turns in serving. We learned that, once a plate was filled with food, everyone had to eat what was on it, and it had to be finished. There was never leftover food; only enough was cooked, neither too much nor too little.

One day, pumpkin soup was served for lunch. I had never eaten pumpkin soup. I did not like the smell or the taste of it. I left it untouched, figuring I'd like the second course better. My bowl was not removed. I was given to understand that I had to finish what was in that bowl before anything else would be served to me.

I figured that no one ever starved from skipping lunch. My sisters did not like the soup either, but they managed to gulp it down. I tried and tried, but it would not even go as far as my mouth; the thought of it made me gag. I gave up. When everyone was finished and the after-meal prayers had been recited, I was ready to file out with the others and join them for the afternoon recreation when Mother Superior stopped me and said, "Olga, by now you must have realized that we do not waste food, nor do we indulge in what one prefers to eat or not. Everyone eats what is placed in front of them. That includes you." She was speaking softly, yet she sounded quite stern. "You will sit here until you have finished your soup. Only then will you join us."

She departed swiftly, leaving me to struggle with the uneaten soup. I sat down again, tried to give it another go. . . but the aversion only grew stronger, and I couldn't bring myself to eat it. I got up, walked around the table, hop-scotched back and forth, listened to the clatter coming through the kitchen. I looked out the window for a while at a few finches that had remained behind, the others having already flown south. They were hopping around, hoping to find some stray crumbs between the pebbled walks of the garden. I wished I could give them my soup. I went back to my seat, pushed the bowl away, folded my arms on the table, and rested my head on them. I dozed off dreaming of chicken-noodle soup, of another time when I hadn't finished what was on my plate. My mother had reproached me, too.

"Goldale, don't take so much food on your plate—you won't be able to finish it all. Take a little less next time." She'd taken the plate away from me and eaten what was left. She would never throw food away.

I woke up realizing it had only been a dream, and that my pumpkin soup was still there. The sisters, returning for their evening meal, found me still sitting in front of the soup. They said grace for the fresh food they were about to receive, but I had yet to contend with the old one. By then, what had been a liquid had hardened, and a crust had formed on top of it. My sister Berta, who was sitting next to me, kept nudging my arm, motioning that I should eat. She even managed an audible whisper: "You are an idiot, making a big deal over nothing. Eat it and get it over with."

Dinner ended, and everyone filed out once again without me, and as if I weren't there; the lights were switched off, the door closed, and I was left behind in the dark. Tears began to run down my cheeks. I started to feel sorry for myself and bemoaned the predicament I was in.

After a while, the noises that had kept me company coming from the kitchen stopped. Stillness surrounded me, and I grew afraid. I reached for the spoon and gulped down, without taking a breath, what had once been soup. I can't remember the taste of what it was like, all I remember, afterwards, I hardly made it upstairs to the bathroom before I threw up all over the place, which, of course, to make the punishment worse, I had to clean up—I didn't want anyone to know that it had all come back out, and maybe being scolded for that, too.

After the evening meals, the sisters congregated in the recreation room. It was a lovely place to relax in. It had big alcove windows from which lace curtains were loosely hanging. A black grand piano graced a corner; usually Sister Eugenia performed at the keys. When she played, she transported each of us to our own fairyland for a while. A harpsichord stood next to the piano. Sister Regina would accompany the pianist and Sister Lavinia join with her violin. There was no telling what the trio would create. Lots of books printed in different languages sat on shelves fastened to the other walls. Not all nuns were Italians; there were quite a few foreigners among them. Even while relaxing, no one sat idle; some would mend socks, knit gloves, or sew something. We were taught how to sew at those times, and to mend so perfectly that no one could tell where the damage had been. I loved those evenings, because I would then be able to talk to anyone I wanted, listen to their favorite stories, or play a game or two with my sisters. At times I took my homework along, where I could get help and explanations. Each and every one became a mother to us, each telling us about the various temptations in life and how to judge the result of one's actions or, better yet, how to avoid them. Some things I understood; some others were too incomprehensible for me—I was too young; nevertheless I loved to listen and felt very grown up that they included me as if I were an adult.

After recreation, the vesper bell would summon all to the chapel. Each sister had her place, and so did we. We sat in the last row. At first we did not know what to do, it was all so new and awesome. As time went on, we were taught the prayers and were expected to participate in their devotion. In time we felt quite at ease kneeling on the wooden benches. It became natural to pray with the rosary and kiss crucifixes. At the beginning, we clung tenaciously to the Hebrew prayers Berta remembered and made us recite with her in the morning and at night before we went to bed, as my mother used to do with us at home. After a while, they became all mixed up; it was easier to recite the prayers the nuns taught us. I enjoyed listening to the sisters when they prayed and sang in unison, their voices rising in chorus, sweet, sad, and joyous. We were taught to sing with them, and began to believe that Jesus had died for us, too.

When prayers were over, the sisters filed out quietly in procession to their dormitory, where each disappeared into her barren cell in silence until matutinal prayers were said, and silence descended again till breakfast ended. We, in turn, would go to our quarters where we could read or talk some more with one another.

Sister Matilda was assigned to Mina and me to teach us literature, grammar, history, and math. My other two sisters, since they were older, were taught at a different level by another sister in a different room. We studied catechism together, since all four of us were considered beginners (I was the only one with an edge over the others, since Sister Maria Angela, at the farm, had crammed all she could into my head).

We took our lessons upstairs: The outside children were using the classrooms downstairs. I used to hear their voices reaching me in our makeshift classroom, distracting me from my work because I wished I could join them. I would have liked to be in their midst, join them in their games, laughter, and songs. I would have liked that very much; it wouldn't have made me feel so isolated and different from the others. I even fantasized having a girl friend and had imaginary talks with her.

In the afternoons, when school was over for the children and they had left, we had the run of the house once again. At that time, we had our chores assigned. We took turns with the work alongside the nuns—at times, helping wash the floor in the chapel, dusting the pews, polishing the candlesticks and making the brass door handles shine that adorned all the hall doors and the ones of the confessional chambers. On other days, we were helping in the kitchen, cleaning vegetables, peeling potatoes, washing and drying dishes, pots, and pants. We were taught how to make our own starch and iron shirts.

Sunday was a day of rest, a day when mass was held at midmorning, a day of reflection and discussion for the nuns, and for us to do as we pleased without much supervision. That gave us a chance to take care of our personal needs. We washed our hair, made sure our clothes were in order for the coming week, wrote letters to our parents which were never mailed. We had found out from Mr. Lucca, who came visiting us from time to time as he had promised, that my parents had made it safely across the border into Switzerland, but it wasn't wise to post letters—if they fell in the wrong hands, they would have given us and the nuns away.

More and more, life regained a sense of normalcy. We began to accept the sisters as our family; they in turn took us lovingly into their fold, affectionately calling us their "little novices." The only thing that detracted from the serenity of the cloistered life was the constant rumbling of airplanes reaching us from the distance. It made us apprehensive. Mother Superior explained to us that the Allied forces were bombing important points the Germans were holding; we were not to worry, the bombs would not hit our area, the convent was not centrally located. After a while we grew accustomed to the sounds and did not give them any thought. Life went on. . .the season changed from fall into winter, and with it another year passed. We were approaching the spring of 1943; I had reached the ripe old age of eight.

The persecution of the Jews was still in full swing, more adamant then ever, a last hurrah to rid Europe of the last of us. His henchmen always found ways and means to haul them from their hidden places. The Gestapo dragged them to their headquarters for questioning before they were deported, more dead then alive after going through torture, because the Nazis wanted to find out where else people might be hidden, and who helped them. They were beaten and clubbed like rats. Many committed suicide rather than give in or endure more punishment. All this was revealed to Mother Superior by her brother when he came visiting. He never wanted us to be present on those occasions when he gave his report, but Berta always insisted that we had a right to know what was going on on the outside. She used to tell Mr. Lucca that, even though we partook in the life of Christians, we were a part of those Jews, and that our parents had told us when parting that we had to remember who we were.

ONE NIGHT A jolting sound assaulted the stillness, waking us from our sleep. Sirens screeching from alto to basso over and over again, piercing the darkness. It seemed that all hell had broken loose, that the heavens had opened up, letting the thunder and lightning come crashing down. In horror we realized that it wasn't thunder or lightning but bombs raking the area. A moment of abrupt silence followed, making us believe for a second that it was all over. Then the explosion—a shuddering blast the likes of which no human ear should ever experience; a tremor, shaking beds, falling crosses, shattering glass that finally gave way under the impact.

"*Down*, kids, under the beds!" Berta screamed. We threw ourselves to the floor and did as we were told. I could not resist looking up. The window was broken, through it I saw flashes from erupting fires where the shells had hit the buildings beyond the convent walls. The fragments shot up, sharp pieces of metal cutting the air, shredding all things in their radial path. No more could those convent walls keep the world shut out; finally, it had reached the solitude of the nun's domain.

The door to our room flew open. Sister Antonia rushed in holding a lit candle.

"*Children!*" she screamed. "Quickly, grab a blanket. We have to rush to the cellar before another blast blows us up!" She lifted the candle to be able to see better through the poor light it gave out. She saw the wrecked window. "*O, mio dio!*" she crossed herself. "Children, are you alright? Anyone hurt?" she cried out in terror, trying to see us. She cupped her hand around the candlelight, which had started to flicker dangerously in the cold air pouring in through the broken window. She saw us crawling out from under the beds and gasped, bending down to touch us. "Are you alright?" she asked again, searching for my hand to help me up, since I made no motion of standing. I was petrified. Berta stammered, "Y-yes, yes, I think so."

"Thank God. For a moment there. . .never mind, let's go." She grabbed the blankets off our beds and handed them to us, pushing us toward the door.

We met with the other sisters in the hall, rushing down the steps in formation as usual. Some were holding lit candles and others oil lamps. The electricity was off. The nuns were clad in their nightgowns, identical in their appearance at night as in the day time—gray tunics with black cloaks over their shoulders, hoods covering the ruffled night caps that concealed their shaven heads. We reached the cellar, where cold air hit us and made us shiver. In our haste, we had forgotten to put our slippers on; thus we were standing barefoot on a cold stone floor.

"Wrap the blankets around yourselves, you'll be warmer," Sister Antonia urged us as she saw how we shivered, while we stood around impatiently waiting for the iron door of the shelter to be unbolted. The noise of the withdrawing bolts resounded like an echo in a catacomb. I held on tight to Sister Antonia's hand; she looked at me with a smile and gave me a squeeze to assure me that everything would be alright. I looked behind me to make sure my sisters were there. They looked like scared mummies with their blankets over their head. Berta gave me a faint smile and whispered, "*Coraggio, piccina. Everything will be over soon.*"

I bent my head, feeling so sorry for her. She was so scared too, yet she wanted to be brave for me when all I wanted was to be cuddling together with my sisters and give vent to my terror, to yell and to cry out loud. But we had to be brave all the time. We had to be grown up. I don't know which was worse, not showing emotion or the circumstance we found each other in. I even felt anger. For the first time I felt that my parents had abandoned us. I had forgotten the reason they had to leave. I had forgotten that it had to be. Why couldn't we be together, safe, wherever they might be. . .we wouldn't be here now in this terrible circumstance, scared and alone with strangers. Parents were supposed to be with their children; otherwise, why did children need parents, if not to be protected by them?

Finally the sisters were able to open the massive door. We entered the shelter, followed by Mother Superior. The heavy door closed behind her. A wild thought came to my mind: What if we were not getting out of here alive?

"Sisters, please blow out your candles," Mother Superior called out, interrupting my thoughts. "The oil lamps will give us enough light." She spoke calmly. "Let's save the candles for an emergency. We don't have that many. Take your seats. The benches along the wall will be comfortable enough to let us rest until all this blows over."

We sat down quietly. The nuns had regained their composure, outwardly at least, even though their eyes gave them away.

Sister Antonia sat between Mina and me. She put her arms around our shoulders, while Elena and Berta sat huddled with one another. We could no longer hear the shelling as clearly as before; it sounded muddled and faint. The bunker was well insulated and strongly built, although no one could tell if it would hold up if the convent building were hit. The walls were reinforced by heavy metal pipes. A row of iron beams crisscrossed the ceiling, and sturdy pipes stood upright every few feet through the room. Shelves along the walls were filled with cans of food. Big water canisters were standing in the middle of the room, which also served as tables. The oil lamps were placed on them. A small makeshift infirmary had been set up at the end of the shelter, separated by two folding doors. A few folded cots leaned against the wall. Two white cabinets containing whatever would be necessary to give first aid. Sheets and blankets were piled up on a table in the far corner.

After a long silence, Mother Superior intoned a prayer. The nuns joined in unison. After that, they sang as they always did in the chapel; it alleviated a lot of anxiety in all of us. When they were finished with their chants, they all prayed quietly some more, moving their fingers through the beads of their rosary while we closed our eyes to try to get some sleep that wouldn't come. Thus we sat half the night, until we heard the faint sound of the sirens signaling that the danger was over. Now people could return to their homes, if they had homes left to go back to.

Mother Superior got up and knelt on the floor; so did the nuns. They crossed themselves and gave thanks for having been saved thus far. She got up and opened the door with the help of another nun, turned to her flock, and said, "I will go first to check if the house has been damaged." She took an oil lamp and, with another sister, disappeared. Tensely, we awaited her return. She came back to announce that all was well; a few paintings had fallen off the walls. "Take the oil lamps with you, and watch your steps—the electricity has been shut off. We will return to our dormitories to get some rest for whatever is left of the night. In the morning we will proceed with cleaning up and make repairs where ever needed," she added matter-of- factly. With her last words, she turned, ready to leave. The door was bolted shut once again. We followed her back upstairs, relieved that nothing more had happened.

As we entered our room, cold air engulfed us from the broken window. Sister Antonia told us to wait in the hall while she and another sister tried to do something about the shattered windows. They fastened a few blankets above them while they stood on some chairs and someone else brought in a broom to sweep away the glass from the floor. Sister Antonia came back to us with our slippers. "Be careful not to get splinters in your feet. Next time, you must be better prepared," she scolded us gently. "Now let's check your beds to make sure there is no glass on them." Diligently we went through the beds, shaking out the linen, pillow, and blankets. When Sister Antonia was satisfied that everything was clear she said, "This will do for now. Make sure not to go around barefoot until tomorrow. There may still be some glass left on the floor."

She gave a deep sigh. She was exhausted and tired. "In the morning we'll see to it that the windows are repaired. Cover yourselves well. It's cold in here. Let's get some rest now."

She kissed us on the cheek and made the sign of the cross on our foreheads. On an impulse, I threw my arms around her neck and kissed her on both cheeks. For a moment I felt as though I was embracing my mother. I couldn't have loved Sister Antonia more. She gently took my arms down and looked at me in surprise. We never gave into such outbursts. We kept a certain distance between them and us, even though we knew they cared for us. We just felt that that was the right thing to do. She took my face in her hands and smiled with a glimmer in her eyes. Then she left without a word leaving the room in total darkness since she took the oil lamp with her.

Berta made her way to my bed to tuck me in. "You were quite brave," she said. "You didn't cry or give way to your fear."

She straightened out the blanket on my bed and gave me a big hug.

"Wait a minute!" I held her back.

"What is it? "

"Tell me something." I paused for a second, trying to find the right words for what I was about to ask.

"Yes?" Berta was waiting.

"If we should die. . .would. . .I mean, *how will our parents know?*" I exclaimed.

"Oh, silly, no one is going to die. Why, is someone after you?" She was trying to sound jovial.

"No, I mean it, *I mean it!*" I insisted, sitting up and tugging at her nightgown. I wanted an answer. It was important; I needed to know. That was all I had been thinking about lately. "If this build- ing got hit, and we ended up under it, how would Mama and Papa find us? How would they *know?*"

Berta realized that I was not about to give up, that I was dead serious. She sat down on the bed. "Yes, Olga, they would certainly know. They'd find us. They know where we are and exactly what's happening to us."

She spoke with assurance, but I still wasn't convinced. "Berta, *how* are they going to know? We aren't allowed to write to them. They may have forgotten us by now. Maybe they think that we're dead already!" I insisted.

"Silly, parents don't forget their children. Why, have you?" she asked in turn.

"Of course not," I answered positively, feeling a little remorse because, though I thought about them, the images were getting blur- ry. "I often think about them," I added. That was the truth. Lately I had thought about where they might be, what they were doing.

"Well, then, why do you think that they're not doing the same? You may not know it, but Mr. Lucca has connections. He's sending them reports about us. I don't know exactly how, but he does, so don't worry, they'll always know what is happening to us."

She hugged me and kissed me on the nose, then gently pushed me down. "Go to sleep now. I'm freezing. Let's get some rest."

Later I found out that Berta didn't really know what she was talking about. She told me, instead, what she herself wanted very badly to believe.

The bell sounded the next morning to waken us up, as clear as ever, as if nothing had happened. I felt rested. I had fallen asleep at once after the talk I had with my sister, while my sisters rose more tired then when they went to bed. They hadn't been able to sleep; they'd thought about my questions, and it made them toss and turn. They never talked about it, but they too had the same thoughts. While I was sleeping serenely with my questions answered, they were worried that the sirens might go off again. The bombings were over, even the distant rumbling which we used to hear and learned to ignore, had subsided. Everything seemed to have calmed down. Had the planes left for good?

I put the pillow over my head; I didn't feel like getting up. But I had to. I went through the morning routine without talking much. No one felt like it. We joined the taciturn nuns, who were going down to the chapel. They began to recite their prayers and sing their hymns without their usual vibrancy. The sisters looked like shadows, which fit the ambience of that morning. The electricity hadn't been restored; we sat in the dismal gray of the dawn. The sky was overcast, promising a nebulous day which suited the mood we were in. It did   n o t help either listening to the recitations of the nuns. Usually it uplifted everyone's feelings listening to their voices jubilantly invoking their deep spiritual vocation and belief, which culminated in sonorous singing rising up to the painted frescos on the ceiling that displayed angels with outstretched arms, who seemed to receive their voices unto them. One perceived that their hearts and souls were not in the chanting. It was depressing. The bombardment had shaken them more then they led on. When the prayers were over, we filed out of the semi-darkened chapel into the hall, which was illuminated only by a few oil lamps that gave off an amber light. Our shadows reflected on the walls.

An eerie silence accompanied our walk to the refectory. There too, it felt as if the room had changed its aspect to accommodate our mood. It was cheerless and depressing. We went through the motions of eating, not looking at one another. A heavy lassitude seemed to settle over the nuns. Mother Superior sat at the head of the table. When I timidly looked up, I saw her intently watching her sisters.

At long last breakfast was over. As we prepared to recite our after-meal prayers, Mother Superior rang the little bell that was always at her right side. In surprise, all eyes rose, focusing in her direction. The bell was rung only when a dispensation was to be announced, and that had not happened while we were there.

"Sisters," she called out. "I am saddened by what is transpiring here this morning." Her eyes, calmly but full of pain, wandered around the room and rested for a moment on each of them. "I don't seem to feel the spirit of *Jesu Christo* in you. Your prayers were not joyful in the praise of Him. I am grieved to see that you have faltered. He is testing us, and we have failed miserably. He, who died for us and suffered more then we can imagine because of our sins, did not fail us. Terrible things happened last night. We never fathomed that such wrath would be unleashed from above. Terrible things are being done by human beings to human beings. We had no idea how this war would affect us, but these children do."

I felt heat rising to my face. I furtively glanced at my sisters. They too seemed to feel uncomfortable. "It does not seem to have affected *their* spirits." How little did she know about our feelings, I thought. We never ran to her with our apprehensions, fears, and terrors. We were lucky. We had each other and were able to extract comfort from each other as best we could. By living through the past and those infinite particulars, our lives were being shaped. How could she ever know about our spirit!

She continued speaking, her voice flowing over the bent heads of her nuns. "We had no idea how it would be like or how it would happen, even though we made all the preparations. We should be grateful that our convent has been spared and pray for the less fortunate."

She rose from her chair. "Now we shell go to the chapel and pray for guidance and faith." She led the nuns out. She stopped at our seats. "Children," she said in a warm tone, "you have some free time for now. Busy yourselves with something while we are in the chapel," and glided graciously out of the refectory.

We went upstairs to our room. We decided to take our jackets and walk in the immaculately tended garden. We walked carefully, always apprehensive when we were outside, always fearing that someone was lurking behind the walls of the convent.

As we strolled about, we saw that the wall at the end of the garden had been hit. There was a big hole in it, bricks were lying all around, and a pile of debris had formed a mound in front. Mother Superior must have forgotten to warn us about it, or maybe she didn't know it had happened.

We cautiously approached. We could see out. We hid hunched behind the remaining wall and peeked. We saw what destruction had occurred during the night. The old elm trees, which had graced the length of the street, were lying scattered across the road and buried under the rubble of fallen houses. Some charred stumps were still standing here and there; others had been ripped out of the sidewalk by their roots, leaving big holes in the ground.

We stared aghast at all the devastation that had spared us. We saw people's belongings thrown about—a pink crib, which had remained intact, was hanging from a pipeline. I gasped. My sisters poked me. I could have been heard by someone. I was thinking of what might have happened to the baby that had lain inside it. We saw groups of people huddled together, gesticulating as they spoke. Some others were climbing over the mounds of fallen brick, looking for any effects that they could salvage.

Then we saw two covered trucks pulling up; our instinct told us to run, but we stayed hunched behind the wall as if glued to it. The trucks came to a screeching halt almost across the street from us. Fascist soldiers and SS men jumped out the back, unloading prisoners by pushing them off the truck. The prisoners had shaven heads—men, women, and children alike. They were holding picks and shovels. The soldiers ordered them to clear the streets of debris and closely guarded them with pointed bayonets. The prisoners' clothes were completely inadequate, ripped and dirty from long wear; they looked haggard and disheveled. We cringed. They were wearing the Star of David on their clothes, as we had seen once before on the way to the convent. These people looked worse, more emaciated. We wondered what the fate of the others had been.

We could not stay any longer. Mother Superior came running toward us. "Children, for the love of God, what are you *doing* out here?" She took my hand. "You know you can't be seen. How could you be so careless? Hopefully, no one saw you." She was speaking in a whisper, to make sure her voice didn't carry.

We walked away reluctantly with the picture of those prisoners imbedded in our minds. It has revisited my memory very often. It has stayed in my mind more vividly than any other moment while I was growing up in search of my identity as a Jew. Subconsciously I always felt I owed something to those prisoners. They were part of my people, doing our share while we were safe. We should have been with them, not tucked away safely in a convent. I felt an unexplained guilt. I had witnessed their plight. I promised to myself that I would never let them down. They did not know of my existence, but I had seen them; I would carry on for them and make myself count when the time came. My father's voice came to my mind, and I knew then what he had meant. I remembered who I was, and I knew I had become their inheritance. I must have grown up all at once.

From then on, we made sure never to be caught unprepared. We went to bed dressed, our shoes at the foot of the bed, ready to be put on at a moment's warning. The terrible storm of bombardment ended for a time. Our days went by in the hope that the bombs had caused all the damage they intended to do and would leave us alone.

Meanwhile, Mina had acquired ESP, because a few days after the last air raid, she woke up screaming just a few minutes after we had fallen asleep, and started shaking each of us until we were fully awake. Then she ran down the hall, stopping at the entrance to the nun's dormitories, yelling like a raving maniac, "Get up! Get up! The planes are coming! They are going to bomb again! " She turned around and came flying into our room again. "Let's *go!* Get the blankets!"

Berta got up, grabbed her by the shoulders, and shook her. "Mina, Mina, nothing is happening. You had a nightmare, a bad dream. Calm down!" She turned to Elena. "Go, run to the bathroom, get her

some cold water and a towel—she's all wet from perspiration. *Hurry!*"
Rushing out, she encountered Mother Superior.

"What is all this commotion about?" she wanted to know, following Elena.

"Mina must have had a bad dream. She woke us   up screaming, telling us that the planes are on the way to bomb the city again."

"Poor child. I didn't realize how much all this must have affected you children," said the old woman sympathetically. "I haven't had much time these days to sit with you, to talk about the past events and about your feelings. I'll—"

Before she could finish the sentence, we heard the air-raid sirens.

"My God!" Mother Superior paled and crossed herself. "I can't believe it. Hurry, go back to your sisters and gather your things! I'll get the others." She hurried off while Elena came running back. She found Berta still holding Mina's shivering body. "You were right!" we told Mina. "We're all ready, thanks to you. We'll go down at once where we'll be safe. Calm down, please!" She stroked Mina's hair and kissed her over and over again, and then helped her on with her shoes.

Mina's body relaxed again; she grabbed her blanket while Berta went to get hers, thinking of the role she had assumed. At fifteen, she had become a mother to us. She had to comfort us, be an example at all times, be there to reassure us when we were plagued by doubts; she felt the heavy burden. But hadn't she promised her parents to watch over us, not to rely on strangers alone to do the job? She was scared too, and overwhelmed by that responsibility.

It took no time at all; we found ourselves downstairs with blasting noises trailing after us and the sirens still wailing. The whole building shook. We made it down before the nuns. They were soon rapidly descending the stairs. "Remember, stay in the middle of the staircase!" Mother Superior was warning them when we heard another blast, and the window on the landing blew open, and glass shattered into a million pieces. The force of the explosion hurled it in all directions. The statue of Jesus that stood at the head of the stairs split in half, and the head came crashing down on Sister Antonia as she was about to cross the platform.

She let out a piercing scream and fell. We stood frozen, looking up in disbelief.

"Oh, no! Not Sister Antonia, no, not her!" I cried. I freed myself from my sister's grip and ran upstairs, pushing aside the nuns, who had stopped their descent. I forgot the shelling. I wasn't scared any longer; another fear had taken over. *Please, God, don't let anything happen to her!* I prayed. We had adopted her as our mother for the time being. She had been put in charge of us and had become very dear—fun to be with, as patient as she had to be to cope with us. She had showered her love on us in a hundred ways.

Sister Antonia was lying motionless on the floor, the fragments of the statue strewn beside her. The blow should have smashed her face, yet no bruises were apparent, only a trickle of blood flowing slowly from her temple.

Mother Superior had reached her before I did. She was kneeling beside her, holding her hand to feel her pulse and then placing her ear on Sister Antonia's chest, hoping to hear her heartbeat. "Thank God! She's still breathing, though it sounds shallow." she looked up at the nuns, who had formed a circle around her. "Sisters, please," she exclaimed, "keep on moving quickly! The whole building may be hit. You must reach the shelter without further delay." Rising from the floor, she coaxed them on. "I need the nurses to bring up the stretcher at once."

She had hardly finished the sentence when the nurses came up the stairs holding one. They must have rushed down at once when they saw what had happened. I knelt down beside Sister Antonia and seized her lifeless hand in mine. I kissed it over and over, praying silently to myself, "Oh, dear God, don't let her die! I promise to be good. I'll study hard. I'll do all my work in time. I'll do anything that's expected of me. Just let her be alright!" My lips were moving without a sound.

Mother Superior lifted me up. "Child," she said softly, "You too must go down with the others." She looked at me with pleading eyes, holding me tighter when I tried to bend down to Sister Antonia again. The last thing she needed now was to have a hysterical child on her hands. "Come on," she coaxed me. "Be brave. Be brave for her. Right now, we all must be." She loosened her hold on me. In a daze I knelt down again to kiss Sister Antonia's hand; then I put the arm on her chest and got up, thinking it was not happening, that it was all a bad dream.

A nun reached for my hand and took me downstairs to where my sisters were waiting for me.

Meanwhile, overhead, the roaring noises of airplanes flying low over the buildings grew louder and closer. It felt as if the whole building was shaking. Paintings and other hangings were falling off the walls. Objects on the table in the hall lost their balance and fell crashing to the floor. Behind the closed door of the kitchen we heard the sound of pots and pans striking the tiled floor and making all kinds of noises.

No, this was not a dream, it was all happening. My fear set in again that we might never reach the safety of the shelter this time. But we did.

A cot had already been prepared, covered with white linen sheets, to receive Sister Antonia. Silently we sat down. A few moments later, one sister began a prayer, timidly at first, then with growing strength and assurance. Then all the others joined in, their voices becoming one, stronger now, with fervor and supplication for the welfare of one of their own.

I couldn't shake the vision of Sister Antonia's pale face as she lay there motionless, with closed eyes. I was wondering if their prayers and mine would really help and be heard by whoever was supposed to be up there. I had already prayed so often, and nothing had happened. I had been told many times to pray for the safety of so many loved ones, and for those who had helped us thus far.

I remembered my father including, in his liturgy, all those people by their first names when he recited his daily prayers, a ritual he performed in the mornings, when he put on his phylacteries, and in the late afternoons. Yet most of them had died. The son of the rabbi in my parents' village, who had come to Mr. Savino's place to give us the route to escape, had been shot in the woods while trying to get back to the partisans. Paulo, the dear friend who had come to our rescue so many times, had been caught and tortured; he was dead, too. My grandparents, and all their neighbors, were dead. All the sisters and brothers of my parents, our numerous aunts, uncles, and their children we had prayed for, were they dead, too? They had disappeared from the face of the earth. I remembered my parents talking about them, wondering about their fate. He'd included them in his prayers, too; and what had happened to my mother's youngest sister? I don't recall how we found out that she and her husband were trying to escape on foot across the Alps into Switzerland. The Swiss had not let them in their country. At the border, they had been sent back, since they had no valid papers. It had happened to others, too, Jews who had destroyed their papers so that, if they were caught, their identity wouldn't be known. Some had been lucky, had had enough money to buy falsified papers for themselves, but most had none. Those who couldn't show the proper papers had no other choice but go back. The Swiss operated with full knowledge that they would be caught by the Germans.

My aunt and uncle had thus been captured by the Gestapo. They'd taken my uncle away for "questioning," they led my aunt to believe. After she waited for two days in a detention depot, a Gestapo officer had brought her a shoe box that contained my uncle's ashes. After he enjoyed his excellent prank, they'd deported her to one of their labor camps, where the front gate greeted her with the words *Arbeit macht frei.* Yes, she had been set free quite soon after. They'd worked her to death, that is. My parents had heard the story from one who survived and had known her.

Those parachutists who landed in the woods had been captured too. Paulo had told us that, after being questioned and tortured by Gestapo intelligence, who had been unable to obtain the information they wanted, those boys had been shot. They were gone, too.

Surely those prisoners who removed the debris must have prayed also. Was that the will of God? The nuns always ended their prayers by saying, "Thy will be done." I was too young to dwell upon the meaning of those words in depths. All I could think was, *Why would God want this?* Among the images of my past that return to haunt me, the question arises often. That constant *why?* still gnaws at my mind.

I was becoming very skeptical about the power of prayer. I didn't want to pray anymore, but since it was expected of me, I mumbled along, thoughtlessly and without feeling. When the nuns cried out, "Thy will be done," I was thinking, *Why Sister Antonia?*

Finally they brought her in. Two nuns were carrying her on a stretcher, with Mother Superior following close behind, holding her rosary in her hands, praying. Sister Antonia was motionless, a cross between her folded hands. It could only have meant that she was dead. They placed her behind the divider.

Mother Superior nodded. The prayers changed at once. Incantations for the dead were recited. I still couldn't pray. I'd been right. . .they hadn't helped after all. My eyes burned, and I was getting tired.

Mother Superior's gentle voice brought me out of my lethargy. "Olga, you have no prayer to offer for the sister you loved so much?" She was bending over me. "It may help, you know? Come, pray with me. Sister Antonia would have liked that very much." She sat down between Mina and me, her arms around my shoulders.

I almost hated her for making me pray. I bent my head so she wouldn't see my tears. She started to lead her flock in prayer. That's all they know how to do, I thought. "Pater Noster, thou who art in heaven, help us in our need, help us to understand and accept your will," I repeated after them, but that was all I did.

SISTER ANTONIA WAS laid out in a simple casket in front of the altar for two days. Two nuns took turns to sit vigil at her side day and night. Two large candles burned at the foot of the casket. The monsignor came to give a special mass for her.

Then, in procession, they went to the burial ground that lay behind the convent garden. The order had its own cemetery.

We were not allowed to follow them. The wall that had been hit hadn't been repaired yet. Mother Superior did not want to take the chance of us being seen, now that everyone could look into the garden. It was thought best to stay behind.

We watched her departure from behind an attic window that overlooked the garden and the cemetery. We still could not believe that she had gone.

The convent did not seem the same without her cheery presence. Someone else had been assigned to us. Sister Magdalena was so very different from Sister Antonia. She did not have the sweet disposition of her predecessor, nor did we ever feel at ease with her. She was tall and slender. She told us she had come from Germany. She had an accent when she spoke, and her voice didn't sound as melodious as those of the other sisters. She looked at us with cold eyes, I thought; she was always so serious. Sister Magdalena expected more of us than Sister Antonia, too: Everything had to be perfect. She did not have the ease and understanding of us as the nun who had been so like a mother to us. She treated us more like adults, and we, it must be admitted, couldn't stop comparing her. Many times she chided us for not having completed our tasks to her liking, and made us do them over. That certainly did not militate in her favor. Why couldn't life ever go on in the same way it always had? I thought. As soon as we adapted ourselves to our surroundings, something happened to change them. Life went on, although not as satisfyingly as before. We tried very hard to get adjusted to Sister Magdalena.

The shelling continued on and off, each time making us think that the final bomb might fall. At times it caught us during the day and lasted for shorter periods. The night raids were the worst.

We began having nightmares. Mina started to wet her bed each night, which she tried to conceal by putting extra towels under her bed linen when she thought no one would notice. At night she lay there in her wet bed.

We never made a fuss over it. We never told her we knew.

She always knew when the raids would occur at least a few minutes before the sirens went off. At night, she would be the first to wake up screaming and run across the hall, crazed with fear, to waken the sisters after having jolted us out of bed first. We had long since learned to heed her warnings.

December of 1943 was one of the coldest winter months in many years. Coal and wood became hard to come by. The stoves were used very sparingly—the one in the kitchen only for cooking, the one in the recreation room only in the evenings for a while, when we all gathered together. We wore extra sweaters and shawls. We even wore gloves at times when our hands seemed to freeze up and couldn't hold a pen when we wrote our lessons, because our fingers were frozen.

The convent was immersed in a somber atmosphere. We started to sleep two in a bed to keep warm. Thus we entered a new year.

January 1944 was just as cold when, one afternoon, the silence of the convent was interrupted by a sudden spurt of activity coming from the street—shrill voices, loud whistles, and, abruptly, a loud, heavy banging and thumping from the main entrance and kitchen door, followed by forceful voices shouting, "*Aufmachen, aufmachen!*"

We were upstairs, studying in our rooms. Our heads, bent intently over schoolbooks, shot up. We paled and automatically brought our hands to our mouths to keep from screaming. A second later, a few nuns came storming in. "Quick!" whispered one, out of breath. "Take your books and your clothes from the closet, and follow me!"

She ordered the others to remove anything else that might indicate that the room was occupied. We ran after her to the attic. As we entered the room, we almost fell over stacks of chairs and a few tables. It was dark and musty; a few rays of light were sneaking through broken windows covered with black shades. She took us scrambling to the farthest corner of the room, where she pushed aside some old paintings and ran her opened hands up and down the wall until she found a small door. Turning around, almost knocking us down, she whispered, "Quickly! Get in there."

Before we knew what was happening, we found ourselves in a black hole. We heard the door closing and shuffling noises against it. We banged our heads against the ceiling because it was so low. Terrified, we dropped what we were holding in our arms. We felt for each other in the dark. There was just enough room to hold us.

We broke out in a sweat; it did not seem possible that, a few minutes before, our teeth had been chattering from the cold.

I think it was Mina who whispered, "They're coming for us!"

Up to that point we had not reacted; we had done everything automatically. Now fear set in as we crouched on the floor.

"Shush. No one will get us." This time it was Berta, whose whisper sounded harsh. "No one will get us. They won't *find* us! Now, *quiet!*"

I felt a hand searching for mine. It was Elena. We held each other. I could hardly breath, and thought in terror, We'll suffocate before they get us!

Silently, I prayed, "I'll be good, dear God, just let us not be caught. I'll practice my handwriting. I'll prepare for my lessons. I won't talk back to my sisters." I think I promised to become a saint if He helped us.

I don't know how long we were in that hole. I was busy promising our lives away when we heard heavy footsteps. My sisters hand, sweaty in mine, started to squeeze it so hard I almost yelled out in pain. I pulled my arm, and luckily she let go, her hand searching once again for me. We held each other, trembling, squeezing against the wall. My eyes were shut tight; I could almost feel my cheeks over my lids.

I heard someone yell,"*Licht! Licht anmachen!*" The voice was demanding, brutal. Then it seemed that things were being thrown about, walls banged upon, glass shattering, boots coming closer, stopping, and an eternity passed before they began to move farther away. Then silence. . ..

We didn't dare move. When the door finally opened, the dim light from outside the room hit us. I could hardly make out the figure who was bending down at the door, calling for us: "Children, you can come out now. It's safe." I recognized Mother Superior's voice. We scrambled out on our hands and knees, and she held out her hand to help us up.

We could hardly get up and stand straight. We had sat so long on the floor, cramped in that hole, every bone in our bodies had stiffened, and we were aching so, we cried out in pain.

"Move slowly," Mother Superior advised us. "Massage your legs up and down to get the blood circulation flowing again." there were other nuns with her who helped massage our backs.

After a while we felt better and started to slowly make our way through the attic and out to the stairs, but not before heeding Mother Superior's warning to avoid the debris scattered all over the floor.

We went down to our room. Mother Superior told us to lie down for a while. "Someone will be right up with some warm milk and some extra blankets. You'll feel better soon. We'll talk later."

She looked drawn and pallid. The others didn't look any better. They all left. We did as we were told—took our shoes off and went to bed with our clothes on.

The warm milk and blankets made us feel comfortable. None of us spoke. For the first time, we had nothing to say to each other. What was there to say? For a while, we had felt safe, even with the bombings and all the precautions we had to take. We felt the nuns would protect us. Those high walls surrounding the cloister would keep all the evil out. We'd never thought of tomorrow. We anticipated that, one day, the war would be over, and that our parents would come for us and we'd live happily ever after.

WE FELL ASLEEP. We woke up at the sound of the usual matutine bells. For a moment I felt disoriented, until the occurrences of the day before returned to my mind. We sat up on our beds, not believing that we had slept through the afternoon and the whole night. Silently we went about the morning routine. We changed our clothes and washed up, joined the nuns in the chapel, and went in for breakfast. We still hadn't talked about what had happened.

After breakfast, Sister Magdalena told us that Mother Superior was expecting us in her office. Apprehensively, we went to see her. Her office door was open, and she was sitting at her desk. She called us in. "I'm so glad that you had such a good rest, after such an ordeal. No wonder! . . .This is exactly what I wanted to talk to you about," she said, smiling at us. "Sit down, girls." She still didn't look well. She had dark circles under her eyes, which we had never noticed before. As we took our seats in front of her desk, she started to talk to us in a very calm and soothing voice. "We had a big scare yesterday. I do not want you to be preoccupied about it. I am certain that the soldiers went away believing that we were not harboring anyone. They thoroughly searched every possible place in this convent." She paused, looking pensively at us, and then continued, "I've talked to the sisters, and we've all come to the conclusion that we will go on with our lives as normally as possible. We will not change our routine. I just wanted to reassure you that we will keep you as safe as possible. This war can't go on for ever, and with God's help and our prayers, we will get through it."

She paused for a moment and continued. "We have decided that, for the time being, you will stay confined to your quarters. You will only come down after dark. Your breakfast and lunch will be brought up to your room. I want to emphasize that no one at any time must go near a window. . . . This is just a precaution—just in case soldiers are watching our convent. I hope you understand that this is for all our safety."

She got up, came around to us, and made the sign of the cross on our foreheads to give us her blessing. "Now, girls, go up to your room and start your lessons."

With this, we were dismissed.

"Well, I think we can relax. Mother Superior sounded very confident," Berta said.

"I am still scared," I told her.

"I understand, but I'm sure that Mother Superior won't let any-thing happen to us." Berta gave me a hug. "Think about something pleasant. Look, you won't have any more chores to do. You always complained about all the things you had to do."

Before Mina or Elena could say anything, there was a knock at the door and Sister Magdalena entered the room. "Well, are we ready for our lessons?" she asked, trying to sound jovial.

We thought that our confinement to our quarters would be hard to handle, but it didn't turn out so bad. We were busy with our les-sons.

We still had our upstairs chores to do, and the nuns came up to visit with us—sometimes reading to us, playing games, or telling us what was going on downstairs. We were greatful that at least we could join the sisters at night in the recreation room.

ONE DAY, MOTHER Superior summoned us to her office. She was once again sitting at her desk. "Sit down, children," she said. We were hoping that she hadn't called us in to lecture us about some misbehav-ior. I immediately tried to think of events in the recent past. Had we done something wrong?

"Don't look so guilty." She smiled. "Or is there something I should know?" She didn't wait for a reply. Besides, we wouldn't have had anything to tell. She became serious. "We have to make a deci-sion," she said gravely, coming right to the point. "Two men have been here inquiring about you. They said that they were sent by people you knew. They were worried about you. They also told me that convents were no longer a safe haven. They knew from reliable sources that the Nazis know that parishes and convents are hiding Jews. Many such places have been searched as ours was. Most likely any day now we will be searched again." She paused, studying our reaction. "These men want you to leave with them the next time they come. They said that it has been arranged for you to be smuggled across the border into Switzerland." Her hands were in her lap, holding a crucifix, her fingers absentmindedly tracing the figure of Jesus carved on it. She added pensively, "These people who would take charge of you are smugglers. They deal in contraband. As of late, for money, they have started to deal in human cargo. They are unsavory characters who do have no morals and don't believe in causes."

She got up and, laying the cross on her desk, started to pace back and forth. She turned around and asked, "By any chance, do you have any idea of who they might be?"

"No—why should we know of them?" Berta asked. "We were told by Mr. Lucca that, if my parents made it safely across the border, he would try to get us there too, through his contacts. Hasn't he told you anything? Hasn't he been in touch with you? I'm sure he'll clarify everything."

"The problem is, I can't get in touch with him in order to confirm their story," Mother Superior said in distress. She hadn't heard from him or seen him in a while. "I. . .I can't be sure of anything," she lamented. "My brother has told me on numerous occasions, and made me promise, that if I didn't hear from him, and if he hadn't been in touch with me, there would be a reason. He made me promise that I would not try to contact him, that any inquiries about him then would only lead to us and put us in danger."

She stopped speaking, her thoughts turned to her brother. She had a premonition that something awful must have happened to him. He had made it a point to visit with her and be in touch regularly. He had told her, when she last saw him, that if she didn't hear from him any more, he'd most probably had to go underground.

We waited somewhat impatiently for her to continue. We didn't want to intrude in her thoughts, though; she had such a distant look in her face.

After a long silence, Berta cleared her throat. It seemed to bring the old woman back to the problem at hand. "Ah, children, you must forgive me. I was thinking of Mr. Lucca and the meaning of his absence. . . . As I was saying," she said hesitantly, trying to remember were she'd left off, "they said they will come back once more to give us instructions, and the next time they expect you to be ready to leave with them." At that, her voice took on an unhappy cast. She looked at Berta. We sat quietly, thinking of what she had just told us. "I am confronted with a dilemma which is weighing very heavily on me. I thought I should share this responsibility with you, even though you are so   young and inexperienced in these matters." She walked to the pew and asked Berta to join her. "These men may or may not be who they claim to be. They told me that they work closely with the partisans, and that they've made the connections with the smugglers to take you. I know that this is being done. I also know it hasn't always worked. People haven't been safe with them. I feel that smugglers who deal in contraband and with human lives are not to be trusted."

We listened intently to every word Mother Superior had to say. Berta's mind was racing. She had a feeling that she knew exactly what the nun wanted of her.

"I don't know whether I can allow you to leave under these circumstances," Mother Superior continued. "You may be captured. You may be forced to tell them where you have been all this time.

These men may be spies. . . . We would like you to remain here. You have adapted yourselves admirably well to our lives. There would be absolutely no problem for you to stay. Monsignor could baptize you. He would give you baptismal papers, and you would be safe. . . . What do you think?"

Berta had made a split-second decision. "Mother Superior, I have a feeling that these men can be trusted, and that they were sent by your brother, since he works with the partisans. I remember," she explained, "my parents promised to send for us as soon as they were able to. It could only have been them asking to send these men. Otherwise, how could they know that my parents escaped to Switzerland, and how would they know where to find us? Mr. Lucca has been so careful to keep our identity, and the whereabouts of my parents, hidden.

"Yes. Yes, you are right, of course. I have asked myself the same questions. Yet I still feel you ought to remain here." She looked at Berta. My sister knew what she had to do, but she said she wanted to talk it over with us.

"*Naturalmente*. Of course, my child. I want you to think carefully about this, and understand that a hard and long journey will be ahead of you, and by no means without danger!" Mother Superior emphasized. "You were meant to come to us. It was meant that we would save you." She rose, and the meeting was ended.

We left, but not before Berta told her, "No matter what happens and what our decision will be, we are so very grateful to you for having given us shelter and kept us as if we were your own." She kissed her hand and motioned us to leave with her.

As soon as we were in our room, we bombarded Berta with questions.

As far as I was concerned, we could leave immediately; since Sister Antonia's death, nothing was the same. I was no longer happy there, and the bombing didn't make it any easier. We were constantly scared. I loved Mother Superior very much and would miss her, but she'd never come as close as Sister Antonia to my heart. I still hadn't come to like Sister Magdalena. She reminded me too much of Sister Maria Angela at the farm, whom by then I had almost forgotten. Sister Magdalena brought her back into my mind, and though it was hardly her fault, I disliked her that much more for having done so.

"Just a minute, please!" Berta lifted her arms in exasperation.

She did not know half the answers to the questions we posed to her, either. She too had her doubts. But to tell this to us would not have helped the situation; it would only have made us more anxious. One way or another, she would have to cope with yet another responsibility.

She knew instinctively that to leave was the right thing to do. "Let's sit down and reason this out. I'm a little confused about this, too. I thought, when the time came, Mr. Lucca would be here to tell us all about it and accompany us to the men who were going to take us to Switzerland."

We made ourselves comfortable on Berta's bed. "Who do you think these strangers are?" Elena asked.

"Do you believe what you told Mother Superior?" Mina wanted to know. "What makes you think they may not be spies after all?"

"No, I don't think so," Berta answered. "If they were, the Gestapo would have been here already. These men would have gone straight to them and reported that the nuns were indeed hiding us. Since this did not happen, I must believe they were sent by the partisans."

As she continued to talk, her voice became more assured. "If you remember, Mr. Lucca said that, as soon as possible, he'd work out a plan to try to get us to Switzerland."

"But Mr. Lucca hasn't shown up!" Elena pointed out. "These men didn't mention his name to Mother Superior. How do we know Mama and Papa even *are* in Switzerland?"

". . .Well, this is what I think," Berta answered, undeterred. "Mr. Lucca must have gone underground. The Gestapo must have found out about his clandestine activities. We are not the only ones he has helped. You know?"

"Yes, yes, we know," Elena said impatiently. "Go on."

"He must have worked out a plan with the partisans, and since he couldn't come himself, they sent these men. In any case, we have no other choice. We *must* leave the convent. The nuns feel they're in danger now. You heard their plan to safeguard us and themselves. That plan is unthinkable. . . .We must trust these men and be ready when they come again. We must believe that our parents have something to do with it," she said resolutely.

In her heart she knew that this was right. She believed what the men had told Mother Superior. The Gestapo would come and search the convent. Again we had to leave.

Mina made a last attempt. "Won't it be dangerous to be smuggled into Switzerland? Didn't Mother Superior point that out?" Her eyes darkened and widened as she visualized all sorts of things. She had become more nervous than ever since the bombings started again. She hardly slept for fear of being too late to warn us before the sirens sounded the alarm.

Once again Berta emphasized that we were in danger no matter what. Finally my sisters understood that, too. I sat there listening.

No one had asked for my opinion. I wouldn't have known what to say. I only knew that Berta was in charge, and that she knew best. . .but that didn't mean that the uncertainty over what would happen to us did not disturb me. It was all so *frightening*.

As if Berta had read my thoughts, she put her arm around me and pulled me closer to her. "Olga, dear, I wish I could assure you that everything will be all right. I can't. All I can say is that we're all in this together. What will happen will happen to all of us. Besides," she said teasingly, changing the mood, "didn't you say a while back that you were sick and tired of this place?" She lifted up my chin.

"Yes, I did complain, but I didn't mean to leave *this* way!" I was whining, on the verge of tears.

"I know. No one did," she replied simply.

"Berta," Elena asked, hoping not to have to be present, "I guess you will go to Mother Superior to tell her about our decision, right? No need for all of us to go?"

"Yes, I'll go alone. I might as well go now and get it over with." Berta got up, straightening her clothes, approached the door, and stood there for a moment; then she said, "*Ciao*," and left.

She went downstairs full of apprehension. She stood a while in front of the door to Mother Superior's office, plagued by a bout of indecision that had suddenly overcome her.

Should she, or shouldn' t she? Was she right? Could these men be the enemy after all? They could deliver us to the Gestapo and buy someone else's freedom.

What if?. . .God, no! She had to believe that this was right, that we had to leave. With this ultimate conclusion, she knocked at the door. When she heard Mother Superior's voice calling to enter, she straightened herself out and walked in.

"Ah, *cara mía*," the old woman said. "I didn't expect you back so soon!" She was sitting behind her desk as usual with a stack of papers in front of her. "Come, take a seat."

Berta sat down. She tried to speak, she formed the words in her mind, but she was voiceless—a knot had formed in her throat.

Mother Superior, sensing the struggle, smiled at her and waited patiently, folding her hands on the table. "Take your time."

Finally, Berta, her voice raspy but steadfast, said, "We must go. We may never have another chance to see our parents again." (She had no way of knowing how true that statement was—soon after we left, the Gestapo searched the convent again.) "It would break their hearts if we didn't follow their wishes. We *must* assume that the partisans are behind this." She was speaking quickly: She didn't want to lose the momentum. "I hope you understand," she added apologetically. "We must go. We do love you!"

"*Va bene!* Very well, then." Mother Superior looked gravely at her. She knew she couldn't insist. She had wanted so very much to save us *and* our souls, she thought, resigned. She had to come to love these children who had been brought to her looking like lost little lambs. "For now there is nothing much we can do but wait for these men to return." She rose and came around her desk towards my sister, who also got up, and made the sign of the cross on her forehead. "We all hope you made the right decision. God be with you. We will pray for your safety." She took my sister's face between her hands and stood still for a moment looking down at her. "Now go, my child." She went to her altar and knelt at the pew to pray.

Berta left, closing the door quietly behind her.

WE WERE WAITING impatiently for my sister, unsure of what to hope for: that Mother Superior would talk her out of it, or that Berta had stuck to our decision.

Berta entered slowly, then burst out, "We are leaving. Mother Superior is giving her blessings."

A moment of silence followed.

"I guess they're glad to get rid of us after all," Elena exclaimed bitterly. "All that sweetness was to entice us to be baptized."

"Are you *crazy*?" Berta was surprised at the outburst. "Didn't we agree to leave? What did you expect Mother Superior to do? Yes, she would have loved for us to stay and be baptized and save us. But what would our *parents* have said?" She was annoyed. "You are wrong! They *do* love us. I'm sure of that. They took a chance hiding us, too, no matter what their motive was," she added.

Almost instantaneously Elena realized how foolish her outburst had been. "I'm sorry. You're right. I don' t know what came over me," she said apologetically, wiping the tears off her face with the palm of her hand.

Mother Superior gave us the rest of the day off. We went about aimlessly; we didn' t quite know what to do with our free time.

We came downstairs to eat when the bell rang. We prayed automatically. We ate without knowing what we were eating and felt awkward sensing the nuns gazing at us. To fill some time. we asked to help in the kitchen. In the evening, after vespers, we joined the sisters in the recreation room. It did not feel the same. We felt as if we had already left. The nuns sang some songs for us as a farewell.

They told us to take care of ourselves and not to forget to pray, that prayer would help us alleviate our fears. We listened to all the well-meant advice until the time came to go upstairs to our room. We didn't feel like going to bed. We knew we wouldn't sleep very well. We made up games, and Berta quizzed me on my multiplication table and spelling. For the first time, I welcomed the testing; it took our minds off things.

There was a knock at the door, and Sister Magdalena walked in. "Children, it's way past your bedtime." She went to the windows to make sure that the curtains were drawn properly. "Let's hope that we'll have a peaceful night."

She waited until we were under the covers to shut the light and, as she walked out, bade us good night. "Don ' t forget to say your prayers."

A few days later Mother Superior summoned us. We knew at once that this was it. We entered her office and, sure enough, saw her in the company of two men. Without much ado, she introduced us. "These are the young girls."

The men nodded in acknowledgment. "We understand that you were expecting someone else to notify you when the time came for you to leave. It is understandable that our sudden appearance frightened you," one of the men said. While he talked, we had a chance to glance at them. They both were middle-aged, stocky, with ruddy complexions. They wore dark, worn-out suits that fitted them very badly. One could immediately tell they were not city people. They seemed quite uncomfortable in their tight suits, which most likely they hadn't worn in a long while. "Let me assure you we come from the right source. Mr. Lucca sent us. We were contacted by the underground."

Mother Superior's eyes widened, and her serenity evaporated. "Wait a minute! Why didn't you tell me this when you first came?" she asked, raising her voice.

We were stunned. We had never seen her lose her composure. She must have realized it, because she changed the subject for a minute. "Well, let' s not stand around. Please sit down." She herself took a seat at her pew. ". . .You have no idea how much anguish you caused us by not telling me this at once," she said in the voice we had become accustomed to hearing. "How is Mr. Lucca? Have you seen him?" she asked.

"He had to go undercover," the man said. "The Gestapo became suspicious of him. He too had to run. We don' t quite know where he is right know, but we assure you he is safe."

"Thank you. Thank God he's out of danger!" she replied, relieved. "I hope he stays put, for his own good. Now, tell us how you propose to get the children out."

"Luckily," he said, "you haven't had a chance to get the rubble removed from the one wall surrounding your building that was hit. We will use this unfortunate incident to our advantage. Under the pretext of coming to remove the debris, we will drive up tomorrow, in the late afternoon, with a truck. It will look inconspicuous and per-fectly normal. We've already received the permission to do so. Otherwise, the office in charge of your district would eventually have sent prisoners under guard to clean it up. The rubble is obstructing passage in the street." He stopped to look at us, to see whether we were following him.

"Go on. What next?" Mother Superior said, hanging on his every word. We too, were eager to hear the rest.

"While we are doing the work," he continued, "the children will be waiting behind the opening of the wall for our signal; then, one by one, they will approach the truck. We have built a hollow space under the floor of the truck, which is covered by a heavy wooden platform.

The debris will cover the surface. The space below is just big enough to hold you," he said to us.

We sat there horrified by what we were hearing. We all had the same thought: What if the floor caved in under that heavy load of soil and brick? We'd be buried alive!

As if he had read our minds, he said reassuringly, "I know what you're thinking. The platform won' t give in. We've made sure of that. We've tried it out."

"How are the children going to get into this hidden space without being seen?" asked Mother Superior, aghast.

"Now, listen carefully. The door of the truck will be open. Each child will have to work quickly. When we give you the signal to move, you will be fully exposed. You will lift the seat, under which you'll find the crawl space. Just slide under. The seat will close behind you." He gesticulated with his arms to emphasize his words. "You won't be comfortable, but it will be all right. We will arrive late at night at a small mountain village. Two guides, who will take you across the Alps, will meet with us there. They're very experienced mountain climbers and know the terrain. They've succeeded in taking many people safely across the border. It will be a hard road, but you are young and strong. You' ll make it!" He had ended the last sentence reassuringly. He added, "Don't look so downhearted! This is a very sound plan."

Utter quiet had descended on the room. What was there to say? We were petrified. Mother Superior looked at us with sorrow in her eyes. Those poor lambs! she thought. "Is there anything else we should know?" she asked.

It was the turn of the other man, who had sat quietly all along, to speak. He told us that we couldn't take anything superfluous along, just the bare necessities. "The children must dress warm, and they need sturdy boots. It is rugged and cold on the mountains. You have to dress accordingly. Do you have trousers?" he asked. "You can't wear skirts."

"Yes, yes," Mother Superior assured him with a smile. "Fortunately, we didn't throw away the clothes the children came in. Everything will still fit them—they haven't grown that much."

"Good. Do they have small knapsacks? They need their hands free when climbing."

"We have those, too," she said.

"Now, one last thing." The man raised one finger. "This is very important," he said gravely. "We are almost positive that this convent will be searched. The Gestapo has been raiding all convents. They suspect something. You must make absolutely sure that no trace remains of the children having been here. If those people find any-thing, anything at all, all of you will be in the gravest danger. You must advise the sisters, so that they may prepare themselves." He paused for a second.

"Is this clear?" he asked.

Yes, it was very clear to her. Her brother had already warned her of the consequence should any of this be discovered. She had already discussed it with her nuns.

"I think we have covered everything, then," he said. "Do you have any questions?" he asked us.

Stupefied, we shook our heads.

"Well, then—" they both rose— "be ready when we come. We must go now."

Mother Superior got up, too. "I will see you to the door."

We just sat there. A million horses wouldn't have been able to lift us. We were glued to our seats.

"*Arrivederci*, then, until tomorrow," both men said to us, and left, accompanied by Mother Superior.

We hardly heard her coming back. "I know you have lots to think about," she said. "Go upstairs, relax a little, and talk it over. You'll feel better," she added softly, standing in front of us.

We came out of our stupor. "Yes, of course," Berta stammered. We rose and made our curtseys.

"I'll be coming up as soon as I find the clothes for you," she said as we were leaving.

We entered our room quietly, each in our own thoughts. We did not talk about the day to come, though, as Mother Superior suggested; there was nothing to discuss. The men had explained everything in detail. We threw ourselves on our beds. "Now we have something else to think about!" Elena mused.

Mina rushed to the bathroom. "All I can think of is, how I will manage when I have to pee so often," she said when she came back.

"Don't think about it. You'll be fine," Berta assured her.

"That should be the *last* thing to worry about," Elena added.

Before long, Mother Superior arrived, followed by Sister Magdalena, their arms filled with clothes. "Remember these?" she asked as they laid their loads on an empty bed. "We found knapsacks too, just big enough to hold one change of clothes, underwear, and toiletries. We'll leave you alone now to try everything on. I'm sure everything will still fit you. You'll join us later for dinner." She nodded to Sister Magdalena, and they left.

We busied ourselves trying on the clothes. They fit as Mother Superior had predicted, a little tight, but they fit—only the boots were not as heavy or as sturdy as they should have been for mountain wear. But they were all we had; they would have to do.

Packing did not take long. "Do you realize that we'll never pass through here again?" Berta mused. "This is the end of a chapter in our lives."

"I guess you're right," Elena answered.

"Won't we come back after all this is over and bring them a gift?" I asked.

Berta smiled. "Sure we will!"

As it turned out, Berta went back to the convent a few years after the war, only to be turned away. The nuns whom we had been with were no longer there. They had been sent to other convents.

The Order requires them never to spend too long a time in one place, so that they won't become too attached to anyone or any place. The new Mother Superior didn't know about events that had taken place during the war, and she couldn't help my sister in finding anyone. . . .

THAT EVENING IN the recreation room, we had a chance to say our good-byes to the nuns and receive their blessings.

After a restless night, we welcomed the dawn. We showered and dressed silently. We still had some time before heading to the chapel for morning prayers, so we decided to go up to the attic to glance through the window and take a last look at Sister Antonia's grave. We looked furtively through the dirty window pane and whispered our last farewells. "She was like our mother!" Berta said in a low voice.

"*Si*," we answered simply. We still missed her.

When we came back, we met Sister Magdalena in the hall, who was coming to see whether we were dressed properly and check that we hadn't forgotten anything. We entered our room together. She examined our knapsacks. "You forgot your toothbrushes, toothpastes, soaps, and combs." On her fingers, she counted the items we hadn't packed.

Berta and I volunteered to fetch them. When we returned, my sister said, "We didn't think we needed all that much. We could share most of it."

"I think it best each of you should have her own. One never can tell. Take your jackets and knapsacks downstairs with you. We'll put everything in the kitchen, so that you won't have to come back up."

We gathered our things, followed her to the door, and turned around to take one last look at the room we had spent so much time in. Once again I felt that, as soon as I became adjusted to one place, I had to move to another. On to another station. Would the time ever come when we found a place to call our own, our home? I tried to picture what home would be like. The one we once had seemed as if it had never been.

After we left our things in the kitchen, we entered the chapel. The sisters had already begun their matutinal prayers. We filed quietly into the last pew. I didn't pray. I was thinking, I won't hear them singing their hymns anymore! I loved listening to them.

As the prayers ended, Mother Superior left her seat and went to kneel in front of the altar. She invoked a special prayer for our safe journey. The sisters joined her incantation. I felt a deep sorrow then; I was already distancing myself from the place.

When breakfast was over, we helped with the usual chores. Before we knew it, the time had come for us to leave. We heard the truck driving up to the gate and hurried into the kitchen.

Mother Superior came in soon after. "It's time, girls! I'll say my good-byes now, my children." With tears in her eyes she embraced us and made the sign of the cross on our foreheads. "You must be brave. You must be strong. God be with you."

Sister Magdalena, with a few other nuns who were working in the kitchen, helped us with our jackets and silently gave us their last embrace, and we left.

We crouched behind the wall, waiting for the signal as was arranged, huddling together like thieves on the prowl. We had come clandestinely, and we were leaving the same way. Mother Superior was standing at the opening of the wall, as if supervising the work. We heard the sound of shovels slicing through the rubble, and the dull thud when it landed on the platform.

The waiting seemed to go on forever. My heart froze when I saw Mother Superior's head incline slightly. It was our signal. Instantly, I felt sorry that it had taken so fast. "Elena, you go first," Berta whispered. "Mina and Olga will go next, and I'll go last."

Without a word, Elena made her way to the truck following the instructions the men had given us. I stared tensely at her back. I thought my teeth would crack, I was keeping my mouth so tightly shut. I felt Berta's hand gently massaging and patting my back. "Be brave. It will be over soon," I heard her murmur.

How I made it into the truck remains a mystery to me. I must have blotted it out of my mind. All I remember is finding myself in the hollow of the truck, packed like a sardine among my sisters, and the men still loading the debris. I felt every stone they were shoveling over us, as if we were being buried alive. I lifted my arms and covered my ears with my hands to try to block out the noise of the falling rocks. I felt the vibration of each shovel load as it was emptied. I remembered the men telling us that the platform was sturdy. It brought little consolation. A tremendous fear came over me. I kept

❈ PART FIVE ❈

on thinking, We'll be buried alive. We'll suffocate! I gasped for air. My head went this way and that. Panic was setting in. I felt nauseous, and fearful I would throw up. "Please, God," I started to pray, "Don't let it happen, not now!" I put both hands over my mouth and kept on repeating in my mind, "Not now, later. Not now, later," and the rhythm of my unspoken words seemed to alleviate the sick feeling in my stomach.

The truck started to move.

FELT EVERY bump the car drove over. We stopped quite often. At first, we heard Italian spoken. The road was patrolled by the Italians. They wanted to know where we were headed and asked to see some identification.

As we moved further north, the roads and check points were controlled by German soldiers. "*Halt*," they yelled. "*Papiere*." Each time, a tremor went through us. Each time, the same thought occurred: *What if?* At one check point, after the German soldiers asked for papers, we heard them approaching the back, their heavy boots hitting the asphalt. "Where are you taking this *dreck?*" someone asked in broken Italian. We held our breaths, bracing ourselves for the worst. Our drivers had rehearsed the answer well in advance, knowing that, at one point or another, this question would come up.

Without hesitation, the driver said, "We were working in the city, at the bomb sites, clearing the streets. We have permission to haul the debris."

"And what do you think you are doing with this *schmutz?*" the same voice asked.

"We thought it best to dump it down the mountains. There's noplace to get rid of it in the city," our man answered positively.

"Shovel some of the *dreck* around," the soldier ordered. "Let's see what else you carry underneath."

The men complied. We heard a lot of movement and shuffling. Then, once gain, "*Halt!*"

My heart was racing and pounding so loud against my chest that I automatically put my hands over it to ease the pain, while my sisters put their hands over their mouths so as not to let an involuntary sound escape. "Get down from there!" the voice snapped . "We'll take care of it." With the butts of their rifles, they pawed through the rubble. Then they shot a few rounds into the debris. I closed my eyes tight. Silence followed. Finally we heard boisterous laughter. "If anyone is under that *dreck,* we made the burial easier!" one of the soldiers said mockingly. "*Weiter,* go, go !" came the final command.

The truck pulled slowly away; they didn't want to move too fast and attract attention. "Those bastards!" we heard them exclaim. At a safe distance they stopped the truck. The hatch opened, and the face of one of the men became visible. "Children! Are you alright?" he asked.

"*Sí, sí,*" Berta assured him.

"We'll be there soon." The hatch closed again . "Those pigs! Those *bastards!*" we heard them curse once more as the driving resumed.

AFTER THAT I lost track of the time. The motion of the rumbling vehicle lulled me into a light sleep; I dozed on and off. The air was heavy; some dirt had come through. The bullets had penetrated the platform through the debris. The soil must have stopped the impact and set them firmly in the wood instead of letting them come through, though they had cracked some of the surface. Dirt was covering us like a layer of dust.

"I am *hungry!*" I heard Berta mumble.

"Me, too," said Elena. "My stomach is making noises, and I have earth in my mouth! *Pfui!* Yuck!" She was making spitting noises. I chuckled. She heard me. "I don't think it's funny!" she snapped.

"I don't think so either. I just couldn't help it," I told her.

"Never mind your grumbling," Mina whined. "I have to *pee*. If we don't stop soon, I'll make in my *pants!*" Ultimately she did; she couldn't wait.

Finally, the truck came to a halt, and the hatch opened. "Kids, we have arrived," said the man in a low voice.

Berta was the first to sit up. "*Ouch!*" she exclaimed, having forgotten how low the platform over us was. "I don't know whether I can move, I'm so stiff!"

"Here, I'll give you a hand," he said. With some exertion, she struggled through the opening. It was one thing to get in, but another entirely to get out. It seemed our bodies had swelled or the hole gotten smaller. We were aching, and we cried out as we squeezed ourselves through. Two strong arms helped me down from the truck. Cold air hit me as I reached the ground. It was dark.

I almost fell off my feet; they were numb. I rubbed my legs up and down to get some circulation flowing into them. As I straightened out, I looked around in curiosity. A half moon was casting some light over our surroundings. I could barely make out the silhouettes of tightly clustered houses. The air was cool, the stillness interrupted only by a distant sound of a barking dog. No lights came through from any of the windows. "Follow us," one of the men hissed. "Try not to make much noise when you walk on the cobblestones. Around here, even the walls have ears."

We followed the men, hugging the walls, feeling our way around the corners. We didn't have to walk far. We stopped in front of a house where one of the men cautiously rapped three times at a door, waited a second, and rapped three times again.

A ghostly silence followed. I was almost afraid to breathe. I was shivering and clutched my jacket closer to my body. Without us seeing anybody, the door opened a crack from the inside, issuing a soft, moaning squeak we slid through it and found ourselves in a courtyard. We were told to stand against the wall, and a flashlight made a signal in the dark.

Out of nowhere, a man appeared in front of us, holding a lantern above his had. "Salvatore, Roberto, glad to see you back," he said in a muffled voice.

We followed them across the yard and through another door, which was already open. The stranger put his lantern down on the table. It was the only light in the room. He turned around to shake hands with our guides. "Did you encounter much traffic?" he asked. "Was there much movement out there?"

"No, not really, just lots of controls—more patrols than usual."

We seemed to have been forgotten for the time being; no one paid any attention to us. We just stood there at the door, following their conversation.

"What are they looking for this time?" the guide asked wearily, sitting down.

"From what I understand, ammunition being smuggled to the Resistance hiding out in the hills," the host answered. "A very inopportune time for us," he added.

Finally, he looked at us. "Please forgive my manners. Come, sit down. Take off your knapsacks and your jackets." He pulled up some chairs for us.

"*Grazie*," we whispered.

"My name is Gustavo." He was younger than our guides. He was tall, dressed in baggy black corduroys and a heavy sweater of the same color. Unkept dark hair was falling over his unshaven face. His eyes were black as charcoal.

He turned once again to the men he had called Roberto and Salvatore. "Rest a bit, have some food, and then you both better get going—otherwise, we'll have the whole damned *commando* breathing down our necks by morning, checking the truck."

There was a faint tap at the door. "Ah, this must be the food arriving!" He opened the door. A woman came in holding a big tray. "*Grazie*, Regina," he said, taking it from her. "You can go now. We won't be needing you anymore."

"*Buona notte*," she replied in a low voice, and left.

He put the tray, which was holding a covered pot, some wooden bowls, and silverware, on the table. "Regina kept this warm for you. She prepared one of her specialties! Her lamb stew is fit for a king's palate," he boasted, handing us the bowls and forks. "She even baked fresh bread." He broke off some pieces of the large, coarse loaf and offered them to us. As he uncovered the pot and proceeded to serve us, an exquisite aroma rose from it, reminding me of long-forgotten succulent repasts. We had never gone hungry in the convent, but the food had been adequate and simple, nothing like that stew. "Dig in! This food ought to strengthen your weary bodies," he urged us.

We ate in a silence interrupted only by the sounds of the forks striking against the bowls and the healthy slurps of Salvatore and Roberto.

"*Hm! Molto buono!*" said Roberto as he pushed aside his empty bowl after having a number of helpings.

"*Sì, sì, molto buono.* Grazie," agreed Salvatore, giving a satisfied, sonorous belch.

"Here, wash it down with some wine." Gustavo seized a bottle standing beside the table. "You too, kids. It'll make you strong," he chuckled, grabbing a few tumblers from the tray. He poured some red wine into them. "To your health and our success!" he called out, handing us the drinks and pushing the bottle towards the men. We sipped it slowly. It was good, strong-tasting, and flowed past our palates like honey, warming our insides.

"Where'd you find this treasure?" the men asked, looking appreciatively at the bottle.

"Ah! We hid our wines in the empty wells right in the middle of the courtyard. The mice and rats are making good cover. We can get to those bottles by a secret passage way from the stone wall in the basement." Gustavo uttered a robust laugh, as if he had made a good joke.

The wine had an immediate effect on us; we felt a little drowsy and started to yawn. He must have notices how tired we were, because, soon after, he said, "Well, you two must be off. These ladies need to go to sleep. They'll need all the strength they can muster for what lies in front of them."

At once, the men got up and stretched their bodies. Then they took some of the leftover bread and shoved it in their jackets. "*Sì, sì,* you are right. It's time. Give Regina our compliments." They turned to us, extending their hands in a firm handshake. "You are in good hands. Don't worry."

Without waiting for our response, they headed to the door, followed by our host. "Have a safe trip back. I'll see you soon with a new cargo, huh?" He slapped their backs while they muttered clipped good-byes. They swiftly opened the door and disappeared into the darkness.

How odd, I thought. I'll never see those men again. I wouldn't recognize them if they passed in front of me the next minute. They risked their lives to bring us here. Shouldn't I *feel* something for them? Did *they* feel something for *us*? Were *we* some of the cargo he mentioned?

Gustavo bolted the door after them. "*Signorine*," he said, turning back to the table, "I'll show you where you're going to sleep tonight." He picked up the lantern. "It's not a palace, but it'll do. Come."

We followed him across the room. A ladder stood against the wall.

"I'll climb up first," he said, raising the arm that held the lantern; it threw some light on the ceiling. "I have to remove a board, so that we can get into the attic." He handed the lamp to Berta. "Hold it up so that I can see what I'm doing." He climbed up, stopping at the third step from the top to give him space to maneuver the board. After some strenuous effort, he was able to slide it along the upper surface of the ceiling, creating an aperture. He climbed up the few remaining steps and slid himself through the opening. "You can come up now. Just be careful with the lamp!" he called down to Berta.

She led the way; clumsily and cautiously we made our way up, taking one step at a time, hoping that we wouldn't miss one and that the ladder wouldn't move, even though Gustavo was holding one end of it. It'd looked so easy when he went up. "Don't worry, she won't give way. She's sturdier than she looks!" he chuckled. He reached out an arm to help us into the attic.

The room was cold and spooky. The ceiling was very low. Cobwebs were hanging from the rafters. Gustavo had to bend down as he walked across the floor, sweeping the cobwebs away with his hand. He came to a table, barely standing on three legs against the wall. Before he put down the oil lamp, be blew at the dust that was covering the surface of the table. He swept the rest of it away with his arm. We started to cough as the particles of the dust reached our nostrils.

He lit another lamp, which was standing on the table. With better lighting, we could make out our surroundings. There was a big bed on the other side of the attic. "I would leave the lamp on if I were you," he said matter-of-factly. "It'll scare the mice and rats away." We automatically moved against the wall.

"I also advise you," he continued, "not to undress. It's cold up here, and the covers may not warm you enough. Under the bed, you'll find night pots. We have no toilets in the house. They're across the yard. It wouldn't be wise for you to venture out. At daybreak, we'll be off. I'll wake you." He grabbed one of the lamps from the table and turned to the ladder. "You must put the board back where it was after I go down. It's just a precaution, in case someone comes unexpectedly. And I will remove the ladder, too. *Buona notte!*" He descended the ladder, leaving us with a lamp that barely illuminated the attic.

We stood there, eyes wandering about. I was afraid to look around too much, so as not to run the risk of seeing a scurrying mouse. I knew I would let out a scream, and that would have been unsafe.

Elena tiptoed around the room with her arms behind her back. "Not a castle, huh?" she mumbled.

Berta seemed annoyed. "What did you expect?" she exclaimed. "You heard the man. Let's go to sleep." She strode towards the bed, and we followed her.

There were a few blankets on a soiled mattress, no linen, and no pillows. It wasn't much of a bed, and not too big either, but it had to do unless someone was willing to sleep on the floor. "We'll use our knapsacks as pillows," Berta said. We took our shoes off and climbed into bed. The spring gave way under our weight, each move answered by a weary squeak. We snuggled close to one another and covered ourselves with the blankets, which smelled old and musty.

I MUST HAVE FALLEN asleep at once. A gentle, consistent tap at my shoulder woke me. I didn't feel like releasing the sleep that still held me comfortably in its fold. I shifted position, unwilling to give in to the pleading voice of whoever was trying to awaken me. I just wasn't ready to get up yet.

I was shaken back and forth a little more urgently, and the voice asked for my immediate attention. I finally remembered where I was and jumped up, rubbing my eyes, fully awake. "Come on, Olga," Berta called out impatiently, removing the blanket. "We have to go. Everyone is already downstairs." She shoved my shoes in my lap.

"All right, all right! It feels like I just went to bed," I whined while I put on my shoes, then followed her down the ladder.

"Be careful," Berta said, looking up to me.

"Good morning, *signorine!*" Gustavo greeted us. "Slept well, I hope?"

My sisters were already seated at the table. "*Mangiate!* Eat heartily," he urged, "because this will have to be enough for a while."

We sat down, and Gustavo offered us fresh bread and homemade goat cheese, and poured milk into our cups. The milk was fresh and still warm from the cow. We thanked him for the food and started to eat in silence.

I glanced furtively at Gustavo. I hadn't had a chance to see much of him the night before. He was of medium height, and he had broad shoulders and almost no neck. His face was still unshaven, and he had an aquiline nose and a firm chin. His hair was thick and black, as I remembered from the previous night, and a hank of it was falling over his left eye. He was wearing the same woolen cap as the night before, rolled up so that it sat on top of his head, as sailors sometimes do. He wore a dark flannel shirt over a black turtleneck, the sleeves pulled up, revealing strong, hairy arms with bulging veins. He wore a lambskin vest, too. His heavy boots were soled with thick nails, like the ones worn for mountain climbing. When he walked, the wooden floors squeaked under his weight.

He sat down with us and started to eat his breakfast, making all kinds of noises while doing so. He finished with a big belch, removed a pocket watch from his vest pocket, and scrutinized the dials.

He shook his head a few times before replacing the watch. "My partner should have been here already," he grumbled, taking a pouch of tobacco out of his breast pocket. He slipped a pinch of the tobacco into his mouth and started to chew on it. "There will be two of us to take you across the mountains," he added.

A few moments later, three short taps at the door almost made us jump. Two more followed. In a split second, Gustavo retrieved a gun from the back of his belt. He motioned for us to get up and go to the back of the room. Weapon in hand, he crept to the door. Another two taps followed. Before he unbolted the door, he put his face next to it and asked, "What day is it?"

A muffled voice answered, "It's night."

Satisfied, he shoved the gun back into his belt, spat the tobacco onto the floor—it had lost its taste—threw open the bolt on the door, and opened it just wide enough to let in the man he was waiting for.

The new arrival was tall and clad in a lambskin vest just like the one Gustavo wore. He closed the door behind him and took a moss green beret off his head.

"You're late," Gustavo muttered grumpily. "We should have been on our way already. It's almost day break."

"I know, I know," the other answered. "Believe me," he answered sarcastically, "I didn't stroll around. I had to dodge all those soldiers patrolling the streets—and you're forgetting that the curfew is still on," the man explained. "There are too many soldiers around. More than usual. I don't like the smell of it." He shook his head as he said the last part.

Gustavo offered him a chair. The stranger took it, turning it around, slid it between his legs, and sat down. He rummaged in his pockets and retrieved a beat-up brown leather pouch tied with a string, from which he took a thin little white paper. He spread a thin line of tobacco onto the paper, which he held between the fingers of one hand, pulled the string with his teeth to close the pouch, and put it back in his coat pocket. He rolled the paper around the tobacco to form a clumsy cigarette. He sealed the edge with his tongue. He did all this with deliberate movements and his utmost attention, as if he had no other care in the world. He looked at the cigarette appreciatively and found a match in his pocket, which he lit by scraping it against the sole of his boot. The flame reflected against his unshaven face. He inhaled and exhaled deeply, and watched the smoke fade away.

Gustavo introduced us. "This is Loreto, my partner."

The man looked at us with dark, penetrating eyes. His aquiline nose and sunken cheeks made him seem an unsavory character; he made us very uneasy. He acknowledged us by raising his hat, then turned to Gustavo. "You know why there are so many soldiers around?"

"Salvatore and Roberto asked me the same thing last night," Gustavo replied. "My guess is that the Resistance must have done quite some damage at the railroad station. Now they're looking for the culprits. They also found a shipment of arms. I think there's a traitor among the boys," he concluded. "They found the weapons, but luckily none of the men."

"Do you realize this isn't good for us?" Loreto asked, shaking his head. "I think we should call this whole thing off. Postpone the trip." He drew deeply on his cigarette.

"It's a bad omen to change plans. We're going," Gustavo told him just as firmly. "We have to be extra cautious, that's all. Besides, I don't think it'll get any better—and then, what do you think we do with the kids meanwhile?"

While this conversation went on, we felt more and more uneasy. Our fate was being decided, and we had no say in it. "Here, have some coffee while I get my gear," Gustavo added. Without waiting for a reply, he went to the door.

He glanced about cautiously before disappearing into the street, leaving a pensive Loreto behind.

"Do you expect a lot of trouble?" Berta finally asked, not knowing what else to say.

He looked us over. His full lips parted, as if he wanted to say something, but he just gave us a grin.

"Well?" Berta wanted an answer, not that it would have mattered much either way.

"Maybe! We always have had trouble around here. Being so close to the border." He exhaled, blowing rings of smoke in the air. "We live in troubled times. We have learned to deal with them." He got up, throwing the cigarette butt on the floor, and stamped it out with his boot. He took the coffee Gustavo had left for him and gulped it down. "Only, lately, our lives have become more perilous, since we've undertaken this new line of work," he added.

We immediately understood what he meant. We sat there listening to him with anxious foreboding. Mina got up and ran to the bathroom. Berta took my hand. "We will make it," she whispered.

Loreto must have heard her. "You must leave the worrying to us. You just have to do what we tell you to. We want to get out of this alive, just as you do."

Gustavo returned, wearing a gray hooded jacket that almost covered his face. He was carrying two knapsacks and two rifles on his shoulder. He handed one of the rifles and a knapsack to Loreto. Across his chest, he wore a coil of heavy rope.

At the sight of the guns, Elena's eyes widened in terror "*Mamma mia!* Wh—what are you going to do with *those*?"

"Girls," Loreto replied curtly, "we aren't going on a picnic here. We may be getting shot at, and if we do, we'll have to shoot back."

Our situation hit us all at once. When Mother Superior told us about our voyage through the Alps and how dangerous it would be, we'd never realized how it would actually unfold.

Gustavo sensed our consternation and told us calmly, "Put your jackets on, your hats, and your gloves. Don't forget your knapsacks, and let's go. This is not our first time."

His icy calm subdued our fears for the moment. We quickly readied ourselves. Gustavo crossed himself and quickly opened the door.

WE STEPPED OUT into a beautiful dawn, the sky orange pink, sign of a clear, bright day to come. The air was crisp and fresh. Loreto muttered, "It had to be a clear day. I was hoping for fog to impede the visibility."

We stood against the wall, waiting in silence. A man on the rooftop was waving his cap, a signal that everything was quiet. Gustavo whispered, "We can move on now."

Loreto took the lead, with Gustavo covering the rear. We moved swiftly across the yard and rushed around the corner. We were facing open space. As far as the eye could see, valleys and mountains stretched before us, everything covered with a mantle of snow. The houses seemed so small and vulnerable in the distance, scattered about under the scintillating sky.

We hurried down a steep ledge. There was no sign of movement. The first light of day had begun to slant down from the mountains toward the valley we were approaching.

Soon the scenery changed, and we were making our way through thickly wooded terrain. We followed the fast pace Loreto had set. Gustavo was constantly looking behind him to make sure that no one was following us.

The small knapsacks we were carrying started to feel heavy. one step of Loreto's were two steps for us. But we went on as if the devil was after us. It was too soon to feel tired. We had to overcome any thoughts of fatigue.

It became more difficult to walk on the uneven terrain as the ground rose toward the mountains. The soil grew rocky. The sun was shining bright and clear, as predicted.

We took our jackets off and wrapped them around our waists; it must have been high noon by then. It seemed as if hundreds and hundreds of kilometers had slipped behind us. Jasmine was blossoming on the sides of the cliffs.

Our leaders never uttered a word. We passed shepherds with bearded faces moving their flocks with bells that tinkled at their necks as they dawdled across the mountains. They were coming down the valley in search of better grazing. The shepherds seemed to know Loreto and Gustavo and greeted them as they passed.

We climbed steeper and steeper, using our hands to help pull ourselves up over especially precipitous ledges. At times Loreto offered us the handle of his pick to give us a final push. "Don't look down!" That was the constant warning from the men.

When it became dangerous, Loreto stopped and fastened us one by one to the rope he was carrying, hooking either end to a heavy belt he and Gustavo wore so that, if we lost our foothold, either one of them would be able to pull us back onto the trail.

I didn't dare to look down, I was so scared at the tremendous abyss that seemed to draw me to it. At times, when the path became too narrow, we had to slide upward with our backs against the sheer rock. It was a blessing that we had our knapsacks on; otherwise, our backs would have been in shreds.

"Use your hands, and dig in with your heels for support," Loreto ordered once in a while. Laboring hard and breathing heavily, we advanced slowly. We stopped ever so often for a drink while the men peered through binoculars to assure themselves that clear passage was ahead, that no soldiers were crossing our way.

At one point we heard gunshots in the distance, sending us lunging for cover. "I think they've sent out the patrols and may have spotted us," Loreto muttered.

"I hope those bastards don't have dogs with them," Gustavo added in disgust, spitting and cursing.

"What are we going to do now?" Berta asked.

"We stay here for a while," said Loreto, "even though we're losing precious time. We only have so much daylight left. We can't walk at night—the mountains are too treacherous, even though desperate people do cross them, and many have ended up at the bottom," he added without expression. "But we'll play it safe."

A few meters above us, we found a crevice in the mountain where we found shelter for a while. We sat huddled and shivering; it had become cold as the day progressed into late afternoon. Our thin jackets did not give us much warmth. I was trying to picture those people Loreto had talked about at the bottom of the mountain. How desperate had they been?

The men scrambled out of the hollow to check the situation once again. Everything seemed quiet, and they felt it safe for us to go on.

We did. Fatigue started to set in; tears of weariness came to my eyes. I hoped no one, especially the guides, would see them. I was scared they would get annoyed with me or think I couldn't cope and slow them down.

As cold as we were, we found ourselves soaked in sweat and didn't know whether it was from the climbing or the fear of being caught. Loreto, looking back at us, realized how worn out we had become.

"We'll stop soon. Take heart," he said encouragingly. "One more hard climb, and then we'll stop for the night. Then you can rest."

Once again we fastened the ropes to our waists and continued the climb, gathering what little strength we had left in the knowledge that soon we'd be able to rest.

By then, there were no more paths—it was all rock. Loreto showed us how to master it. "Before every move, find a hold with one foot or knee, then lift yourself up with your hands till you're sure that the rocks will hold you. Don't go on till the person behind you has found a safe foothold, too. And only then go on to the next step. Take all the time you need, and concentrate only on your next step."

We worked our way ever so slowly. I had to dig my nails (whatever was left of them) into the ground tenaciously, till it had to give in, till it had to hold me.

Gustavo had changed position for that part of the climb. Rather than stay at the rear, he was following right behind me, so that when we used the rope I was fastened between Loreto and him. My sisters seemed to have the situation better in hand.

As we were moving around a bend I lost my foothold and felt myself slipping without being able to hang on to anything. I screamed. I was hanging suspended between the men, paralyzed with terror; senselessly, I started to swing my legs to and fro.

"Stop dangling your legs!" Gustavo yelled. "Push them *forward,* and try to find a footing. You won't fall. We have you securely by the rope. *Concentrate!*"

I tried desperately to swing myself onto the solid rock and grab it. My mind was racing. Oh, God, I thought, what if they can't hold me? Oh, please, God, help me! With whatever strength was left in me, I tried to do as I was told, yet each time I thought I'd found something solid, the rock gave way under me.

"Try with the tips of your boots," Gustavo coaxed me on.

"I can't, I *can't!*" I cried. Yet I went on trying, tapping at the rocks till finally my hands seized onto something. Slowly I felt the rope tighten and help me to stay on the ground. The strong arms of Gustavo and Loreto had gotten hold of me. I was pinned with my face against the rock.

"Move your leg and feel for a cavity to hold you." Loreto was holding my arm by then. My face was chafing against the mountain wall; my pants had ripped at the knees. I gave it one more effort and found a protruding ledge. I could stand on my own, and the grip of the men loosened. "You're doing fine," Gustavo called out.

When I realized I had found my equilibrium again, I started to sob uncontrollably.

"Come now, get hold of yourself. No need to cry. Let's go on," urged Loreto. My hands were bleeding and I had no nails left. It didn't matter. I cleaned the blood off against my pants.

All that counted now was to watch out for the next step, and then the next. Each advance without incident was a conquest.

The day was almost coming to an end. The sky grew orange-red in the distance, and our endurance was almost at an end when we heard another shot ring out from below.

We stopped climbing. Gustavo had once again taken the rear to be of help to my sisters. Loreto yelled to him, "Can you see anyone below you?"

"No, I can't see anything!" he yelled back. "We can't stop here. We must reach the other side. We're a sure target here. They'll pick us off one by one."

More than ever, we had to pull ourselves together, though the challenge wasn't of our making. Somehow, we made it up to the clearing as dusk fell.

MOST OF US carry an image of ourselves standing on a mountain, hiking along a trail, experiencing the majestic natural harmony and peace that nature radiates. Not for us: All we could feel then were the bumps, blisters on our feet, hunger, and chest pain. We hadn't eaten the whole day.

"This is it," Loreto called out. "There must be a cave around here." We walked a few more steps, tapping rocks, moving stones aside, till he found a hollow that would give us shelter for the night. He crawled in and, with the beam of his flashlight, looked around to see if the place was free of snakes and other threats. When he found neither, he called us in. We clambered in on our knees and lay down numb on the floor, almost falling asleep.

"Oh, no, *care mie*," said Gustavo. He was standing over us, grinning. "Oh, no. First of all, you have to go outside and try to do your business. Once we secure the exit with rocks, no one goes out anymore. Afterwards, you wash your hands and faces from the water bottle as best you can."

"Yes," agreed Loreto. "Then we will have to take care of the scrapes you have on your hands and knees so that they don't get infected, and then—" he grinned deeply, knowing that we could hardly hear him from exhaustion— "we will eat and drink, and go to sleep."

The magic words *eat* and *drink* made it easier for us to get up and, as quickly as possible, do what Loreto had told us. We had forgotten how hungry and thirsty we were in the exhaustion that had set in.

There were reasons for all the things Loreto told us to do right there and then. Once the night set in, the mountains were no longer glorious but full of danger. Walking about and taking a wrong step could send us flying down the precipice to our deaths. Patrols were out in full force, even at that altitude. They knew that desperate people were trying to reach the border; therefore, we couldn't have used a flashlight if we needed to relieve ourselves later on. We tried to clean ourselves as best we could and attend to our cuts, which, neglected, could have become quite painful by next morning, impeding the last *etape*.

Gustavo had quite an impressive first aid kit with him. He put some cream on our sores and bandaged our hands and knees. "Let me tell you, girls," Loreto said to us while he was rolling himself a cigarette. "Let me tell you, you are quite a quartet. You have shown resilience. Hopefully this will help us tomorrow on our last course."

Gustavo was nodding in agreement as he sliced slivers of bread and cheese he had produced from his knapsack. He came up too with a leather bottle filled with wine. "I surprised you, huh?" he laughed at Loreto. "I thought that some good wine for the road wouldn't hurt." He drank some of it and tossed the bottle to his friend, who quickly caught it. "Damned good wine," Loreto commented, gulping unceremoniously from it, making loud gurgling sounds. "Here, girls, drink up—it's better than water." He offered the bottle to Berta, who took it reluctantly; she would have preferred something hot at that moment, since the cold night air had started to set in. She didn't want to insult the men and took the wine, but not before furtively cleaning the top of the bottle. After a few swallows, she offered it to Elena, and so down the line. We drank the wine till the bottle was empty, passing it back and forth. It gave us a warm feeling.

After the food was gone, Loreto managed to get a small fire start-ed with some branches he had found in the cave. We all sat around it to warm up a bit. We finally stretched out on the ground and imme-diately fell asleep while the men were still talking to one another.

WHEN I OPENED my eyes, for a moment I couldn't remember where I was. It took me a while to make the transition back to reality after having slipped for hours into a dreamless void. I felt stiff, and my muscles were aching. Slowly, my awareness returned. The cave had acquired a damp, mildewy smell overnight. My eyes, still dazed with sleep, adjusted to the semidarkness of the hollow. Looking around, I noticed that my sisters were having a hard time getting up, too.

Loreto came over to us. "*Buon giorno!* I was just about to wake you. How are you feeling?" he asked.

I tried to get up.

"Not so good," we moaned in unison.

"C'mon, I'll help you up."

He reached his two strong arms out to me and pulled me up like a feather while I cried out in pain.

He went over to my sisters, who were in the same predicament, and got them off the ground, too. We put on our footgear and approached the entrance. Gustavo had already removed the rocks.

We looked out into a cold, drizzly morning. A gray mist hung in the air.

Loreto poured something lukewarm from a thermos bottle into tin cups. "This is supposed to taste like coffee, ladies. It is boiled-over chicory, our '*caffee ersatz*,' as the Nazis like to call it," he said sar-castically. "But it is better then nothing, and it is still warm. It'll hold you over for the few hours we have till we reach your destination."

We looked at each other in surprise when we heard those last words. They hadn't told us that we were so close. "We thought we had another full day ahead of us," Berta said.

"Well, we thought so, too. But we pushed very hard yesterday," Loreto explained. "We were lucky to be able to use a short cut to minimize an encounter with the mountain patrols. Not too many know about it. Besides, we never thought you could do it at such fast pace. Therefore we gained quite a bit of time."

"Let's not be too hasty now," Gustavo cut in with a word of caution. "We are almost there—if your legs will not hurt you too much."

"And," Loreto added pensively, "no unforeseen incidents occur."

"Such as?" Berta wanted to know.

"Patrols, *patrols*, my girl!" he answered almost angrily. "Drink up, and here—have some bread and cheese. The bread got stale, but it'll have to do."

The ersatz coffee tasted bitter and awful. We knew it would be better then nothing, though, so we gulped it down like taking a potion, making faces and crinkling our noses. It did warm our stomachs a bit, while it made our insides contract.

Before we set out again, Gustavo checked our hands and knees to see how our cuts and bruises looked. He rearranged our bandages and put some more on. "You have to keep them on your hands," he said. Since you have no gloves, they'll protect them and keep the dirt off. In five minutes, we're going. Do whatever you have to do to get ready." He pointed to a clearing. "There, behind the rock, you can do your business."

We took combs from our knapsacks and tried to make ourselves a little more presentable while each of us took a turn behind the rock. We took out the change of clothes we had left in the knapsacks and put it over the ones we were already wearing to keep us warmer. Thus we bundled up against the chilly morning air. The wind stirred; we tucked our noses into the upturned collars of our thin jackets. I wished I could do something about my torn pants, to protect myself against the cold air that was hugging my legs. The nuns had given us what they could, but had no second pair of pants to give us.

Soon we were on our way down the other side of the mountain, mastering the downhill slope. We were a little more in control of our steps than on the previous day. We still had to be careful not to slide, and to secure each step forward. The constant awareness of that one slip of the foot that would have made us lose control and slide down over the cliff was always present, our nerves and minds laid bare by the continuing consciousness of having to beat death.

I found myself playing a game, it seemed, to keep me more alert and less afraid. I have never told this to my sisters or anyone else. I never thought about it again—a fugitive notion lost amid so many thoughts and events that took place in those years. It puzzles me that I remember it now. It puzzles me that I feel I have to write it down. I won't try to figure out why. I know that at times I created an imaginary world inside me to ease the fright and the pain I felt. I already knew then that, while there's a big world out there whose inhabitants made bad things happen at times, we can create another world to live in for a while where dreams come true, one that is obscure and secret, hidden from everyone, which at times make it easier to go on.

I had in this fashion created an image of death: a tall skinny, scrawny figure with hollow eyes and two big holes for a nose indented in the face, whose lips were two thin lines that grinned unceasingly. I even imagined hearing deep, hair-raising laughter coming from within that skeleton of a figure each time it thought it had caught me off guard. It had long, skinny hands with bony fingers, too, most likely to better catch its victims. All the skeleton wore was a black cloak around its shoulders, and black tights; the cape waved like a banner in the wind. I could not figure out whether it was male or female.

It was gliding behind me, daring me to make a false move. Before each step I took, I said to it, "I guess you'd like me to take this one, eh?" while proofing the ground with my foot for the resiliency beneath it. Whenever I thought the image had nodded or become too eager, I immediately pulled my foot back to step onto safer ground.

Gustavo led the way now, and Loreto would lift us down to him when the going got too difficult. Thus we reached the half-way point. We stopped when we found a trail wide enough to allow us to sit. Gustavo produced a map from under his shirt and consulted over it, gesticulating often, with Loreto.

We looked around; the clouds were still hovering over the mountains. That day, there would be no sun; there was fog below us. We tightened our scarves closer to our chins.

Where was the pleasure and the enjoyment that comes with an awareness of nature, to heed the call of the outdoors, to discover, to experience the majestic harmony and pride of mastering the elements, all of which should give one a feeling of being free? Where was the excitement of standing there and seeing spring coming on—a time when the bare hills were waiting to show off their resurrection after the snow had melted? Where was the sensual gratification of seeing it happen while hiking along a trail? It didn't even enter our minds. How different that trip could have been! (Yet I experienced those feelings twenty years later; when I went back, as on a pilgrimage, to try to relive the past, it was a bittersweet experience.) It certainly inspired no joy in us then, only consternation.

Loreto clasped his temples. "Ah, my friend, I could use some grappa!"

No sooner had the last word been said than Gustavo slipped the load off his shoulders, rummaged through his backpack, and came out with a canteen. "Here." He handed it over to his friend. "Be quick about it. We have to figure something out." He pointed to the map. Loreto took a good gulp of the drink and then went back to examining the map with Gustavo, who kept on pointing up and down with his finger.

They started to talk to each other in a dialect we couldn't understand. At once we sensed that there was something wrong. We sat up straight, our backs rigid, ready to receive the blow.

Berta couldn't wait any longer. "Well, what are you talking about?" she finally asked.

Gustavo took off his cap and scratched his head. They stopped talking and looked about.

"Well?" she asked again.

"Girls, we have a problem." Gustavo turned to us and showed the map to my sister. "This doesn't show this crevasse you see in front of us. We are confronted with a crack in the ridge. Something has separated the mountain."

"Yes, yes," agreed Loreto. "Quite unusual." He scrutinized the fissure, measuring it with half-closed eyes. "I would guess it's a good two meters," he finally concluded. "What do you think, Gustavo?"

"I am in agreement," the other answered, taking another gulp of the grappa, and giving the canteen back.

Loreto reached for the canteen and took a swallow of grappa too, cleaning off a few drops of the liquid that had nestled in the stubble on his chin with the back of his hand. "We have to get across it in order to reach the plateau that lies behind the slope."

"We don't have the time," Gustavo continued, "nor will you have the strength, to go all the way to the bottom and climb up again to reach the other side." He paused, looking at us.

We hadn't the slightest notion what he was getting at.

"You don't understand, do you?" he asked somewhat rudely.

"Should we?" asked Berta in surprise. "We have a problem, that's all I understand."

"We have to reach the crossing within an hour," Loreto said with a glance at his wristwatch. "At mid-day, the border patrol switches sentries. For this, the guards must return to their sentry boxes. It also happens to be the only time of day you can try to run across the Swiss side. While the soldiers exchange formalities and give their reports, they won't be guarding the area that closely."

He stopped, took out a dark checked handkerchief from his pants pocket, and started to wipe his face. It was obvious that whatever else he had to tell us was not going to be pleasant, and it was making him uncomfortable. We sensed that there was more to it.

"Well, go ahead, let's have it." Berta looked directly into his eyes. "And don't leave anything out, please," she added, "We don't want any surprises."

Loreto gave him a push. "Tell them the rest. . .go *on!*" he urged.

"You'll have to make this by yourselves," Gustavo said at last, staring at the gap to avoid Berta's eyes, which were directed straight at him.

"You'll have to make the jump across this here aperture, and then go on the few kilometers that are left between here and the Swiss border." He wiped his face and blew his nose.

"*What?*" Berta jumped up as if bitten by a snake. "Did I hear you correctly? We are going on *alone* from here?" she yelled, terror-stricken.

"You're screaming," he whispered hotly. "The mountains have ears. Let me explain." He pulled my sister down to him, and told her to calm down and listen.

"You see," he continued, "we can't go any further with you, because if we should get caught with you, we'll hang no matter who gets us. Whereas if you were caught alone, you could tell them that you're orphans and have relatives a few miles across the border, and that you had no other choice but try to reach them."

He put his arm around Berta as if to console her. "If they ask for your papers, you tell them you lost them on the trip. Maybe, seeing four young kids, they'll let you go on. If not, if they don't. . .God help you."

For a while, everyone sat quietly. We needed time to digest that piece of news. Already pictures of doom were swimming in front of our eyes. Why hadn't they told us this before? It would have been easier having been prepared.

I was still playing my game; I looked behind my shoulder; Death was, as previously, lurking there. . . .

"And how do you suggest we get across?" Berta pointed toward the crevasse.

"We'll put a rope on each of you, around your waist, while you make the jump, and we'll hold the end of it so that we'll be able to catch you if. . .believe us, it's safer than the climb we've had up to now. There—there is no other choice," he added, apologetically shrugging.

"When you reach the other side," Loreto said, picking up the explanation where Gustavo had left off, "the terrain will be flat. No more climbing or descending. You'll have no problem walking around the ridge. . . .

"You'll be able to make out the barracks on each side of the border. You'll make a run for it, and don't stop till you reach the other side of the barrier where the Swiss flag is standing, and you'll be safe."

The long speech was over. It had been cold and impersonal. They had done what they were supposed to do.

We were wondering if we really had heard all that, or were we dreaming?

"Oh, yes, all we need to do is make a run for it and we'll be safe," Berta replied mockingly. "Maybe you'll be so kind as to tell us how *long* a run you think it is? Supposing we make it to the other side, that is! Is it a long-distance race that will take an hour, two, or less? How many kilometers are we talking about?" She threw these questions at them one after another, without waiting for an answer. "Oh, and another thing. Tell us, while we run for it, what do you think the Italians or Germans will be doing? Aren't they patrolling the area too, or will they conveniently look away as soon as they spot us, and calm their dogs down and order them not to chase us and attack us?"

Berta had stood up and planted herself firmly in front of the men. She became increasingly angry while she spoke. The guys looked in surprise at one another, not having expected such an outburst from one so young.

"There you go again. Calm down, young lady," Loreto said, trying to appease her. "I'll try to be as accurate as possible. This is what we calculated. We don't think it'll take you more than an hour at the most to make the crossing. When I said 'make a run for it,' I meant you'll walk briskly, straight toward your target, and you'll only run the last few hundred meters. Somehow, you'll know what to do. The whole distance is about five kilometers. . . . What the Italians or Germans will do is anyone's guess. All we know from our sources is that they're changing guards, and that it's their lunchtime. So we hope they won't be as alert either. That's all we can tell you. We all knew the risk involved, we all took a chance, and this is it."

Berta turned to us and shook us out of our stupor. "Let's take our knapsacks off," she said. "Take only your rosaries and the prayer books the nuns gave us, and put them in your pockets. These will be our passports, if the Fascists or the Nazis should catch us. The extra baggage will only hinder us. Let's go. No sense prolonging this. Time is of essence, and the less we think about it the better it'll be." She spoke like a commander.

To this day, as I think back, I can't imagine how she had mastered the courage and resoluteness to make us do what had to be done without a word of resistance.

She gave us a few moments and then turned to the men. "We are ready. Let Olga go first. It should be no trouble for her. She's very athletic. She used to take the steps down four or five at the time on the staircases in our home and at the convent. She'll make a perfect jump." She smiled at me.

I was holding my breath, stunned. A fleeting recollection of our house appeared before me, with my mother, at the bottom of the stairs, shaking her head and scolding me when she had caught me once again jumping down a flight of stairs or shooting down the bannister like a tomboy. She'd say, "It'll be your undoing one of these days if you insist on keeping this up. You'll break your neck!" She would give me a whack on my behind. Oh, God! I thought, she was right. She had foreseen the breaking of my neck, but neither of us could have known it would happen this way. But these weren't steps. Before I could protest, wanting to watch someone else go first, the rope was tightened around my waist.

"Step back and give yourself enough room to get momentum, then run and jump." Loreto went through the motion, showing me how it should be done.

"*Avanti,*" Berta yelled. I had no choice. I'd learned to obey. I felt the wind in my face. I mumbled to myself, "Mommy, you wouldn't be mad at me this time." I took a few steps backward and looked around me. Berta nodded. I bent forward a little, took a long breath, ran, picked up the tempo, and jumped. I had forgotten the game I played to look if death was following me. The game was over.

I fell as I reached the other side. But I'd made it. I lay in the dirt and could not get up. All strength had left me; I felt faint. No matter how hard I tried to lift myself up from the ground, I couldn't get up. My arms were trembling, and my legs had lost the strength to sustain me. I heard all kinds of voices swarming in my head. They were urging me on to do something.

"Get up! What do you think you're doing there? *Move!* unfasten the rope around you. The others have to jump, too!"

"I am getting sick! I'll throw up!" I heard myself answering back.

"A fine time to get sick. Just don't think about it. You must free yourself from the rope. Your sisters will help you as soon as they reach you. Come on, be a good girl."

Now I recognized Loreto's voice almost begging me to do as I was told. Finally I succeeded in getting up, and as I did, I became sick. I made funny noises, I heaved, but nothing would come up. What could one expect from an empty stomach? All we'd had that morning was that horrible black liquid reminiscence of coffee. My stomach contracted violently all the same. I fell back on the ground again, my head spinning.

"Here, this will make you feel better." I felt something cool being wiped over my forehead and softly cleaning my face. I opened my eyes and looked up into Loreto's.

"How did you get here?" I managed to ask him, dumbfounded.

"The same way you did, *cara mia*. I jumped. Someone had to help you." He undid the rope that was still around my waist and propped me up against a rock. I wanted to say something, but he stopped me. "Sh. Don't say anything now. Just save your strength and clean yourself up. Here's a wet handkerchief. That'll do." He undid the canteen that was hanging from his belt and gave it to me. "Here, sip some of this water, and then spit it out. It'll take the bad taste from your mouth." I did as I was told. My mind was clear now. All I could think was that he had jeopardized his safety to help me. "Now, take this piece of bread. You children haven't eaten anything this morning from all the commotion."

I gratefully took the bread and the water. I felt a little embarrassed for having caused such a dilemma. Loreto must have read my thoughts. "It's alright, these things happen. The body can take only so much, and you kids did your share. You did well." He squeezed my shoulders, and before I could answer him he jumped back to the other side. I sat there watching in awe while, at the same time, petrified to see my sisters making the jump over the crevasse. I couldn't believe I had done that, too. Berta was the last; as soon as she too had made it, the two men waved to us, we heard them faintly say, "*Buona fortuna,*" and they quickly disappeared behind the mountain.

We never found out what happened to them. Berta was still furious. She felt they had deserted us, leaving us too soon alone to march the last distance, however logical their reasons may have been. We kissed and hugged each other with tears in our eyes. The wet handkerchief Loreto left behind helped the others too to clean themselves after falling in the dirt as I had.

"Do you feel well enough to continue?" Berta asked me.

"We really should get going," said Elena.

"Oh, yes, yes," I answered, getting up, "I feel fine now."

For a moment, though, I felt as if everything was spinning around me. Berta caught me. "No, I don't think you are quite well. We will wait a few more minutes." She took my hand, pushed me down again, and dabbed the damp kerchief over my eyes and face. We removed the bandages from our hands. We had no more need of them, since there would be no more climbing; besides, they were dirty and tattered.

We scrutinized the new area and started to walk in the direction Loreto had shown us on the map. This time, the ground was easy. The slopes leveled off to an even trail. As easy as it was to walk it, though, so much more dangerous the walk would be. We could be seen quite clearly for miles through the binoculars in use at the observation posts. But on we went for a few miles.

At last we came upon a meadow from which we could see the barracks in the distance. We stopped to figure out how to go about reaching our next station. We could see barracks scattered in groups, some to the left and some to the right, with flags on either side waving back and forth in the breeze. Narrow buildings, taller than the others, were standing next to the flags. They must be the watch towers, we thought. We could make out the gates in front of them hanging horizontally from massive hinges to protect the entrance.

"Well, here we are," Berta said. "Thank God there's a bit of wooded area up there. We should start crawling till we get closer. Then we'll run as if the devil were after us, and not stop until we reach the other side of the gate. You understand?" She looked at us, expecting some questions. When she saw there wouldn't be any, she continued, "We will not stop or look behind us once we start running." We all nodded. "Now, for the most important part, and if it happens, the hardest. . . ." Her voice lost its tone, but soon she was once more in control. "You must swear that, no matter what happens, *no* one is going to stop for any of us till we reach the Swiss side. We wouldn't be able to help each other anyhow if something should go wrong. Our aim is to stay alive. Remember what Papa told us? One survival is better then none." She made us swear and repeat after her, word for word, that each was on her own once we started the run. "You see there, to the left of us? That's the Swiss border. It has the red cross on the flags. That is the direction in which we must proceed."

After that, everything went so fast. It was like watching someone else going through the motions, Berta's voice once again commanding, "*Avanti*, good luck," and all of us going down on all fours and starting to crawl between the trees that separated us from the border. I began to regret having discarded my bandages too soon. The cuts on my hands had reopened as soon as I touched the rough ground. They started to burn.

All of a sudden we heard voices in the distance. "Let's hurry," Berta whispered. "Whoever they are, they seem to be too far to have

PART SIX

spotted us. We don't have far to go, and then there will be no more trees giving us cover." She paused. "Then we'll make that run. I don't think it's wise to wait till those voices fade away. They also could come closer. What do you think?"

We agreed to go for it. We tried to make our movements as inconspicuous as possible and not to crack any branches from the bushes in our way. As my sister had said, it only took a few more minutes till we reached the last trees that gave us some cover. Now it was time for the most important run of our lives.

"Kids, we've come too far for anything to go wrong now. You can almost reach across. So take a deep breath, and don't stop for any thing. Remember?"

We took one last look at each other, our hands bleeding, our faces wet with sweat, and began to run straight towards that horizontal bar that stood between life and death for us.

The impact of our bodies broke the bar. We fell against two guards who had come out of their posts to stop us. Too late for whoever was yelling, "*Halt!*" we were on Swiss soil.

THE FOUR OF US

THE INITIAL SHOCK over, we stepped back from the surprised guards. We looked at each other, breaking out in laughter; impulsively, we embraced, and for a moment we stood silent.

"We are *free!*" Berta shouted. "*Free, free!* . . ." We could still hear the soldiers on the other side yelling, "*Halt!*" and firing warning shots in the air.

The Swiss soldiers found themselves in control again.

"*Na*, let's see what we have here," one of them said in German. It had an odd accent.

"Young ladies, will you explain what on earth are you thinking of doing?" He stood in front of us with legs spread apart and arms folded across his chest, fixing his eyes menacingly on us, waiting for an explanation— trying to act with authority yet not knowing how to handle the situation. They were new recruits at the border position and had not yet encountered something like this, refugees bringing down the gate in plain sight of the border police from where the shots were coming.

Now the surprise was ours. We were not ready for, had not even thought of, what would happen after we got through safely.

In our innocence we assumed we would be welcomed with open arms, no questions asked, and congratulated on having accomplished such a dangerous feat. Surely the Swiss knew under what peril we found ourselves in. We would ex plain and, without a doubt, find our parents, and after that we'd start a new life and live happily ever after. Yet this soldier was asking us what we were *doing*. Wasn't it obvious?

Berta, as usual, was our spokesman; besides, she was the only one who still spoke German fairly well. "We have been lucky to make it safely to your border. We are Jews. We had no other choice but try to escape. We know that our parents escaped too, and made it safely inside your borders."

"*Ach so*, you have a mama and a papa here. Do you know where?"

"*Nein*, but surely—"

"Let me see your papers," he demanded, not letting her finish the sentence.

"We don't *have* any. I just told you."

"Never mind what you just told me." He unfolded his arms and waved his hand at her, giving her to understand he was no longer interested in what she had to say. He turned to the other soldiers who had been standing around, curious, watching, and asked them if something like this had ever happened before. They shrugged and looked away. They knew very well what it was all about, since refugees of all sorts arrived at the border begging to be let in on a daily basis. The soldiers orders were to turn everyone back unless there was a proper passport or valid paper.

"Alright, let's go to the captain's office," the soldier finally concluded. "It's up to him to decide what to do with you. Follow me." Relieved, thinking that a captain would be more understanding and knowledgeable in these matters, and wouldn't give us any problems, we followed.

He led the way across a patch of grass to where another barrack stood, and knocked at the door.

"*Herein*," a voice answered briskly. The soldier shoved us nonchalantly through the door. Inside, he saluted his superior, who was seated behind a gray desk half covered with papers and maps. The other half was taken up by a black box from which all kinds of knobs and buttons lit up in quick flashes of red and yellow. A glass stood next to it filled with pencils, standing upright, with sharpened points. The walls were just as gray as the desk, and bare. In one corner, a Swiss flag hung limply from its wooden pole; two large lockers stood side by side along one wall. A closet door was open, through which one could see shelves full of boxes and stacks of papers. Another had a heavy padlock hanging from the handle as if guarding some deep secrets. The desk stood between two windows with bars, like the ones in a prison cell. Not looking up, the captain asked, "What is it, Lieutenant?"

The other came to attention. "These *frauleins* came charging through the barricades, sir, and have no identification papers on them, sir."

The captain finally looked up, took off his spectacles, and pinched the bridge of his nose, closing his eyes for a second; then he contemplated us thoughtfully without a change of expression in his pale face.

"At ease," he said at last. He rose from his chair and came around his desk. He must have stood six feet tall; so at least he appeared to me. He placed himself in front of us, gazing at us with cold blue eyes. I felt the heat rising in my body. Yet my blood froze. I searched for my sister's hand while standing at attention, too. I looked up at a clean-shaven, angular face. He had almost no cheekbones and was sucking at his lower lip, which lent his features a grotesque look. He had a high forehead and a crew cut; his dirty blond hair stood brightly at attention, too.

Oh, my God! I thought. We will not get any sympathy from this man; he scares me. He feels like an icicle in uniform. At last, the icicle spoke. "*Keine Papiere*. You cross the border without identification, what do you expect us to do?" His question hung in the air.

We had grown smaller by the minute, till we felt like worms crawling on the floor, waiting to be trampled on at any moment. No one answered. The icicle spoke again, this time louder; maybe he thought we hadn't heard him the first time. "*Keine papiere*, no identifications. I guess no tongues either, huh?"

"Sir, if I may answer for them, they said they are Jewish and threw their papers away, sir. They didn't want to get caught with false papers by the Germans, just in case. One more thing, sir. They said that they have parents here too, sir."

"Aha, so they have tongues after all, if they were able to talk to you," the captain said sarcastically. His attempt at a smile resembled a grimace. "Maybe you'll tell me all about it too, whenever you are ready, of course!"

Berta, finally goaded by his sarcasm, came to life again and looked him straight in the eye. "We walked and climbed our way across the Alps," she said, "with the help of smugglers who showed us the way. Our parents have found refuge in this country. We were told that they had arranged to get us here, and to find them through the Red Cross. Now, all we ask is for you to get in touch with this organization. They will verify everything I have told you, and find our parents, so that we may join them."

The captain was neither moved nor impressed. "Why should I believe you? Parents don't leave their children behind, that's unheard of. If anything, they would have stayed behind with you and not be here," he replied curtly. He had figured it all out, and was pleased with himself for it. We looked at each other. Had we heard correctly? This man hadn't listened to a word my sister had said. Was it possible he didn't know what was going on? Surely we weren't the first ones to have crossed the border under these circumstances?

"Our orders are not to allow entry to any foreigners anymore. Our orders are specific, especially for those without papers. We can't make any allowances." He started to pace back and forth. "We've had to turn back quite a few people already. This is a small country. We have exhausted all the facilities were to place newcomers. Besides, we are a neutral country and have to live in peace with our neighbors. Can you imagine," he continued, "the chaos that would result if we opened the border to everyone who seeks asylum?" Once again he stopped in front of us. "And don't think for one moment that, because you are children, we can be persuaded. We have rules, regulations, and laws to abide by." He emphasized these last remarks by gesticulating with his arms.

The world had really gone mad! How could this man talk about laws and rules? Was there a law to kill Jews? Mr. Mazza came to my mind. Would he have been able to explain this to me? Oh, how I wished I could have been able to ask him, or the priest who taught me to pray. Was God testing us here, too?

"What are you telling us?" Berta asked, incredulous, turning pale.

"*Mein Fraulein*, what I have been telling you, if you would have had the courtesy of listening to me, is that you can't find entry into this country." The captain had bent down toward Berta, speaking to her as if she were hard of hearing.

"But—" she involuntarily took a step backward, since she could feel his breath on her— "I already told you, *our parents are here*. All you have to do is to get in touch with the Red Cross. They are the ones who set all this in motion and know exactly where to find them. They know our story. Our real names are Berta, Helene, Mina, and my little sister Goldy Silbermann." She had used our real names—there was no more need to use our alien ones. Our parents had surely used their real names too, and had given ours to the Red Cross.

Yet the icicle wasn't about to melt. In fact it seemed he would stay frozen, more determined than ever to follow all rules and regulations.

"So you think that, if I call the Red Cross, they'll produce your parents at once, just like that?" He snapped his fingers. "Do you know how many refugees we have in this country as of late?"

"Well, no," Berta answered, still in shock. "But you must! You *must* call the Red Cross and tell them our story. They are the only ones that can help us. You can't send us back. You know that we'll be *shot* out there, and you won't be better than *they* are," she said brazenly. "That's not what neutrality means!" Her voice was starting to quaver, and that was the last thing she wanted him to notice. "It is your *duty* to let us stay," she insisted, getting the strength back in her voice. My mouth stood open.

"Young lady, I am very well *aware* of my *duty*!" the captain yelled at her.

Mina started to cry. "You—you *can't* send us back!" Her body shook from sobbing. Helene's face took on an odd look, too. She'd start bursting out in tears any moment. She had tried to repress them, but now there was no more will in her. We are finished! she thought.

What was I to do? I felt I had to do something. This was serious. This could be the end. I saw my father in front of me demanding, and yes, expecting us not to fail. I remembered the cellar in Mr. Mazza's castle, and heard my father's voice telling me, "There may come a time when it'll be up to you. . . ." Right there and then, I forgot that I had felt like a worm and that the captain scared me, and shouted, "We *won't* go back! We *can't!* Don't you *see?* Please! I want my *parents!* I *miss* them so. They are waiting for us, honest." I turned towards Berta, put my arms around her waist, and began to cry, too.

We will never know what changed the icicle's mind. Was it the intolerable noise we made with our sobs and sniffles, or the unbecoming sight of us?

"*Ach, Gott,* this is *impossible!*" he hollered angrily. "Lieutenant, get these kids out of my sight. Lock them up till I decide what to do." He motioned with his arms for us to leave and returned to his desk without looking at us again.

The lieutenant seamed relieved and jumped to attention. "Yes, sir, right away, sir." He clicked his heels and turned to us. "Let's go. Quickly." He was smiling broadly. Once outside in the corridor, he said, "I think you have done it!"

He marched us out of the building and into another one that stood near by, and ushered us into an empty room that also had barred windows.

"Sorry, ladies, you must remain here till the captain decides what to do next and calls for you." He turned on his heels, locking the door behind him.

"Do you think that was necessary?" asked Helene, "To lock us up? Where did the captain think we would go?"

The room was dismal; the walls were cracked and dirty, chips of paint were hanging loose; names, crosses, and Stars of David were scribbled and smudged on them. The room was cold and ugly. Yet we knew that, as long as we were in it, we were safe. We had come so far and found ourselves in so many worse predicaments. It did not matter.

While we were no longer scared, to be locked up in that cell gave us an eerie feeling that did not lift our spirit. Forlorn, we looked around. There was a foul odor in the room; most likely the windows were never opened to let in some fresh air. We couldn't open them even if we wanted to—they were much too high for anyone to reach them or be able to look out. There were no chairs or anything to sit on, so we sat on the cold, filthy stone floor, hunched together closely for warmth and comfort. We still had no understanding why they would do this to us.

"I hope they won't keep us here long," Berta grumbled.

"I have to go to the bathroom!" Mina announced. She always had to go to the bathroom at the most inopportune times. We knocked at the door to get someone's attention, but no one came. We called out and yelled as loud as we could, and still no answer.

"I hope that someone else knows that we are here other then the lieutenant and the captain," Mina said. "Now what will I do?"

We looked about to see how we could accommodate her. There was a pail in the corner. "Here, use this." Berta handed it over to her.

"You must be kidding!" she cried.

"Do you have a better idea?" Berta asked. "We made it in worse places. Remember?" We all managed to laugh at last, and realized that it would have been worse having nothing. Mina went about her business, moving to the far corner of the room. In the stillness of the cell the noises she made sounded loud and crass.

"Can't you go about it more ladylike?" Helene snapped. Then realizing where we were, and the circumstance, we burst out in laughter again. It was better then tears. We sat on the floor, leaning against the wall. "When will all this come to an end?" Berta wondered.

"What do you think will happen?" Helene asked her.

"Your guess is as good as mine."

"Will they send us back, like they did the others?" I asked this time. No one answered.

"I am getting tired," Berta said. "I think we should try to rest and close our eyes for a while."

We fell into silence, each lost in thought. I tried to remember all we had learned the past year in the convent. I heard Mother Superior's voice; she used to say that patience was a virtue, and that to forgive made you a better person. Why those words came to my mind, I couldn't say. I went on thinking of the war. What was war in the long run? Who benefitted from it? War was treachery. It made you cease to be a person.

Sleep eluded us and denied the well-deserved rest that would have taken our minds off things that night. We shifted from one side to the other. We couldn't find a comfortable spot. We rose from the floor, walked around a bit, and sat down once again. They must have forgotten us, since no one came to bring us food or water. No one came to see if we still were alive or needed something. Yet ever so slowly the night passed. The dawn found us cold, dirty, and hungry. The morning approached us weary with new hatred and sick to our stomachs. We had exhausted our minds with thoughts and memories.

Finally our locked cell was opened. A soldier made his appearance. He stood at attention. Berta smiled sarcastically and said, "What do you say, someone is standing at attention for us!"

"I am Corporal Stream, *gruss Gott*." The last part of it meant "greetings to God" or "God should be greeted" or whatever. I remember my sister commenting on how inappropriate that hello was. God had nothing to do with it. He wouldn't have wanted four kids locked up for the night in such a hole without food, water, or a latrine. God wouldn't have wanted to see his children this way, or having them treated like this.

"Ladies, I have breakfast waiting for you, and some good news!" He seemed to be quite happy to be the bearer. He had a round, healthy-looking face, and was of medium height and quite good looking. "You are going to be allowed to stay in this country, and you will be sent to the quarantine detention center, which is on the other side of the camp. They'll also try to find a place for you to stay after that."

We had no idea what he was talking about. "Will you please explain to us what *quarantine* means, and what a *detention center* is?" Berta asked. "Oh, and please speak slower, we can hardly understand you."

"Well, I really don't know all the details. Every one entering illegally and having retained permission to stay must go through a quarantine. To make sure that you are not carrying diseases with you. Furthermore, anyone coming into this country must have a place to live. Since you have no place to go, you will be detained in the camp while the Red Cross finds families willing to take you in."

What the corporal thought was good news it did not sound so good to us.

"What about our parents?" Berta said. "Surely we don't have to be *placed* anywhere. When you will find our parents, we'll live with them,"

"I really can't answer that. Right now I am to take you to the mess hall for some food. I told you only what I overheard. I thought it would make you happy. Let's go," he concluded, a little annoyed that the news he had brought hadn't brought the reaction he expected. Feeling this annoyance, Berta did not want to press him for more information, and asked for a bathroom.

"Later, girls. Right now we have to get you some breakfast, before the kitchen closes."

He herded us through a hall and out the front door. We inhaled deeply; after the stale air in the cell, our lungs craved fresh air. We crossed a narrow alley that separated the barracks from one another, and entered the mess hall. No one was there. It was a big hall with a long row of tables with benches on either side. The silence and emptiness of the hall gave us an eerie feeling.

The corporal led us to a set of double doors across the hall, where we found the kitchen.

Three men in white pants, white jackets, and starched high hats were busy peeling potatoes and cleaning vegetables. A big pot stood in front of them. They were having a spirited conversation, laughing loudly every so often, slapping each other on the shoulder when something funny was said. As we came in, they stood at attention and saluted.

When the formalities were over, they sat down again and continued with their work. One of them said, "We were expecting the girls. You'll find three trays set up for them. You don't mind eating in the kitchen, I hope?" The others laughed.

The corporal motioned with his arm toward the table. "Go ahead."

We devoured everything on the tray. We had not eaten since the day before. . .when they locked us up for the night, no one had bothered to ask us if we had eaten.

When we were finished we asked once again for the bathroom.

"You must hurry up," said the soldier. "A truck is waiting to take you to your quarters."

"Truck or no truck, we simply must *go*, if you know what I mean!" Berta said, angry now that the guy could not understand our needs after having seen the cell he picked us up from.

"And we need to wash up too," she snapped.

Finally the corporal understood and took us there. Little things started to mean a lot. We were so happy to be able to wash up and tidy up and at last use a real toilet once again after having done without for such a long time. What a pleasure!

We WERE REMINDED to hurry by a knock at the door; they were waiting for us, we had to leave, and then on to another station. . . . Would this be the end of the line? Quarantine, and then free? Free to do what? It had been such a long time since we had been free to do things that pleased us. For me such times were almost forgotten, as if they had never been; I'd been too young then to understand what it meant to be free to choose your time. I only remembered the years of forced things to do. Strangers telling you what you could or couldn't do. Musts and must nots, when and where and how, always being on guard, always watching behind you. I tried to imagine how it would be like to be able to relax, not having to look over your shoulder or having the feeling of being watched.

I thought about the new language I would have to speak. I spoke it at home (actually it was our mother tongue, even though Italian had taken over). This German had a different accent to it, however. I guess one would get used to it; even if I had forgotten most of it, I still understood it and would pick it up. What worried me most was, how would I adjust to all this—the people, the ambiance? My thoughts were interrupted by the corporal calling for us impatiently outside the door.

"Let's go, *meine Damen*. The truck is ready and waiting. We don't have all day!"

"Are we ready?" Berta asked. "No sense letting them wait. Let's go and meet the future." She opened the bathroom door.

Now more relaxed, we followed the corporal through the hall door into a glorious morning. We were surrounded by mountains, the snow melted and only the very peaks, still capped, glittering in the distance under the rising sun. Narrow roads, etched in the grassy meadow that spread before us, curved away inland in different directions.

The truck was parked in front of the barracks, motor running, waiting for us. The same group of soldiers we had seen the day before was standing by, waving at us. They helped us into the vehicle. When we were seated, they lifted the tailgate and saluted us. The corporal waved the driver on, and with a jolt, we drove off. This time, in comparison, we were transported almost elegantly. With no cover over us or hay to hide us under, we rode openly, without the old angst of being caught or asked for our papers. On each side there were benches to sit on. Silently, we looked around and scrutinized the surroundings we were traversing. We descended the mountain and were soon driving on paved roads. More houses appeared. We came closer to civilization. In the distance we could hear the rumbling of planes and the noise of falling bombs. There was no mistake. We had been accustomed to the sound of dropping bombs. We were close to the border, and the raids of the adjacent countries could be heard.

But what had scared and concerned us yesterday was no longer of importance to us. We were out of it, though yesterday was still a reality. The spirit of the mind is a wondrous thing.

We drove past factory buildings with high smokestacks emitting black fumes. Neatly dressed people walked along or rode on bicycles. They looked different from those we had left behind. Their faces were not shadowed by sorrow and hardship. Their eyes did not look spent. They were smiling; they looked happy, well fed, and well dressed. Ever so often, they nodded toward an oncoming person in greeting. Flower pots with blooming blossoms decorated the balconies and window sills. It came to my mind that I hadn't seen too many flowers in Italy other than those cultivated by the nuns. Where had they gone?

It was a short ride to our destination. We drove to the outskirts of Basel. We knew we had arrived when we entered a barbed-wire gate. Soon after, we came to a stop in front of a barrack where sentinels were guarding the entrance to the main building. When the truck came to a halt, so did the guards. They stamped their feet and stood at attention, dropping their rifles from their shoulders, to rest along their right flanks. The driver jumped off the truck, saluted them, and handed over some papers. One of the guards leafed through them and, after assuring himself that everything was in order, came to the back where we were, unlatched the tailgate, and helped us down. The driver saluted once again, climbed back into the truck, and drove off.

The guard opened the door and led us into a very lively busy office. A line of desks occupied by uniformed men and women filled a large airy room. Telephones were incessantly ringing. Receivers picked up and banged down; buttons pushed in and out with lights going on and off accordingly. Voices came through intercoms, barking out commands, while others were summoning someone or bending down at a seated soldier to ask something or show some papers. Typewriters were in audible use, busy fingers harmoniously striking keys. The office was filled with a haze of smoke coming from so many lit cigarettes. Books and papers crammed the surface of the desks. The shelves that lined the walls were filled with all kinds of books, an impressive Swiss flag covered the width of one wall, and various maps hung from others.

A soldier approached us as we entered. The guard saluted and handed over the papers our driver left with him. It was now someone else's turn to scrutinize their contents. More and more, I felt in awe of those documents: Would they free us or doom us? The soldier dismissed the guard and told us to follow him.

"I'll take you to the reception depot, where you'll meet the camp director," he said dryly.

We traversed an asphalt yard through another gate and yet another barrack door. He let us standing in the hall.

"Wait here while I announce your arrival to the commander in charge." After knocking, a command to enter came from behind the door.

"To hand over those papers once again, no doubt!" Berta said sarcastically.

We began to feel uneasy regarding those documents. What could they possibly contain, and what important things could they divulge?

We had just arrived without a shred of identification. Yet there were pages and pages. To occupy my mind with something else, I took a look out the window. The area, enclosed by barbed wire, brought a chill. We were imprisoned once again, I thought.

There were many rows of barracks. Some were lined with trees, which cast big shadows against the walls and streets.

There was quite a bit of traffic out there—people on bicycles, people walking about, people stopping to chat with one another. They wore drab gray clothes. The women wore kerchiefs on their heads, and most of the men painter's hats. They all seemed to look alike.

What struck me was something in their faces. No one smiled, even while talking with each other; there was no expression in them. They looked sad and empty. I knew they had to be refugees as we were. Otherwise, they wouldn't have been there. So why that sadness? It must have been that barbed wire that affected them. It perturbed me, too.

A terrible thought occurred to me. What if I too get to look like that? What did I have to smile so much about? They too must have gone through a lot before they reached this place. Would I ever forget? Who would care, after all? Wouldn't it be embarrassing to those who let it happen? Why hadn't the grown-ups put up a fight? I wondered. Why had no one stood up for us and not let us be persecuted? We wouldn't have been there, begging to let us stay and pleading to find my parents. Had these people risked their lives too to get there?

Did the partisans know that the Swiss had sent back people knowing what would happen to them? Hadn't they almost sent *us* back? How had these people gotten to stay?

"So this is going to be our shelter for a while," said Berta, interrupting my troubled thoughts. "Looks pleasant enough, don't you
think?"

"Look at the barbed wire! We're in a prison!" I said, worried.

A door opened behind us. We spun around, feeling we'd been
caught like peeping toms.

"*Kommen sie herein*. Come in!"

We entered an office.

"This is Commandant Yaeger, the camp commander!" the corporal explained, introducing us, and asked if his services were still needed.

The commander shook his head and dismissed him with a salute.
We were standing in front of a tall, well-built man with light brown
hair, high cheekbones, and a clean-shaven face from which steel gray
eyes gazed at us. "Please sit down while I familiarize myself with
these papers." He motioned us to chairs that stood around a coffee
table in the corner of the room.

The camp director turned briskly toward his voluminous desk.
He swung his chair toward the window behind it and became
immersed in those documents, giving us a chance to examine him further. He had broad shoulders that contrasted impressively with his
thin waist. He wore his uniform impeccably fitted and pressed; it
suited him like a glove. I whispered to my sisters, "I wonder how he
can sit down, his pants are so stiff," and giggled. Berta put her finger
to her lips, giving me to understand to be quiet, and poked me in my
ribs with her elbow. There were a few medals on his jacket and a few
stripes on his sleeve, insignia of a high-ranking officer.

"So you are the new refugees!" I thought I detected a mocking
tone squeezing a thin smile from his full lips. His voice was strong

and clear. I felt that there was no human sympathy in him. He looked us over. He didn't like us. I perceived that immediately. I couldn't say why. Kids have a sixth sense about these things. He made me feel like a nonperson with his cold gaze. Involuntarily, I looked down and realized how wretched we must appear in his eyes. We were still wearing the same clothes we had worn when we left the convent. By that time, they hung like rags on us, torn, dirty, and smelly.

"I guess we are," Berta answered, looking intently and unashamedly in his face. She too felt that our appearance must seem revolting to him, but she had decided not to come across meekly, and that we had nothing to be embarrassed or ashamed of—it was his problem if he didn't like us, not ours. All we wanted from life at that moment was to be reunited with our parents and live happily ever after.

My sister's answer and demeanor surprised the commandant, because an astonished look came into his eyes. Apparently Yaeger preferred to see us with downcast eyes, afraid and timid, so that he could feel superior and give us to understand that we were under his mercy, which in a way we were. He was responsible for final decisions regarding detainees.

He never liked to look into the refugees' eyes, to see them staring at him with pleading eyes, with the hope not to be sent back. They had come too far. Yet some were sent back and never seen or heard from again. He was uncomfortable in the presence of all these losers. Now too, he preferred to avoid Berta's eyes. He leafed through the documents once again till he found something suitable to say.

At that moment we knew instinctively that he had thrown the book at us. I have never understood what makes people know in a split second that someone likes or dislikes them—what makes us discriminate against or for someone, what that invisible flow is which draws one to another or signals an absence of contact, in short, all that lends a reality and essence to what makes us human.

"Has anyone told you what to expect here?" he asked coldly.

"We have been told that we will be in quarantine." Berta stopped for a moment to look at us. "And then, hopefully, meet our parents and to be able to live with them."

"You were well informed, young ladies. About the latter we will see. We'll have to work that out."

We all had the urge to ask him what he meant by those remarks.

Berta quickly realized, though, that to press at that moment for an explanation would not be the best thing for us, and she quickly suppressed that consideration and squeezed Elena's hand, to give her to understand not to question him either.

"Have you also been told that everyone must work while being here?" he continued.

"No," Berta answered, "we haven't, but it won't be a problem. We have worked before."

My intuition of his dislike of us was right, because, from then on, all the dirtiest jobs around were given to us. By asking others, we later found out that we had been explicitly chosen for those duties by Yaeger.

"Very well, then, we'll see. For now I will take you over to the delousing station. You will meet with another group of refugees who arrived last night. Together you will shower, get new clothes, be told of the routine of the camp, and assigned to your barracks."

The interview was over. He marched to the door. "Follow me," he said harshly.

We looked at each other; Elena smiled at Berta and, in a barely audibly whisper, said, "You didn't make a big impression on this man!"

Berta shrugged. "There will be others." A mischievous smile played around her lips.

We followed Yaeger down the block. To our surprise, we came upon real buildings, not the wooden barracks we had seen so far. There were a cluster of sturdy houses with many stories. The commandant pointed them out to us one by one with his cane, which he carried at his side like a sword.

"We are coming to the bathhouse and dispensary. To the right, the tan building is where our hospital is housed. We are very proud of it. It is very well equipped. We even have a nursery. To the left, you have the laundry room, kitchen, and mess hall, where most likely we will find work for you." For a while we felt like tourists. He pointed out every single building we passed.

"Behind there," he continued, "are the sleeping quarters. The gray ones are for the men, and the brown ones are for the women. We also have quarters for children. And, ah, I almost forgot to mention the auditorium, where our inmates give performances." When he said "inmates," we cringed. We are prisoners no matter what, we are not free after all, we thought.

"We have quite a few talented refugees." Again he had to make sure that we knew who we were. He constantly referred to the "inmates" and "refugees" as if they were not people, but a caste of their own.

"Here we are." He ran up the steps of a whitewashed building. We followed him like little puppies. He opened a big door, which almost closed in our faces. He didn't even bother to see if we were following him or keep the door open for us.

We entered a big hall where we found a group of about thirty men, women, and children. The noise and chaos was quite indescribable. You could hear different languages spoken. Their clothes looked like ours, tattered, ripped, dirty, and wrinkled. When the commander entered, the buzzing stopped. I guess they all had already met him before and felt ill at ease in his presence.

"*Gruss Gott. Meine Herren und Damen*, we have three young ladies joining you."

All eyes turned to us. We don't know why he'd felt he had to make that announcement; it made *us* feel self-conscious and ill at ease.

"Mrs. Reuter and her assistant, Mr. Grundig, with his aides, will show you to the showers. Then, as I mentioned to you before you will be deloused, our camp doctor will then examine you, and when everything is in order you will receive camp clothes. Further instructions will come forth after everyone is finished and ready. I leave you in good and capable hands." He waved and left, glad to get out of there. Each time he had to go through that official procedure, his stomach turned, though no one could ever have guessed it by the looks of him. It took all the power he could master to go through the routine he had to perform each time a new group arrived. Only because of his rigid training could he come across as stern and in control as he did. He disliked the new duty he had been assigned, but he accepted it because of the pay increase and new rank. He disliked these foreigners. How could one deal with them? Who *were* they? Some of them did not even act as they were normal. The only way to deal with them was to act strong and unyielding; otherwise, they might think he *owed* them something. He had a job to do. The camp had to run smoothly. These four kids were a puzzle to him. They looked strong, unaffected, and *demanding* no less. They wanted to be with their parents, and that was that, but no one knew where *they* even *were* yet. Most likely in one of the many other detention camps that had sprung up all over the country since the war began. Who did they think they were, to *demand* anything? Hadn't they just received the gift of life? He was hoping that, soon, the wretched war would come to an end, and all the refugees would return to their countries. Switzerland was for the Swiss, no malice intended. These kids and all the others should have been sent back. Why did he have to let them in? Orders, orders. These kids had no papers, no relatives, yet insisted they had parents here. At least the others could show some documents, even if he knew that most of them were false. Some even could name a few relatives or friends they had living in his country. He could only send back those that he felt were really pushing it too far. Entering illegally was a felony. Rules were rules.

As the commander left, Mrs. Reuter stepped forward—a robust, bosomy woman, followed by Mr. Grundig.

"Please form two groups, males to the right, females to the left," she announced loudly in German, French, Polish, Italian, and some other languages I couldn't place. This was to make sure that everyone understood.

The shuffling and talking started all over again. We were stunned to find ourselves in the midst of such commotion. We hadn't expected anything like it. Some people refused to line up. They knew only too well that to be marched into showers meant one would never again come out alive. They knew because some were lucky enough to have escaped from concentration camps, and others had been told. These people had to be convinced by the aides that this was Switzerland, and that they had to trust them. They had arrived to a safe haven. It was a neutral country.

After that pep talk, it didn't take too long to form the two lines. Each was ushered to separate quarters—and a nightmare began that would be tattooed in my psyche well into adulthood.

We were looking forward to a nice shower, hopefully with warm running water. We were escorted into a long gray tiled room with shower heads protruding from the ceiling. A long bench stood at the far corner with neatly folded towels and heaps of soap pieces in a bucket.

"Ladies," Mrs. Reuter instructed, "undress and put all your clothes in the receptacles standing in the corner. If you are wearing anything of value other than your wedding bands, please give it to me or my assistant."

What a laugh. Who had *valuables?* Some didn't even have wedding bands. They'd been given away as a tradeoff for food or papers. "Everything will be returned to you when you are given your new garments." Once again, the translation in the various languages followed. Surprisingly enough, an array of amulets, pendants, and bracelets found their way in the open hands of Mrs. Reuter and her helper. Some women ripped open the hems of their clothes to get to a few jewels they had been lucky to escape with, in case of need.

Everyone undressed. It was my turn to become distraught. I could not believe I had to disrobe in front of all those strangers. All the lessons taught us in the convent about modesty went to hell. I had never entered a bathroom or shower unless it was totally unoccupied. We had been bathed together sometimes as tots, a long time before. Even in those hard times, however, our naked bodies had always had privacy. I had never seen my mother fully undress, or my sisters naked.

I looked around in anguish. Beads of sweat moistened my forehead. I was nine years old and embarrassed. I hadn't yet been taught to see the beauty and the uniqueness of each naked body, in whatever shape or form it might grow. I hadn't yet begun to show pubic hair or breasts. My sisters' bodies already had, and my disconcertedness rose by the minute. I'd never thought that my sisters would look different then me once they took off their clothes. I thought only very old people looked different. I'd never noticed or realized that my sister Berta's figure had begun to change.

I don't recall if my sisters felt the same discomfort; I never discussed it with them. Maybe now, finally, I will get a chance to ask them after so many years, when we're all together again visiting my father on Twentieth Street in Miami Beach. Maybe now, finally, I won't be embarrassed to tell them how ashamed I had felt then, to be thrown together with all that flesh, all kinds of breasts, young ones, old ones, some emaciated, some shriveled, others sagging, my sisters' firm (I hardly had the courage to look them straight in the face).

We stood almost on top of each other, touching bodies to get under the shower heads, which were too few for so many. It wasn't fair, I thought, to throw us in like that. Even though we were called displaced people and refugees, we still had the right to keep our dignity. It had been taken away for so long. We had been told we had finally made it to a free country, to be free at last. . . .

The aides gave us a bar of soap which smelled like tar, and opened the water knob that controlled the flow of the water. I was leaning against a woman with a matronly figure. She too seemed at a loss, it was obvious; she closed her eyes in order not to have to look at anyone. Her sagging breasts were almost caressing my face. She involuntarily crossed her arms around them. What a pathetic gesture. I felt stultified and suffocating. When I tried to move away to give her a little more room, I only encountered another body that needed more space than anyone: I bumped into a pregnant stomach.

"*Ouch*, be *careful!*" she said in German, touching what I had just inadvertently pushed, as if to feel that nothing had hurt what was inside her. A sickening thought went through my mind. Ugh! *That's how it looks? I* was in something like *that?* My knowledge of sex went only as far as knowing that one is carried in the stomach, but not how one gets there, and how something so big as a baby can enter the belly and get out. I had made myself a mental note to ask my sisters. I knew that they knew everything and would know this, too. (I never got around to ask; too many other things took precedence.)

I panicked and left the showers to get a towel. I walked crouched over toward the bench. I began to breath more comfortably once I had left the group and could cover my body with a towel. The aggregation of mental components, conscious or unconscious, was to surface many a time while I was growing up and way into my adult life, causing me physical and mental unease.

I was told to step into another room. Privacy at last, I thought. I was taken to an aide dressed completely in white. Even her head was covered with a white cloth, almost like a nun, showing a red cross on her arm sleeve. She wore surgical gloves. "Come here, child. Don't be afraid. We have to check you out for lice." She went through my hair with deft fingers, searching, messing, parting, looking for those little parasites.

"I really don't have any," I assured her vehemently in broken German.

"Impossible," she answered, very sure of herself. "From my experience, all refugees coming through here carry lice on them. To make sure, I'll cut your hair anyhow. Everyone coming through here gets their hair cut, men or women."

Before I understood what was happening, she started to crop my hair. She manipulated big scissors and kept at it as if demons were imbedded there. She did not let go till my head looked like a bare ball. Meanwhile, I cried bitterly. "Please *stop*, don't cut anymore, *please*, it's *enough!*" My whole body was shaking. I was convinced that the aide only stopped when she had satisfied her sadistic need. Thinking back, I can still feel those hands going through my hair and the snipping of those scissors. She than spread something that had an awful smell on my head. It took many washings to lose that terrible odor. I didn't dare touch my head or look at the mirror for weeks.

She handed me a kerchief. "Wear this for a while. It won't look so bad, child. In no time, you'll see, it'll grow back." The aide who had held me still while my hair was cut led me through another door, where I was to have a physical examination.

After that, a nurse gave me a dark gray smock, a sweater, some underwear, socks, and shoes. "You'll be given some more clothes and a jacket as soon as your living quarters are assigned to you. You should be pleased to know that you are a healthy young lady and will be able to fit right into the routine of this camp without problems. Now, go and put on your clothes. You are finished here."

I dressed automatically, still feeling unhappy, unwanted, and uncared for; in short they had made a nine-year-old child feel like a worm, an ugly duckling. I was told to go outside and look around while waiting for the others. I stood by the door, not knowing what to do with myself. I sat down on the stoop. hugging my knees close to my body. Here and there a few people walked by. No one seemed to notice me, or look my way. These were free people, I thought.

Then why did they look so dismal? Shouldn't they have looked happier? . . . Little did I know that it would take a long time for many of them to return to normalcy. Some of them would suffer from nightmares, waking up in the middle of the night screaming, bathed in sweat, having just dreamed of being dragged away to jail for questioning. Many would walk around with the images of those they had left behind and of those who had died along the way. Some others would live with the guilt of having survived while members of their own families had not.

Hiding my face in the hollow of my lap, still feeling miserable, tired, and hungry, I felt a tap on my shoulder. I was too weary to pay attention to it. A second later, another, harsher tap followed. I had to acknowledge it and looked up unwillingly.

A young girl stood in front of me. "Don't cry, *ma petite*," she smiled, and sat down next to me. I stared at her and wouldn't talk. I felt like running away, hiding. This girl looked so sweet and smelled so fresh while I smelled worse than a pig and must have looked like a scarecrow. She had curly red hair and was pretty.

The girl, unperturbed, went on cheerfully talking. "Are you Jewish?" she asked in broken Yiddish. I still did not answer.

"I am one. I am Jewish."

"So? What's the big deal," I retorted. "No one *likes* you because of it. You wouldn't be here if you weren't one."

"That's not so. Many people here are not Jewish. I've been telling them that I was Jewish, and no one has yet spat on me or disliked me for it." She waited for a reply and, as none came, went on, "Are you, or aren't you? It doesn't make any difference to me! *Say* something. . .." She sounded annoyed this time. She finally understood that I had no intention of getting into a conversation with her. She continued the monologue anyhow, hoping I'd snap out of whatever I found myself in.

"I've been here almost three months now. Quarantine is over, but they don't know what to do with so many of us. I came with a group of orphans from France. My parents were taken from our apartment in Paris while I was in school, and so were everyone else's."

For a moment I thought she would cry, because tears were rolling down her cheeks. But I was wrong. She did not cry; she continued her story instead. "We fled through the Alps. What a trip! . . . I guess you came the same way, huh?" She waited for an answer, but only dead silence followed. I had no idea what to say to this girl, or what she wanted with me. Yet I hadn't taken my eyes off her. It was the first time that I had heard from another child what she had gone through. For whatever reason, we had started to believe that all that had been behind us had happened only to us. We had had no contact with other Jewish people for such a long time, and knew little of what was happening to them. We knew that things were happening, but they seemed so remote. Now here was a young girl telling me her story. "What do I have to do to get you to talk?" she finally asked. "Did you swallow your tongue? They cut your hair, but certainly not your tongue. Come on. . .*say* something," she coaxed, and gave me a little push with her elbow. "My name is Mirelle. What's yours?"

"Besides talking a lot, what are you doing here?" I asked, surprising myself by being so curt and rude. It was not at all what I had meant to say.

The girl's face turned red, and she rose. "*Pardonnez moi!*" she mumbled, ready to leave.

I realized at once that I didn't want her to go and quickly grabbed the hem of her dress. "*Nein, nein,* don't go away! *Bitte nicht!*" I said. "Please don't!" Not knowing what else to do, I started to cry again, hiding my face in my lap. I felt her arm around my shoulders, searching for my hand. I felt her head near my face. She smelled so sweet, so unlike me, I thought.

Thus we sat quietly for a while. Even though I had been so nasty to her, I felt that I had known her all along. My unhappy mood began to melt away. It almost felt natural to sit beside her. I relaxed all of a sudden, secure next to her. . .we knew each other.

"I am Jewish, too," I said after a while.

"I thought so," she answered simply. "Why were you crying?"

"*Mein Gott,* look at me!" I held my hands to my head. "Don't you smell me? I can't stand myself!" I complained, feeling the tears well up again. "I don't know what a *geschmier* they put in my hair!"

"Oh, non, *ma cherie.* No more tears," she said emphatically, offering me a coarse, crumpled handkerchief. "Here, dry your eyes. If you go on crying, you'll look worse."

I broke out in laughter. "You are absolutely right! I can't go on crying like a baby for the rest of the day. Worse things have happened to me. I'm glad to have met you, and my name is Olga."

Then I remembered, and added, "No, not really. My real name is Goldy. I was called Olga not to attract attention with such a foreign name in Italy." As I spoke, things didn't seem to look so bad anymore.

"Your hair will grow back. Don't worry about it any longer. Look at mine." She combed her fingers through her hair. "It has grown back quite a bit already. It seemed it never would, but believe me, it does. You won't smell it after a while either."

She undid the kerchief around my neck, tightened it around my head, and pushed it back. Overlooking the result of her work she continued, "Now, that looks a little better. I am eleven years old—and you?

My first notion was to lie and tell her I was older. I was afraid she wouldn't want to be friends with me knowing I was so much younger. But I thought better of it. Hesitantly I said, "I am eight and a half—but soon I'll be nine!" I added quickly to impress her. I needn't have worried; it didn't seem to matter to her, and at least for a while, happiness meant a new-found friend.

A shrill whistle broke into our conversation. It made me jump and tremble all over. I grabbed her hand, about to run, and cried, "Let's get *out* of here! They're going to *bomb* this place! We must get inside, to my sisters!" I pulled desperately at her dress.

"No, no." Mirelle was trying to free herself from my grip. "Calm down, calm down. No bombing here. You are in *Switzerland*, remember? No war here. It's time to eat. Every day, when it is twelve o'clock, the siren sounds to tell everyone to stop working and come to eat. I must go now and join my group. I'll see you later."

Before I could say another word, she was running down the street. Since no one else had yet come out of the door, I sat down on the steps once again, looking at the spot from which she had vanished. I repeated her name over and over: *Mirelle, Mirelle!* It was a most beautiful name.

As if to coincide with mealtime, the door behind me opened and the people I was with filed out. I could hardly recognize any of them. I looked for my sisters. I could tell they too had shed a few tears. They tried to smile as they saw me. I joined them in line.

"*Mamma mia*, what a sight we all are!" grumbled Berta. "How are you doing?" she asked, taking my hand.

"Oh, I'm all right," I said, raising my shoulders. I didn't want to get into it again. "I'm fine now, with some help. I'll tell you later. First, put your scarves on the way I have mine. It looks much better."

Berta looked at me in surprise, relieved. She had thought of how to calm me down once she joined me outside when it was over. She was right to have been concerned, I really would have behaved badly if I hadn't met Mirelle. I would have lashed out at my sisters as I had with Mirelle.

"We are going to have lunch there." The aide pointed to the building across the street. People were approaching from all directions. We followed them in. We were led to one side of the dining hall. It seemed to have been set up especially for us. A welcome sign had been laid out on the table.

Slowly the room filled with smoke and a conglomeration of voices, rising in different tones and languages. The moment we were seated, a number of people surrounded our table. They knew we were the new refugees. News like that went through the camp like a torrent.

"Where are you coming from?" asked a bearded, scholarly- looking man. "Is anyone here from Vilna?" I could see a hope surfacing in his eyes. Maybe someone knew his family and their whereabouts, he thought—but, no. . .no one had come from there. No. . .no one knew the Horowitzes or the Goldblatts or the Mendelsons.

A young couple asked if anyone knew the Greenfelds from Vienna. "My parents owned the biggest bakery in town." the man said.

Oh, how we wished we had come from his town. . .but no one had come from there, either. He had to console himself, like the others, with the hope that someone in the next transport would be able to tell him something.

I tried to visualize who all those missing people might have been. Scholars, rabbis, matchmakers, doctors, or artists, were they already victims, or had they escaped? Had they been able to outsmart their persecutors, lucky enough to have found someone who helped them? And for how long?

A scream interrupted my thoughts. A man from our group jumped up from his seat and cried out, "Hanka! . . . *Hannale, mein Schwester!*" He kept on repeating this, pointing his finger at a middle-aged woman standing at a distance with a group of people. He stood there half-crazed, eyes bulging. He seized his head in his hands.

A silence descended in the hall. Everyone's attention focused on what was unfolding. The woman called Hanka turned toward the caller. Now it was she who screamed, "*Oy, gewalt!*" She grabbed at the nearest person because she felt a lightness coming over her, and then she fainted. In that semiconscious state, she felt someone lifting her, holding her, kisses and caresses brushing over her face. She heard a voice she thought she recognized calling her name, the name of her childhood: *Hanka, Hannale.* She didn't want to break the trance she found herself in, but the call became more urgent and pleading. She opened her eyes and found herself staring right into a face she thought she had seen before.

"*Schmuel. . .Schmulkale,*" she whispered tenderly.

"Yes, yes it's me! Try to stand up." He was kneeling beside her, since she had slipped to the floor. Someone was putting a cold towel over her forehead.

Slowly she felt her strength returning. With the help of her brother and another man she was led to a seat. In total disbelief, she continued to call out his name. She took his hands and kissed them, then held his face between her hands and looked into his eyes as if she could read in them what had happened to him after the day he left their house in Lodz, Poland. They had been hungry, down to a few morsels of stale bread. He had resolved to go out and peddle the silver candle- sticks, the only valuables left, in exchange for some milk, bread, or potatoes.

He had never returned, and no one had heard from him since, as if the earth had swallowed him up; and now he was here, holding her, smiling out of a face etched in pain and sorrow.

There was not a dry eye among us. We all shared in their happiness, smiling at each other.

From then on, we were quite a few times to witness such encounters and reunions of lost members of a family or friends. We were also present to hear the heartbreaking stories of some people who knew the unhappy endings of others being sought after.

The rabbis among the Jewish people who passed through the detention camp before us had immediately set out to get permission to form a makeshift synagogue to hold services in. Very often after news came that someone's kin or friend had perished, we went to the synagogue to recite the Kaddish in unison. Did God hear the supplication in the rising voices of the mourners? We all mourned, because if only one among us is smitten we are to remember him or her as if they were our own.

On a daily basis people gathered around a bulletin board filled with news and names that hung at the entrance of the mess hall. Among the lists of the daily agenda there were newspaper clippings and notes asking for information about someone missing. Pictures of all kinds were posted asking if anyone recognized them. Some people left forwarding addresses for the newcomers to see when they moved on from the camp.

At a later time, when yet another group of new refugees entered the mess hall, a young woman approached our table asking the same questions. "Are you from Hungary? I am Leah Suderman. I left my parents behind. Are you from Budapest? If so, you would know them. Rabbi Eli Suderman was well known. Surely someone must have heard of him."

A toothless woman nodded. "Sure. I come from Budapest. Remember me?" she asked. "I am Nadja, the matchmaker. I used to live around the corner from your family. Remember? You were one of the few that never wanted me to find a nice young man for you, like I did for the other fine girls you knew. Remember? You used to look down at me. You may not recognize me the way I look today. Aged before my years, toothless, hairless!" Thus she went on, lamenting her plight.

Leah recognized and tearfully embraced her, rocking her back and forth in her arms, stroking those wilted cheeks. "Sha, sha! Maybe you will be able to find me a good man yet. Tell me, can you give me news of my parents?"

"Oy, oy, oy!" wailed the woman. "Why did I have to meet you? And why was I chosen to have to tell you such news? Why wasn't I killed with all the others?" She was pounding her clenched hand back and forth on her chest.

"Please, Nadja tell me—who knows? Maybe it was to be."

". . .One fine morning those brutes went from house to house, chasing all Jews out of their homes. Those who tried to run or were found in hiding places were shot on the spot or beaten to death. . . . They were all hauled onto trucks. I was told that they were marched to the railroad station." She buried her head in the young woman's shoulder. "I was spared, Leah. Through a miracle, I was spared. I had gone to the cemetery to pray at my parents' grave. It was the anniversary of my mother's death. When I was ready to leave, the gravedigger saw me. He told me not to go back home, and what was happening in all the neighborhoods."

We all hang at every word she was saying, because for most of us she was telling our own story.

"He kept me hidden around the cemetery, bringing me food whenever he could. Locked me in an old forgotten cellar under the chapel to avoid my being captured, swearing each time that this would be the last time he'd come to bring me food, because if he was found out he would be tortured and killed."

Her crying did not stop. Leah consoled her, still remembering in shame how she had never liked her. Nadja had come at least once a week to their house, been less than straightforward, and entered through the back door. She never stated her business at once, but talked around it till someone had to ask her what it was she wanted or why she was there. Only then, after having been asked more than once, would she wipe her hands in an old, oily apron tied around her immense waist and explain why she had come—most of the time about a young man. *A prince of a man*, she used to describe all the suitors she had had in mind for Leah, who mostly turned out to be quite a bit older than she and had no roof over their heads, nor a job or a profession. Nadja had given these prospective husbands her hospitality until she found parents to convince that she had a match made in heaven for their daughters and collect her matchmaking fees, if and when an agreement could be reached. Sometimes, she had indeed come up with a find, but mostly not.

Leah put all those thoughts out of her mind. Oddly enough, she looked back upon those days with love, now that she knew they were from a time that would never return. "Well, now I know. I won't have to dream that I'll see them again. They were not strong enough to have been able to make it for any length of time," she said finally, kissing the old woman, and left the mess hall to cry aloud in pain.

That night another Kaddish was recited for her parents.

After a time there were people who seemed to know someone who knew someone else—a friend's mother-in-law's cousin's sister, say, who was actually a distant relative and had been hidden somewhere outside Munich at the time they left. Hopefully, they'd make it in the end. But no one knew precisely.

A son's close friend had joined the Hitler Jugend, became disillusioned soon after. He had come to warn the Leitners that the Gestapo was going to round up every Jew in their district that night and helped them to get out of town. Years later the Leitners had come face to face, in that camp in Switzerland, with the parents and brother of that young man, to find out that Eric had been executed as a traitor to the Fatherland. Eric's family had had to flee, too. They'd decided to make it to the border.

Over and over we witnessed the unexpected, the unbelievable stories and unheard coincidences of life. By all rights there should have been erected a hall of fame there, a hall of human bondage. After a while, passions subsided, some questions and hopes were answered, some searches came to an end, but more often the searches went on and the questions remained unanswered.

Food was in abundance. It was dispensed through big pots on rolling wagons, pushed through the aisles of tables by those in charge.

There were always baskets filled with slices of bread on each table, with jugs of water and bowls of apples.

At times the camp commander made an appearance in the mess hall. He ate with his soldiers in another place. He blew a whistle to get our attention and demanded absolute silence. He would read us some excerpts of the news and reports from the various fronts. He would announce the arrivals of the new groups and read the roster. He reminded us of the good fortune that had befallen us in being allowed to remain in his country, forgetting to mention how many others hadn't been allowed in and turned back, ensuring their certain death. He would go on lecturing the newcomers of what was expected of them. After a few appearances by the commander, we could recite his speeches by heart; they were always the same:

"*Meine Damen und Herren*, you will receive a work schedule which will rotate at intervals. Everyone will have a fair share of easy and pleasant work as well as hard and unpleasant chores. For those who become ill, we have a very good first-aid station. We frown on those who take advantage of their sick days and will only excuse those who have a real need to be absent from work. If needed, you will be hospitalized right here. We have excellent nurses and competent doctors on call, some of whom come from your midst. If you are fit, you will contribute your share of work to the fullest." He held a crop under his left arm, and used his right to make emphatic, expressive gestures.

"I hope you have understood clearly what I have said. If you did, and follow through, we'll get along just fine. Otherwise, you might encounter. . .hm. . .hm. . .with some unpleasantries from the staff."

His voice came stridently through the speaker, drowning out any other noises. "My aides will help you in any way possible, and will answer any questions you may have. *Gruss Gott!*" And he was finished, waving his leather crop, and marched out with his entourage.

After lunch, most people left; here and there some lingered on to talk to one another. "Where is everyone going?" asked a tall blond man who was a political refugee from Germany.

His countrymen had tortured his wife in order to find out where he had escaped. Back home, he had not ingratiated himself with the Nazi party and had been heard many times to vent his antipathy for Hitler. His sons were in the Hitler Jugend and his most staunch adversaries. He'd had to be careful of what he was saying in front of them. The thought of being called up to report for duty repulsed him. After painful discussions with his wife, they had come to the conclusion that he had to leave his country before risking induction in the army or being reported by someone to the police for his unpatriotic feelings. When they came to get him, he had already fled. His family would be safe, he thought. . .he hadn't thought or known that the Nazis had their own way of paying back, and that no one could outsmart their authority.

"These people have a few hours of rest period left. They are going to their quarters. Now it's time for you to be shown where you are going to be housed. Men, you follow me," Mr. Grundig called out. "The women and children will go with Frau Reuter."

The men left first. Those who were married showed their resentment for having had to separate from their wives and children, and the others joined in sympathy. We. followed soon after. We headed toward the main road and passed the soldiers' barracks. Their compound was surrounded by barbed wire. It definitely told us it was off limits.

We saw the drilling in the back yard, the drill master yelling at the top of his lungs, "*Eins, zwei, drei. . .zwei, drei. . .eins...*"

We passed the hospital. It was distinguished from the other buildings by its white color and the red cross painted on it. A few nurses passed us arm in arm.

"*Gruss Gott!*" they said, smiling and waving at us. They looked so prim in their flawlessly white uniforms with dark blue capes around their shoulders and starched white caps on their beautiful hair. I envied their natural, healthy looks. They did not seem to belong in those surroundings. Even more, what were *we* doing there, in their country?

We were accustomed to seeing emaciated bodies, sad faces in which one could read past history. My eyes followed them till I couldn't see them any longer. Would I grow up to look like them? I thought. Right there and then I wanted to become a nurse.

We arrived at the *Kinderheim*, the children's quarters. We followed down a long corridor and heard noises and laughter. The aide stopped at an open door through which it was coming. We entered a playroom full of children of all ages immersed in various play activities.

"*Gruss Gott,*" a woman in a white-and-blue nursing uniform said cordially by way of greeting. "Are these the new arrivals?" she asked the aide.

"Yes, they are to be shown their living quarters. I leave them with you." The aide turned to us and waved good- bye. "You'll be in good hands here." She smiled and left.

The young kids who were with us looked on with wide-open eyes, mesmerized by the sight of so many toys, building blocks, stuffed animals, play soldiers, dolls, and loads of books. Even a beautiful white piano stood at one side of the room. Instinctively I remembered. . .my mother had wanted us to learn to play the piano. Berta had been just about ready to have lessons. Mother had surprised my father one day by having the instrument delivered at our apartment while he was away on a selling trip.

When he came home, he hadn't exactly been thrilled. He questioned the necessity of it. "The children have enough with their studies in Hebrew school," he commented briskly. "I don't recall having seen such high grades from them in their Torah studies." My mother had replied wisely, "There's a time for everything, Chaim. There is a time to play, and a time to pray . . . !"

My father had never spurned such comments. Maybe there *was* a time for me to learn to play the piano after all. . . .

Some children left our group to check out the toys. They knelt down on the floor to gently touch each of them, looking back at us to make sure no one was going to object. When they saw that no one did, they began to play and smile at each other.

"*Schein!*" said one of them in Yiddish.

"Ya, it is beautiful, *sehr schein!*" the others agreed. The boys had broken the ice. When the girls saw how much they were enjoying themselves surrounded by the other kids, they too timidly approached the big table that stood in the middle of the room.

One girl opened a book bound in a beautiful cover, bold letters standing out and demanding one's attention. It was entitled *Brothers Grimm Fairy Tales.*

Another picked up a rag doll that was sitting on a high chair. She embraced the doll as if it were a baby. She held her tight, kissing the golden locks made of thick woolen threads.

I was watching the children at play. I almost felt like joining them. I hadn't played in such a long time. . .they weren't that much younger then I.

Yet I felt so much older. That thought stayed with me only for a fleeting moment, though; I knew my playtime had passed me by. I felt too old to be engaging in such silly things. I had grown up fast. Little did I know then that I would have a chance again with my three children and grandchildren. The first thing I did when I had my children was to make a playroom furnished like a toy store. They had a playful mother, and, later, grandmother, like none other. Whenever they asked me to play with them, there I was, gladly dropping everything I was doing. I never tired of it. I loved playing with them, and now with the grandchildren. I never gave up that playroom, and I know I'll always keep a little corner as one, needed or not.

The nurse introduced herself. "I am Nurse Gina. We will go to your rooms now. The little ones will stay here. They seem to be happy."

She turned to the other women involved with some children to let them know that she was leaving.

We followed the nurse down the hall. She unlocked a closet door, from which she extracted pillows, blankets, towels, and linens. She piled them up in our arms. Further down the corridor, she carefully opened another door. She pressed a finger on her lips. We entered a semi-dark room where some younger children were sleeping. A woman in a white uniform was sitting at a small desk; a lit lamp gave her enough light to read or write while on duty. She rose as we entered. Sister Gina whispered something to her, then turned to us. "All those empty beds will be for the toddlers, and you will have to make them up. You can divide the chore among yourselves later. Now I will show you to your room.

We dropped the linens and blankets on one bed and followed her sister into an adjacent room, simply furnished and immaculately clean. Ten beds stood on each side, night tables beside each. At the end of the room, a whole series of metal cabinets lined the wall. Some closed ones, occupied and locked, bore owner's names. Many others stood open and empty.

The room was engulfed in bright light coming from the windows, this time without bars. Some girls were sitting on their beds reading, others squatting on the floor talking to each other, sometimes giggling, sometimes chatting.

As we walked in, all the girls jumped up at once, rushing toward the nurse to greet her. Apparently, she was a welcome sight to them, and for good reason. As soon as the girls surrounded her, she offered them chocolates and candies—rare commodities in the camp, and hard to get. Chocolates were rationed because of the war. Whenever she came to visit, she always had a surprise for them—a magazine, ribbons, cologne, or other pleasantries that were not among the offerings in the camp. She gave us a few goodies, too. I couldn't believe that a candy tasted that good. It tasted heavenly. It had been such a long time since I had had one. I held it in my mouth, not daring to suck too much, lest it would melt too soon. I savored it as long as I could.

"Hallo," a blond girl about my age called out to us. Her hair had grown back into a ragged crew cut. Nevertheless, it looked cute on her. She had big blue inquisitive eyes. "Are you all moving in here?" she asked.

"Yes," Nurse Gina answered.

The nurse introduced us and said, "Please help them making the beds," and, turning to us, added, "I have work to do. When you are finished, I'll see you back in the playroom. *Adieu!*" She waved her hand to all and left.

"My name is Ariel," said another girl who had approached us. "I arrived six weeks ago. In ten days, I'll be sent to stay with a family. They will be my foster parents for a while—till they'll find my parents," she said as a matter of fact.

Another girl came up to us. "I am Roza. I'll be sent on to a different camp with some other girls. I am an orphan," she said sadly.

"All orphans stay together," another girl volunteered.

"I think we'd better get to work," Berta pointed out. "Nurse Gina will wonder what happened to us."

"Can I help, too?" someone behind me asked. The voice sounded familiar. I turned around, holding my breath. Yes! It was Mirelle, the new friend I had found that morning and thought I had lost again.

I couldn't help myself and just kept on hugging her, holding her tight.

She disengaged my arms from her neck. "*Oo la, la!* You're *choking* me!"

"Where have you been? I was looking for you in the mess hall," I asked. "It was impossible to *find* you among so many people!"

"I *told* you we were going to see each other later," she reminded me, smiling. "I didn't say I was *eating* with you. Did I? I am working with the children and also eat with them. That's why you didn't see me in the mess hall. We have our own kitchen." Looking around and seing everyone busy making beds, she added, "Don't tell me you're assigned to this room. It's mine, too!" She sounded very pleased. I took her hand and walked her over to my sisters.

"This is Mirelle," I said happily. "She's the girl I told you about this morning."

"Ah, *this* is the friend Goldy spoke about. How pleased I am to meet you," Berta said giving her a hug. "We're finished here. Too bad we can't stay around to talk to you," she went on apologetically. "Nurse Gina expects us back in the playroom. Maybe you can come with us for a while?"

"*Oui*, I can. I still have some free time left."

By the time we returned to the playroom, it had filled with more children. The nurse was kneeling in the midst of a group of children sitting on the floor. They were taking turns showing her pictures they had drawn.

She rose when she saw us. "They're quite a handful! To think that, not too long ago, some of them wouldn't even talk to me, or play. Just sit and stare. They didn't seem to trust anyone or let anyone get close to them. Look at these children now! Aren't they a joy to behold?" she asked, pleased. "Even the language barrier vanished. . . . How did everything go?" she asked. "Did you choose your beds?"

"Yes, we did," Berta said. We had picked ones near each other. Nurse Gina saw Mirelle at last. "Ah, you have met Mirelle! How nice," she said, and gave her a pat on her head. "Now, what's left is your work schedule, which we will find in the office. And to get your personal supplies." She asked us if we would like to work with the children, explaining that she could use more help. We gladly jumped at the opportunity. "Alright, I'll see what I can do," she promised.

We walked down another corridor feeling quite happy. Things seemed to be looking up. We were ready to start our quarantine as prescribed, hoping to pass the forced internment as well as circum-stances would allow.

But it was not to be.

We went back to the main office. Nurse Gina rang a bell and announced us through an intercom; a second later, we were buzzed in.

An officer beckoned us to his desk. "Fraulein, I'll look for these girls' papers. Just give me a minute." He flipped through a pile of folders stacked up on his desk. "Ah, here we are," he said to her. He opened the folder and looked through all kinds of papers.

At once we became apprehensive again. She felt our anxiety. She said sweetly to the officer, "By the way, I could use these girls to work with the children. I am shorthanded. How about it?"

"I would have loved to oblige you, but these girls have been assigned to kitchen duty by the Herr Commandant."

She seemed quite sorprised by the news. "Since when does the commandant engage in giving out jobs to the newcomers?" she asked incredulously.

"Well, I don't know. He seemed to know the young ladies."

"And *what* job are they assigned to?" she asked.

"I told you. Kitchen duty!"

"But this is no job for children. It's much too hard for them!" she exclaimed. "I'll go and talk to the commandant about this."

She rose, ready to intercede for us. The soldier stopped her.

"Fraulein Gina, I am sorry to inform you, but the commander is not available. He went home on vacation and left word that under no circumstances are his orders to be questioned or changed." He shrugged; he seemed really sorry for us.

We realized at once that this was a punishment for us, for Berta having been too brazen over our stay. We approached the nurse. "Please don't be upset. We know why the commandant did this,"

Berta told her, and went on to explain her what had transpired in the commandant's office on our arrival.

The nurse realized that she couldn't help and took the paper from the officer.

"Well, then," she told us, "I'll take you to the kitchen and introduce you to the people in charge. They are a good bunch. You may not like the work, but you'll like the people you'll be working with." Thus it came about that, instead of having an easy and enjoyable time in the camp, we became kitchen helpers of the first order. At least we were allowed to remain in the quarters Nurse Gina had assigned to us. She had her authority, too.

As requested, at five o'clock in the morning, just as the sun was coming up, we presented ourselves before breakfast in the kitchen. The kitchen help consisted, first, of Herr Muller, a Swiss chef who spoke only Switzer Deutch, a dialect that no one understood. Then there was an assistant chef, a French Swiss whose name was François but who was called "Franc," since Herr Muller the chef did not like the name. François spoke a broken German that was also very hard to understand. Whenever he became angry, mostly with his boss, he reverted to speaking French. Muller yelled back at him, cursing that he shouldn't speak French. He felt that anyone living in Switzerland had to speak and understand his dialect. The dislike between them was mutual and knew no bounds. There was a constant upheaval in the kitchen because of it.

Then there were two immigrants doing miscellaneous work, Mendale and Oscar. They were Polish and couldn't have cared less what was going on around them. They could hardly understand what was spoken anyhow. They had lost all their family, and that was hard enough to bear. They did whatever they were told to do.

I almost forgot Mr. Wolf, a pious man, learned man, and the forgiving one. He was a myth among us. No one knew where he came from, where his family was, or if he'd ever had one to call his own. He never let anyone even come close to asking him. His age was somewhere between sixty and a hundred, and everything that happened was God's will.

I remember the arguments my sister Berta often had with him about God's will. She spoke harshly to him, outraged: "And you want to tell me that all those people who died because they were Jews is God's will?"

He used to clear his throat and proceed to chant his answer, swaying back and forth as if he were praying in a temple. "*Kindale*, you are much too young to question God's will. You are not learned enough or old enough to understand His ways."

Berta's annoyance with him would increase by the minute. What answer was that?

"Remember this," he continued. "Nothing happens without a reason. Remember the story of Lot? She turned into a pillar of salt because she disobeyed God's orders. Do you remember the story of Noah? He sent the flood because people had become evil. He punished them for it."

"What has all this to do with us?" she demanded.

"Child, it is happening again to us. Our people have forgotten what it is to be a Jew. Our people have assimilated. They have forgotten the Ten Commandments. They have forgotten to teach their children!"

Chanting away in this fashion, he kept on peeling potatoes, and when he was not peeling potatoes he was stroking his beard; it had become white with age. "History repeats itself," he continued.

"There will be more things happening to His chosen people because we continuously deny him. This is our punishment." When he felt he had said enough, he waved my sister away.

Berta could never reply to such theory.

All this talk sounded very familiar to me. I had heard it once before, not exactly in the same words, from Mr. Mazza. He used to have similar thoughts.

I liked Mr. Wolf. I used to ask him to tell me stories of the bible. He obliged gladly. He spun tales that were somewhat biblical, yet he changed them to fit his judgement. I loved that old man with calloused hands and eyes that used to lighten up whenever he talked about God. I envisioned him looking like my grandfather—he too had had a long white beard.

We also had a woman completing the staff named Mrs. Kowalsky. Her specialty was making borscht. She used to argue with Herr Muller because he never allowed her to make it. He kept on saying he had never heard of such a soup. Borscht did not come from Switzerland or from France, she said; just because he'd never heard of it, that did not mean others hadn't either, she went on. Everyone in the camp knew what borscht was—*almost* everyone, that was, she corrected herself. Every so often she made it anyhow, even though it meant incurring his wrath. The camp was filled with a lot of eastern Jews who craved for her borscht. It brought back memories of home.

She was Russian. She loved to tell us about the Bolsheviks and the revolution. She talked about her father when he was alive. "We were aristocrats, mind you! We lived in St. Petersburg. Those were the days!" She mournfully went on and on telling stories of her past. Some were funny, others sad.

Everyone we came in touch with had stories to tell from those days that might have been my yesterdays.

With the passing days and weeks our hands became calloused from holding peeling knives and carrying full pots back and forth to be emptied and refilled with cleaned vegetables. Our hands looked like those of scrub women, raw and blistering at times from washing the kitchen floors. Sometimes we couldn't sit straight from constantly bending over those big containers that had to be filled with peeled potatoes or some other vegetables.

We were off for three hours starting at lunch time. Most of the time we were too exhausted to wash up and take our meals in the mess hall. We went to our room and collapsed on our beds. We had made up our minds not to let the workload bother us. We had made it thus far; a while longer wouldn't matter.

With every passing day I looked in the mirror to see if my hair had grown some. It seemed I would remain bald forever. My only consolation was Mirelle. I wished the day to pass quickly so that I could rush back to see her, to sit with her and talk. The evenings were ours to do as we pleased. Mirelle had things to remember, too. She told me she used to live in Paris with her family. They were well-to-do. She had been to the theater, gone to ballet school, traveled to different countries. I was dreaming away with her, making believe it was my past, too, while mine started to become vague.

Once in a while I took out the rosary beads that I had managed to save and furtively recited the Hail Marys I had been taught in the convent. I still remembered the nuns telling me that, since I wasn't baptized, I would end up in Hell. Therefore, I needed to recite lots of Hail Marys; it would help. Besides, I had forgotten the prayers my parents taught me.

One day, the commandant called us to his office. "I want to inform you that we have located your parents. They live in a camp for adults."

We almost jumped for joy. "You see?" Berta said, all excited. "We *told* you that they were here. You didn't believe us. . . . When can we see them?" she asked in anticipation.

"Hm. . .well, they were here to see you—but I couldn't allow them to visit with you." As he spoke those words, he looked away from us when he saw the bewilderment in our eyes. "No one in quarantine is allowed visitors. It would defeat the purpose of your being here."

We could not believe what we were hearing. They had *been* here, so close, and yet. . .how could he have been so cruel? Was it that he hated us so much?

"How could you do this?" Berta cried out, while we broke into tears. "Do you know how long it has been since we saw them? We weren't even sure they were *alive*. Couldn't you at least have allowed us to see them through the *gates*?" She broke into sobs. She could immagine the pain of our parents not having been able to see us.

"Rules are rules. Your quarantine will be over soon, and then you'll be able to visit them," he answered briskly, seeming quite annoyed at us. "Here, they left something for you." He opened a drawer in his desk and handed us a package our parents had left with him.

Later on, when we were able to visit them, my parents told us what had occurred on that bleak day. The Red Cross had finally located them and told them the good news of our whereabouts. Their camp commander had immediately issued them a special permit to visit us. They had saved some money from the work they were doing in the camp. It was sort of pocket money they received to enable them to buy a few extra things the camp didn't provide. They used it all to buy cookies, candies, and other frivolities they thought children might like. The commandant had personally taken them to the train. Their excitement and happiness knew no bounds. Mother told us she was so excited she couldn't stop talking to my father. "Chaim, do you think they will recognize us? Will we recognize them?"

"Why not, Dvora?" he had patiently answered.

"Well, we haven't seen them for such a long time. Children change quickly at a certain age. Do you think they are well taken care of?" Not waiting for a reply, she had continued, "We may have become strangers to them!"

On and on she'd talked. By the time they reached their destination, the whole compartment had heard the story behind their trip. The travelers, in tears, gave them scarves they had brought along to give as presents to those they were visiting, and another a bar of chocolate.

"Our friends will understand," they'd said when my parents felt they couldn't accept such kindness.

At the train station, they'd found out that our camp was not close—it was four kilometers away, and they had no extra money for cab fare. But that did not matter—they had walked longer distances before. This would be a pleasure. Even though it was a cool spring day, they did not feel the cold seeping through their shabby coats. They were holding on to each other filled with happy anticipation. They felt neither cold nor fatigue; they would have walked to the end of the world to see their children again. Soon, soon, they would be there. My mother was rehearsing the greeting in her mind a hundred times: *"Meine kinderlach, meine teiere kinderlach!"* Would they still understand Yiddish after such a long time?

They'd finally reached the gate of the camp in the late afternoon, shown their papers to the guards, and, after they were examined, announced to the commandant and led to his office by a young soldier. My mother's excitement had grown ever so much, she could hardly walk; because she started to tramble, my father had had to hold her up as they made their way down the hall.

The guard had knocked at the door, ushered my parents in, saluted, and left the room.

"So you are the parents of those four girls?" he'd said as a matter of fact. "Sit down." He hadn't even bothered to greet them. "You are lucky they made it through the border alive under such circumstances. Do you know they were almost sent back?" He'd wanted to let them know how grateful they should feel.

"But now, Herr Commandant," my father said impatiently, "can we see our children? You have our gratitude for all you have done." He couldn't comprehend the delay. "We came from quite a distance. You must understand how eager we are to see them!"

The commandant cleared his throat. "Hm. . .we have a problem here. You should have called us first."

"What do you mean, we should have called you first? What is the problem? We have papers and special permission to come here to see the children." My father removed the documents from the inside pocket of his coat and, with shaking hands, laid them on the desk for the commandant to see. Surely now everything would be clear to this man, he thought. Just another formality. He stroked my mother's arm to reassure her.

"Well, calling first would have informed you that, while in quarantine, no visitors are allowed," the commandant had answered coldly. "Your camp commander should have been aware of this."

My parents couldn't believe it. My father had repeated the regulation. "*No visitors?*"

"Yes, that's exactly what I said. No visitors. None, *vertig*, finished. You could have saved yourself a trip and some grief," he'd added.

My mother had pleaded, cried, wrung her hands in despair, and almost fainted. But the officer would not be swayed. Rules were rules; besides, he was up for promotion—he was not going to jeopardize that chance to sidestep rules for refugees.

When they realized they couldn't sway the commandant, my father had asked, "Could you at least give them these small gifts from us?" He'd had handed him the precious package and, with a last effort, said, "Tell them we are well and will see them soon. That they are constantly in our thoughts." He had risen then and had to drag my mother out of the office.

For a while a depression set in among us, dark sullen days followed. Even Mr. Wolf, with his infinite wisdom, could not console us. Getting up became a chore. Work became a burden. All we wanted to do was cry out, vent our pain, and tell the commandant how unfair it was. But, of course, we couldn't.

Word got around of what had happened. Everyone felt our pain. In order to show us their feelings, the inmates found a way to express their disapproval to the camp commander's face. When he came to our mess hall to give us the latest news and one of his moral speeches, they greeted him with boos and noises made with the clatter of their silverware. He understood immediately what it was all about. He raised his arms to signal for silence. But when he started to explain the rules, the boos and noises started again. Since his voice became lost in the uproar, he shrugged and left the room in obvious rage, vowing disciplinary action. We were stunned by this show of unity and caring. We felt great knowing that people cared. We in turn gathered our courage to go on with our daily lives and find some consolation that, soon, this too would pass and we'd be able to live in freedom without being told what to do, when to do it, and where to go.

MY HAIR STARTED to grow. Mirelle began to create different hairstyles to make me feel better about myself. To my regret, the hair grew in straight and raggedy, not as curly as before. It did not complement my face at all, it made me miserable, yet Mirelle refused to give up her creativity. Very often she brought tears of laughter to my eyes after inventing yet another new look even worse then the last.

Too soon, the day came when I had to say good-bye to Mirelle. Her quarantine was over, and she was being transferred with a group of other children to an orphanage. We had grown so close, I couldn't imagine life without her. I was disconsolate and moped around. She too felt the closeness we had shared. I had become the sister she never had, and leaving saddened her, too. Our days had been more pleasurable because of each other's company. My sisters had adopted her, too. She never complained about me as did they, who usually had *something* to reproach me for. She was there to listen patiently whenever I complained about anything. She minimized the terrible things I thought I had to endure from my work in the kitchen; therefore, I became less quarrelsome. Thus we spent so many beautiful hours together.

The day Mirelle told me she was leaving without being able to tell me her destination sent me into a frenzy. "When will I *see* you again? How will I know where you *are*?" I cried inconsolably.

"*Ma cherie*, as soon as I get there, I will write you, and you can write me back! I am sure we'll be able to see each other somehow, someday." We hugged and kissed, and then she pushed me gently away. "Now, let me try to do something with your hair." She proceeded to brush it (my hair looked better since it had grown longer, and she could do a nicer job with it). "Promise me not to look in the mirror until I am finished!"

After what seemed an eternity, she said, "*Voila! Now* you can look!"

Glimpsing myself in the mirror, I almost cried out, "Are you *crazy?*" But I couldn't; she seemed too pleased. I felt like a peacock. She had put on a few multi-colored ribbons, making the ends into bows that sat in the middle of my head. I stared at this face that was supposed to be mine. I had swollen eyes and a red, runny nose from crying, and those *bows*. . .in my opinion, I looked like a disaster. "You like?" she asked, growing impatient with my silence.

Ach, mein Gott, I thought, how am I going to tell her? I couldn't hurt her feelings and let it be, even though the other girls were laughing behind my back.

I never saw Mirelle again. My heart was constantly with her. I kept asking if there was mail from her; my sisters assured me that she would write one day, that there must be a reason why she didn't.

Meanwhile, I composed letters so that I could mail them to her at once. I felt lonely and miserable—even the company of my sisters didn't help.

Then, as things happened in our lives, I thought of her less and less. Most likely she wrote to let me know where she was, but we left the camp soon after. . . . Now and then I still think of what might have happened to my first best friend. We imagine that we have put those hard days behind us under layers of new experiences, yet the persecution, the hidden years, the lost youth, the war, the destruction of whole families, the death of so many millions, will remain imbedded in our minds forever. We have the capacity to go on and give birth to new lives; but to forget what happened to us, that will never happen. We can't. We can't let go. We are the survivors of a brutal past that must be told, especially to our children, so that they in turn will be the guardians against future holocausts and stand up for those that cannot—otherwise, all those lives will have been taken in vain.

BERTA BEING THE oldest, took it upon herself to become my teacher and mother. She set up time for me to go with her to the library; she practiced reading and writing with me, and math to boot. While in quarantine, not much importance was given to setting up classrooms or teaching the kids. Everyone did their own thing in their free time. Musicians came together to practice and form a band. Singers gathered a choir. Ever so often these artists joined together to give us a concert. Those affairs remain unforgettable for me. Their repertoire brought us, not only music, but a piece of their home, of their past and culture. Sometimes I recognized songs that my father used to sing on Friday nights or on the Sabbath.

Those were times when nostalgia over what had gone by swelled among the older listeners. Silent tears and moans rose from their lips, and they joined the singers. I cried with them, not really knowing why. I was too young to understand their emotions.

JUST WHEN IT seemed that quarantine would never come to an end, it was suddenly over. We were summoned to the commandant's office one day. "Well, young ladies—" he tried to sound jovial as he spoke— "your stay with us has ended." He looked at us, resting his eyes on us taking in the changes that had occurred to each of us in such a short while. We had lost the gaunt look and suspicious glint in our eyes that are so common in people who have been persecuted. Our scrawny bodies had rounded out in an unhealthy chubbiness due to the daily diet of bread, potatoes, and little exercise. Our hair had grown back unevenly yet was somewhat wavy, giving a more natural look to our faces. All in all, what he saw in front of him were four young girls who could not have been distinguished from any other, normal, child growing up around the country. He couldn't possibly see the invisible scars that would remain and make us different from other children. He didn't see that, in front of him, stood another breed: those who who had grown out of childhood before their time.

"I hope that you have gained some experiences here to help you along in your new life. I hope that you have realized by now how lucky you all are having been allowed to stay in this country."

He forgot about those he hadn't allowed in; he never gave a thought to those he, and other commanding camp officers, had sent back to certain death. Their real numbers will never be known, nor have they been recorded in the archives of history— among them my aunt and uncle.

While the commander was thus immersed in his achievements as a camp director, he had lost our attention. We were thinking only that we were going to be free at last, and excited at the thought of being reunited with our parents and becoming a family again.

We were brought back to the moment when he finally came to the point. We had to live through another disappointment. "Now, I will tell you where you'll be going." He came around his desk, picked up a document from the table, and began to read the devastating news. Berta and Helene were to be sent to different camps for young girls to work and study. Mina and I would be going to Zurich, to different foster parents.

The news hit us like a ton of bricks. We had never thought for a moment that, by then, we would ever be separated again and not remain a family. We thought we had escaped, that we were free. We could hardly hide our feelings of consternation.

I put my head on Berta's shoulder and cried silently. Mina and Helene held hands. "I hope you'll be grateful and humble to those who will offer you a home," he ended, staring at us, waiting for a response.

He did not get one.

"There is no need to cry. You should be happy leaving here," he said, annoyed.

"We thought we'd be going to stay with our parents," Berta said.

"Girls. Who told you that you were going to stay with your *parents?*" He seemed genuinely surprised. "You know that they are in a camp for adults. There are no accommodations for children."

"Oh. No one said anything to us, but we automatically thought we would finally be together," she said.

"Well, I guess it was natural to assume this. But don't be too unhappy. I have another bit of news that will make up for your disappointment."

Our interest rose again. "You will be able to visit with your parents before going on to your destinations. You will also be able to visit with each other once in a while after that." He didn't wait for any reaction from us, turned towards the door, and without further ado escorted us out. "My officer will tell you all the rest. *Gruss Gott*," he said abruptly, and walked away.

THAT WAS THE last time we saw the commander. We never missed him, either. Yet he lives on in the shadows of my past.

The young officer was ready for us. Without waiting for our questions, he handed us written instructions to what would be following. He waited quietly until we were through reading.

"Well, what do you say about this? You'll be staying *two weeks* with your parents. No one has been able to obtain so much time off before going on to their new destinations!" He was excited for us.

As we trudged back to our barracks, no one spoke. I felt so miserable; the thought of being separated from my sisters after such a long time of togetherness, of again becoming a stranger among strangers, seemed incomprehensible. I tried to think of the time we would be spending with my parents and concentrate on the excitement of seeing them again. Even that did not ease my pain. I couldn't imagine the separation, the sense of it. We had left the Germans and persecution behind. Then what was keeping us from being together again?

Wasn't this what it was all about?

Even though I didn't like life in the camp, I had begun to get adjusted to the routine of our lives. The people who surrounded us were no longer strangers. We all had a common bond. Among the multitude of people from all walks of life, with different languages, we understood each other. I felt them; I knew them. I recognized them in later years, and always felt at ease with them, because they were, like me, "the survivors."

It had meant no more running, no more lurking in the dark and looking furtively around you, holding your breath when you heard the sound of heavy boots approaching, hearing the commandoes of German soldiers ordering everyone out of their homes, onto the street, to search for Jews or escapees. The unfortunate ones would be hauled to their interrogation headquarters knowing they would never escape again; they would be dead before the day ended, either by torture or by the noose, as the Resistance reported. While we were hidden in an attic, we had huddled together, with my father praying for those caught and reciting the Kaddish before their deaths. He knew there would not be anyone left to say it for them, and then he went on, "*Shmah Yisroel*, Hear us, O Israel, our God—" and my mother whispering, "*Far vos? Why?*"

For me, who had almost forgotten how it had been before this all started, it wasn't so bad. . .we *were* grateful for having narrowly escaped being sent back when we reached the Swiss border, which would have meant certain death, as had befallen so many others. We *had* been lucky; we had been *spared.*

We'd worked hard, too, to earn the right to stay there and live. I had become friends with Mirelle, whom I dearly loved, at least for a while. She was gone too soon, like a mirage in the desert. Had she really existed? And my parents! The memory of them barely kept alive by my sisters! I was trying hard to remember.

Certain events here and there came back to my mind, like the memory of that night so long before while we were interned in Borgo San Giacomo, Italy, when my sister Helene was bitten by a scorpion and was in unbearable pain. My father, not knowing what to do, had cut open the bite to remove the venom and carried her on his shoulders, trudging back and forth the whole night through, singing to her all kinds of songs to lull her to sleep. He was invoking God not to let her die.

"Dear God, not now, *please!*" my mother was silently praying, too. I could only see her lips moving. Her eyes had no more tears. My father sang, "*Oifen prepetchik brennt a fierel, in steeb is heis, und Der Rebbe lernt mit die kinderlach, chumash, alev beis*"—in the hearth burns a fire, the room is warm, and the rabbi studies Torah and the Hebrew ABC's with the children. . . then my mother was imploring her deceased parents, "*Mamegnu, Tategnu*," to intervene on their behalf with the Almighty to save her child. My father, who had no more songs left, prayed on: "*Ani maamin beemunah in kol-zeh, Ani maamin hamashiach*"—I believe with a perfect faith in you, I believe in the coming of the Messiah, and though he tarry, I believe!

We sat in our room thinking of what lay before us. We hadn't even noticed the entrance of Nurse Regina. She had known before us why the commandant called us. She understood the turmoil we were going through. She had wrangled permission for us to be given the remainder of the day off, and eat in our room. She brought us our trays and left them on the table without saying a word. She looked at us compassionately praying for us: "*Lieber Jesus*, help these poor lambs—you were once one of them!"

She gave instructions that no one was to disturb us or come into the room, in order to give us ample time and opportunity to talk to each other.

The shrill sound of the afternoon siren calling everyone back to work after lunch recess brought us out of our stupor. We looked sheepishly at one another and started to laugh. We told each other it couldn't be worse than staying there, and after all, we would be together with our parents for a while. As youth always prevails, we jumped back to reality and felt hungry when we saw the food that Nurse Regina had left us. We took the trays on our laps, squatting down on the floor and leaning against our beds.

As we started to eat, we spat out our food. The food was disgusting. It was cold. The potatoes were cold and hard, the hardly chewable meat drowned in a mushy sauce, and the vegetables, consisting of red beets (to this day, I don't eat beets), had a terrible taste. The best was the fresh fruit that accompanied every meal with a piece of cake.

"So," Berta began, "are we going to start looking forward to a bright future or not?"

"What king of a bright future are you suggesting? Maybe you know something we don't?" Helene asked, noisily blowing her nose and then, with her handkerchief, boring deeply into each nostril.

"Come on, let's not be so gloomy. Isn't this what we were waiting for?"

After a pause, Berta continued, "Think, my darling sisters! We won't have to see the Herr Commandant any more." She jumped up from the floor and started to mimic him: "Hey, no more speeches, no more communal showers, no more checking for lice, no more—"

We jumped in while she was thinking of more 'no mores'.

"No more sirens for breakfast!" Mina yelled.

"Lunch and dinner," I added.

"Hip, hip, hurrah!" Berta flung up her arms and plunged onto her bed.

"We'll finally see Mother and Father," Mina added pensively. "For a while, anyhow." She moved close to me and gave me a hug. "We'll go together to Zurich. We'll be able to see each other, and I am sure we'll see Helene and Berta, too."

"You'll start a more normal life, you'll be going to school, and we'll write often to each other," Berta went on. "We've heard over the radio that the Germans are losing the war, and this mess will be over soon." She had stopped thinking of what her own future would be like. She had her problems too, focusing on her tomorrows.

"Let's think of Mama and Papa," Helene suggested in a better mood.

"Will they recognize us?" was my usual question and apprehension. It seemed always, and foremost, on my mind.

"Of course, parents never forget their children," Berta answered without hesitation.

"Then why did they leave us?" At the time I could not understand that.

"Goldy, they *had* to. If not, none of us would be alive to day. We spoke about this before. When you grow up, you'll understand better the sacrifice they made when they left us."

I loved to listen to her when she tried to explain why things were the way they were. I wondered again and again what made my sister so wise.

We were not given many days to prepare for our departure. Besides, there was nothing to pack. We had no clothes; we were given one suit of clothing to travel in and another to take along. We had not acquired mementoes of our sojourn. No one even thought of *owning* things anymore. People came, and people went. Some managed to touch someone for a short while, and some others just passed through.

Yet we managed to have left an impression somehow—maybe because we always were together, the four of us. Maybe we reminded the others that a family was still to be had, that families still existed, that children still could grow, and therefore that there was still hope. We were lovingly called *la famiglia branbilla* by the Italians among us. God only knows what it meant; to us it conveyed that we belonged, that we were loved. We knew it had been bestowed in terms of endearment.

Almost too soon, the eve of our departure arrived. The children's ward staged a short play for us, produced and directed by the one and only Nurse Regina. The camp's inmates gave us a farewell party too, after dinner in the dining room. Songs were sung.

"*Avenu shalom aleichem, avenu shalom aleichem*"—peace with all, peace together. Songs reflecting the various cultures of their homelands, other songs that were born in the diaspora and out of despair yet that ended with hope for, and belief in, an end to it all.

Finally, we all rose and held hands as we sang "Auld Lang Syne." We were hugged, kissed, blessed by men and women. We were told over and over again, "Make good, remember who you are, make a good life for yourselves, remember us, bring our tradition forth. Don't ever forget."

Those good-byes and well-meaning words reminded me at once of my parents, especially my father as he left with my mother on that cold dismal morning to cross the border into Switzerland before us, not knowing if we'd ever see each other again. The mood was so somber, so sad. All my father wanted to be remembered by was his teaching to us: "Don't forget your upbringing. If you forget your ancestry, your culture, then soon you'll forget who you are, where you belong—you'll be a nobody, a nobody without pride. All of a sudden, I was remembering, reminiscing over those words that echoed in my mind. I didn't understand them, their meaning, didn't have the slightest idea who I was supposed to be or what I shouldn't forget. At that point all I knew was that we had been different for quite some time. Once I had played happily with other children, had a happy family, smiling parents. I knew that, when I was put to bed, I would get up in the same place. The same routine would follow, except on the Eve of the Sabbath. I remembered the undercurrent of excitement every Friday night. I would take a bath in the evening before dinner and get to wear my best outfit. My mother would polish the silver candelabra on that day and light the candles at sunset to usher in the Sabbath. She'd recite the benediction, covering her face with the palms of her hands, her head adorned with a special shawl. Since I insisted to do the same, I too was given a shawl to cover my hair. I had to stand on a chair in order to reach her height, and thus I repeated the words after her: "Praised be Thou, o Lord our God, king of the universe, who hast sanctified us by Thy commandments and hast instructed us to kindle the lights for the Sabbath."

She would add a silent prayer.

"Mother, what are you whispering?" I asked. "I want to say it too!"

She would smile and say, "When you grow up, you will know what *you* want to add. This is my secret."

"When will I be grown up, Mother?" I couldn't wait to grow up to find out that secret.

Every Friday night, it was the same ritual. "Am I grown up enough now to know, Mother?" I repeatedly asked. I wonder if my mother said the same things that I said when I had grown up and found myself doing the same. I smile sadly now, wishing she could stand beside me and we could together add a personal prayer. Somehow I know we invoke the same petition. Not for us but for those whom we love.

Soon after, my father returned from the synagogue. We never knew whom he might bring home for dinner. There was always some stranger in town who needed food and shelter. In turn, we were blessed by the visitor for having invited him in to share our table. My father gathered us at the table and blessed us all, placing his hands over our bowed heads and saying, "Make thee as Sarah, Rebecca, Rachel, and Leah." Then he would sing joyous hymns. When, and why, had all this changed so suddenly? When had I stopped remembering; when had I started to forget?

How come I was recalling it at that moment? I couldn't say. All I know that it never left my mind again.

I was brought back to it when I heard Nurse Regina saying, "You are embarking on a happy life. Don't worry. Everything will turn out al right."

Tears were streaming down my face. Why was I crying? Why was I so terribly unhappy? Everyone was wishing us well, telling us to be happy. . . .

WE LEFT EARLY the following morning. The air was still moist from the night before, the grass covered with dew that shone like crystals as the early sun tried to hold her own through the clouds. All in all, it appeared that the sun would ultimately come through. The camp was still engulfed in sleep. A few birds ventured to fly criss-crossing patterns in the sky, and the cries of distant cocks were audible greeting the dawn. In the distance one could see a luminous display of colored arcs, banded streamers caused by an electrical disturbance in the atmosphere. The beauty of it enhanced the solemnity of the moment. As the gates of the camp opened, I felt paralyzed for one instant. It came to me suddenly: We had been free, or thought we were. But how could we have been if we had never been allowed beyond those gates? We'd had guards around us all that time. And now they were letting us out, like birds from a cage.

I looked around, and an overwhelming feeling came upon me. I couldn't explain it then. It was the first recognition of freedom. How can it be made clear to anyone who has always been free, even to those who enter a battlefield to fight for freedom and the cause of justice? I couldn't explain. All I felt was this tremendous openness arising from within. We were out from that big Inside. I was walking like other people, *outside*.

We were met by a uniformed woman wearing a white band with a red cross on her sleeve. She wore a green beret with some kind of insignia on it. She saluted the guards, and then she spoke to us. "*Freuleins*, ladies, I am Captain Locke, your chaperone for the duration of your trip." She smiled curtly. "Let's be on our way. My Jeep is waiting down the path. The chauffeur will drive us to the train station. *Gut?*"

The guards offered us a salute. We felt very proud and all choked up; all we could do was look at them sheepishly and smile.

As we made our way toward the Jeep, a chorus of voices interrupted the chirps of the birds, which, startled, flew off in disarray to take shelter in the branches of more distant trees.

We turned around to see a group of inmates lined up on both sides of the gates we had just passed through. They were waving with their arms, some with handkerchiefs, others with their caps. In unison they once again sang good-bye to us. I had the urge to run back to them. I didn't want to leave this place that had become a secure heaven for us. It hadn't been all that great, but we'd managed to get by. I had found a new family with my sisters, a circle of people who, despite our differences, had become quite close and involved in each other's lives.

For some mothers and fathers, we had become the new-found children they had lost, for some others their sisters they presumed dead.

As if Berta knew my thoughts, she took my hand and squeezed it tight.

The red cross officer reminded us that we had to go: A train was waiting. And so we turned, suppressing the urge to run back and hug them once again.

The songs echoed in the air while the car drove off. We'd never again meet those people or cross their path. A new chapter in our lives was beginning.

We saw them again for a fleeting moment as the train climbed slowly through the mountains. In the distance, they stood on the highest point of the encampment. They knew the train would pass and have to slow down while making its way uphill before turning down toward the valley. We were seated at the window, in our own compartment, gazing at the panorama spread out before us. We had opened the window to let in the fresh air, to feel the morning breeze caress our faces. We jumped up and almost hung out the window, waving at them, signaling back, showing them they had been noticed. We distinctly heard them yell, "*Shalom, shalom! Arrivederci! Adieu!*" We watched them grow smaller and smaller until we could no longer see them.

We traveled through alpine meadows shadowed by magnificent peaks enveloped in clouds. We saw waterfalls that tumbled eternally into valleys so distant that they seemed an illusion. At times we plunged through swirling mists that engulfed the entire terrain and cut the visibility to zero.

That's when the train had to move along slowly, to resume speed when we reached the plateau.

Then we were racing faster toward our destination, leaving behind memories to be resurrected far in the future, passing rural towns, stopping at small stations to let passengers on and off. At times one could hear yodeling through the meadows—maybe lovers trying to convey their unending devotion with their refrain?

I finally broke the silence that had settled among us. Our chaperone had tried at the beginning to draw us in conversation but soon gave up, as we only answered in monosyllables. She'd clearly understood that we were not up to conversation. She'd sat back and closed her eyes.

Our tears had long subsided, and we too had nestled back in the seats, watching the ever-changing scenes unfold as we sped along.

"Will Papa and Mama really recognize us?" I asked. How many times in the past had I asked that? How many times had I attempted to recapture their presence when their images became vaguer and vaguer in my memory? I felt remorse and shame for having forgotten how they looked. I could never bring myself to tell my sisters about it, since they seemed to have so many more recollections of them than I did.

I didn't realize that it was only natural, since they were older than I. I could have spared myself much pain if I had asked then why they did and I did not.

I blamed myself for being thoughtless and not a nice person, since I quite often had the tendency to be naughty, as my sisters told me. So now I was afraid that, perhaps, Mama and Papa too might have forgotten *me*. After all, they had left us. I had forgotten, through the years, that by leaving us they had saved our lives.

"Do you think they still love us? They could have adopted other kids, the same way the people in the camp adopted us and loved us, yes?"

I didn't wait for answers, I had so many questions. Berta took my hands finally and put her finger on my lips to silence me. "*Sha!* Keep quiet for a minute, so that I can answer you, and stop *worrying*—Mama and Papa will recognize us, and yes, they still love us. Parents never cease to love their children. It's only through their doing that we got away from Italy." I had heard these answers before. Berta continued, "They worked very hard to find people to take us to Switzerland. And didn't they try to see us? Have you forgotten?"

Relieved, I snuggled against her shoulder. I was beginning to get tired, and my stomach was making funny noises. I was hungry. We had been on the train for almost four hours by then. I was wondering wether we would get some food. "Berta," I whispered, "are you hungry? Because I am, and thirsty, too."

"Well, I'll ask the woman. She'll tell us. Come to think of it, I *am* hungry too." She turned to my sisters. "Mina, Helene, do you want to eat?"

"Oh, I thought no one would ever ask!" Helene was holding her stomach. "I'm famished, but who has food?"

"I'll ask for it," Berta said. ". . .Uh, we have a problem."

"What problem?" I asked.

"She seems to be sleeping."

"Wake her up!" said Mina matter-of-factly.

"I don't know. . .should I?"

"Come on, what are you waiting for?" Mina sounded impatient.

"Then why don't you wake her up yourself?" Berta snapped. It was always up to her to do things that no one wanted to, because she was the oldest.

"All right, I'll wake her," Helene volunteered.

But before she had a chance to, Captain Locke stretched herself and opened her eyes. "*Ach du Lieber*, I must have dozed off. You ladies must be hungry or thirsty, ya?"

"A little!" we all answered at once.

She opened the satchel by her side. After arranging and rearranging its contents, she finally brought out a few paper bags. She handed one to each of us and said, "*Guten appetit!*"

Each bag contained a wrapped sandwich and a small bottle of lemonade.

We ate in silence. When we finished, she took us to the lavatory and told us to freshen up, since we would be arriving soon.

It took another hour, and than we were there. As soon as we stepped down from the train, all those questions that had plagued me seemed so superfluous. As we were standing on the platform, someone swept me off my feet. Two strong arms lifted me up.

All at once it seemed like yesterday. I was looking down at my father. I swung my arms around him; his moustache scratched my chin as it always had before when he kissed me.

"Oh, Papa!" I jubilantly repeated his name. He held me tight. It almost took my breath away. Then he let me down. He was smiling through his tears.

Then it was my mother's turn to hold and kiss me, over and over again. I *recognized* her. A little older, a little grayer, a few more wrinkles—but it was *my mother*.

God had answered their prayers—and mine.

The four of us in 2000. From left, Mina, Helen, Goldy, and Berta